Socializing Land

Socializing Land

Plantations, Dispossession, and Resistance in Laos

Miles Kenney-Lazar

University of Hawai'i Press
Honolulu

Printed in the United States of America

First printed, 2025

Library of Congress Cataloging-in-Publication Data

Names: Kenney–Lazar, Miles author
Title: Socializing land : plantations, dispossession, and resistance in Laos / Miles Kenney–Lazar.
Other titles: Plantations, dispossession, and resistance in Laos
Description: Honolulu : University of Hawaiʻi Press, 2025. | Includes bibliographical references and index.
Identifiers: LCCN 2024059273 (print) | LCCN 2024059274 (ebook) | ISBN 9780824899011 hardback | ISBN 9780824899035 epub | ISBN 9780824899042 kindle edition | ISBN 9780824899028 pdf
Subjects: LCSH: Land use—Laos | Land tenure—Laos | Land settlement—Political aspects—Laos | Plantations—Political aspects—Laos | Environmental justice—Laos | Agriculture and state—Laos
Classification: LCC HD890.4.Z63 K46 2025 (print) | LCC HD890.4.Z63 (ebook) | DDC 333.709594—dc23/eng/20250318
LC record available at https://lccn.loc.gov/2024059273
LC ebook record available at https://lccn.loc.gov/2024059274

Cover art: Villagers ride a motorbike through a Chinese pulpwood plantation (top image). Lowland swidden rice fields among dry dipterocarp forest (bottom image). Photographs by Miles Kenney-Lazar.

University of Hawaiʻi Press books are printed on acid-free paper and meet the guidelines for permanence and durability of the Council on Library Resources.

For Lamphay, Gabriel, and Samia

Contents

Illustrations

Figures

Maps

Preface and Acknowledgments

This book examines the social dynamics and relations that shape how control over land is determined during periods of heightened land investment, often referred to as a land rush or land grab. However, I started the research for this book in 2013 just as the land concessions boom in Laos was beginning to fade. A moratorium on concessions for mining as well as rubber and eucalyptus plantations had been issued by the government the previous year in response to the impacts, conflicts, and misgovernance of land-intensive extractive investments. The research itself looked back on land conflicts that had been taking place since 2007 and had mostly been officially resolved, even if aggrieved villagers were far from satisfied. A similar story was playing out globally. While land grabbing received extraordinary media attention soon after the 2007–2008 food crisis, the land rush started to slow by 2013 in response to falling commodity prices as well as various forms of political and regulatory backlash.

More than a decade later, the political-economic context of land has not radically changed, whether globally or in Laos, especially in comparison to the rapid pace at which intensive land investments emerged in the earlier period. The Lao government has not put in place a new regulatory framework for land concessions although the earlier moratorium technically expired in 2016. Moreover, several plantation companies have sold their concessions because of their inability to acquire the amount of land they were initially granted. Others have moved toward leasing land directly from villages and private owners or engaging in contract farming arrangements. Globally, research and activism on land grabbing have slowed, although there have been periodic reflections on what has transpired.

Considering the dampened climate of large-scale land dealings, what value is there in analyzing the patterns of land distribution among plantation capitalists and peasants during a boom that has now faded? Central to the arguments of the book is the notion that land should be seen not simply as a thing or entity but as a complex set of social relationships. These relations are lively and dynamic. While they may become sedimented for many years, such as in the form of a plantation, in the long run they are shifting and malleable, especially during periods of turbulence and transformation. Bearing this context in mind, there are several reasons why it is critical to analyze and theorize how land access, control, and ownership are produced and distributed during a land rush.

First, land rushes are often cyclical, tending to be associated with larger political-economic trends and geopolitical changes. While they are relatively new to Laos, frenzied periods of land grabbing did not commence in the mid-2000s in many other parts of the world. They can be traced back to the unprecedented waves of dispossession driven by European colonialism starting in the fifteenth century. In Europe, they started before the Industrial Revolution, such as with the Enclosure Acts in England, which were first passed in the early seventeenth century. It is not unlikely that when economic and political conditions shift, and perhaps the immediate memory of the recent land rush begins to fade, large-scale land grants and concessions will be prioritized again as a tool of economic development. In Laos, new regulations approved in 2019 allowed rubber and eucalyptus companies to acquire land in production forests that were historically reserved for logging. Many villages reside on and customarily use land within production forest areas and this new form of expansion may generate fresh land conflicts. And while the granting of land for plantations and mining has slowed, the same cannot be said for infrastructural, industrial, real estate, and hydropower projects, which have continued to be approved and have generated significant degrees of dispossession. In the post-pandemic period, there is additional pressure to facilitate foreign investment in land, infrastructure, and resources to recharge economic growth. Understanding why and how land is possessed and dispossessed by different groups of people under such pressure will remain critical for a long time to come.

Second, the slowing of new land investments does not equal the disappearance of land conflicts. Villagers may continue to contest the boundaries of land concessions for the foreseeable future, especially in areas that companies have yet to develop. Even when such conflicts are officially resolved, they are likely to be socially important for communities for many years and can shape tense interactions with plantation companies and government officials. Furthermore, land investments are shifting in response to the moratorium as well as heightened vigilance by communities defending land rights. As it has become harder to acquire land over time, companies have resorted to other strategies of access, particularly direct land leasing and contract farming. Additionally, while concessions may no longer be in favor, there have been recurrent cycles of cash crop booms driven by smallholders, including in rubber, maize, and, more recently, cassava. These new forms of plantation development are built on farmers' land rights rather than ignoring them as with land concessions. Yet they can still be rife with conflicts over how land is distributed and for what purposes. The question this book sets out to address is thus crucial for understanding the allocation of land for different purposes within new regimes of land control.

♦ ♦ ♦

Working through these questions and transforming them into a book project has been slow scholarship, and not always by choice. Over many years of preparatory work, field research, and the transformation of data into publishable writing, I have accumulated a great number of debts. This book would not have been possible without a supportive network of family, friends, comrades, and colleagues. Of course, none of them is responsible for the misjudgments, errors, or omissions that I have certainly made.

My family has provided me with something much more than the time and space to focus on this work: the emotional and spiritual support to believe in my capacity to complete the project. I am deeply grateful to my wife, life partner, intellectual comrade, and the love of my life, Lamphay Inthakoun. We met in Vientiane as undergraduates in 2008 and have shared a passion for forestry, the environment, rural livelihoods, and politics in Laos and beyond. She has been with me every step of the way, and many of the ideas in the book were inspired by our long discussions about the politics of environment and development in Laos. Further, she has endlessly fielded my queries about plant names, cultural practices, and Lao terms, among other miscellaneous topics. She has also made enormous sacrifices of time, energy, and career development in socially reproducing our household despite my best efforts to share the workload. It has been an enormous relief to partially return the favor over the past few years as she has pursued her doctoral studies.

Our two children, Gabriel and Samia, have been a constant light in our lives. Their growing years are a frequent reminder of how long it has taken me to complete this project. Yet their joy and radiance more importantly take me back to what matters in life, and it is certainly not an academic book. It was a wonderful opportunity to bring them to eastern Savannakhet in 2022 and introduce them to people and places that had been a critical part of my life before they came into this world.

My parents, Bruce Kenney and Ana Lazar, have given me everything that I needed to succeed in life, including a distinctive surname. They instilled in me a profound appreciation and interest in the political and social lives of worlds far beyond our small town in Maine, which has taken me to many corners of the world. To their disappointment, this has also led me to live very far away from them for most of the past decade and more. However, I know they ultimately appreciate that they have enabled me to build a fulfilling life abroad. They have also played a crucial role in helping us to manage the complex intersection of work, home, and childcare in our lives, often traveling across the globe to do so.

In Laos, Lamphay's family has made me feel like one of their own, such that it seems wholly inappropriate to refer to them as "in-laws." Their warmth has made Laos feel like a second home during extended stays and on shorter visits. They have also frequently brought a part of Laos to us, in Japan and in Singapore, and helped us balance family and work demands at critical junctures.

My research in Laos, especially on a controversial and sensitive topic, would not have been possible without the efforts of many. Due to the risks associated with such sensitivity, I unfortunately cannot include their names here. They include the villagers of eastern Savannakhet who generously took time out of their busy days to share their knowledge and experiences with me. Oftentimes they were recounting traumatic experiences of intimidation, dispossession, and deprivation, and I am grateful for their openness. Several Brou research assistants played an indispensable role in the project, not only interpreting between Lao and Brou languages and helping to conceal sensitive information from government officials at key moments but also providing a deeper understanding of villagers' perspectives and ideas. Their life and work experiences in these areas facilitated a much deeper understanding of local politics than would otherwise have been possible. Several provincial and district officials in Savannakhet greatly aided my work by answering many questions about local land governance and by sharing sensitive information. They were also crucial in ensuring that my project had local governmental approval. Appreciation is also due to the managers and staff of the two plantation companies for meeting with me and explaining their project operations.

Fortunately, there are also many people whom I can name and thank for their support, as they did not provide sensitive information for the book. My research was formally hosted by the Natural Resources and Environment Information Center (NREIC) of the Ministry of Natural Resources and Environment (MONRE). I imagine they stuck their neck out a bit to support a project like mine. Unfortunately, NREIC has since been absorbed into other parts of the ministry and their staff have been moved around. At NREIC, I am grateful to Ek Vinay Sayaraj for inviting me to affiliate with the center. He has been a constant intellectual companion—our lengthy discussions of the politics of environment and development in Laos have been very fruitful for my work. I also appreciate Dr. Bounkeua Vongsalath for helping me to obtain the necessary research and visa approvals. Additionally, several government staff provided valuable field assistance during trips to Savannakhet, especially Khammai Vongsalath and Thanousinh Sanethachack.

Many others were generous in offering their knowledge and guidance. My first research projects in Laos were based at the Faculty of Forestry Science at the National University of Laos, which was a formative intellectual environment. I am particularly appreciative of the conversations on forestry that I have had with Achan Sithong Thongmanivong, Achan Thoumthone Vongvisouk, the late Achan Lamphoune Xayvongsa, and the late Achan Khamla Phanvilay. Additionally, Pheang Xaydongvanh has been a great friend since my earliest introductions to the world of Lao forestry. During my doctoral fieldwork, I collaborated and informally affiliated with the Centre for Development and Environment (CDE) at the University of Bern, which was a generative intellectual space. My knowledge of Lao land governance and politics was greatly enriched by Dr. Vong Nanhthavong, a true comrade in the field and office. Collaborations with Michael Epprecht and Connie Hett helped me get this project off the ground. Additionally, there has been a vibrant community of development practitioners and fellow scholars living or conducting projects in Laos who have welcomed me and immeasurably improved my understanding of the political-economic context. Among others, they include Mike Dwyer, Glenn Hunt, Diana Suhardiman, Keith Barney, Juliet Lu, Wanjing (Kelly) Chen, Mariko Hayashi, Honkeo Douangdy, Richard Hackman, Joost Foppes, Andrew Bartlett, Michael Victor, Ian Baird, Chris Flint, Martin Rathie, Andreas Heinimann, and Oliver Schönweger.

I returned from the field to Clark University's Graduate School of Geography, where my professors and fellow graduate students helped ease the transition into writing. My supervisor, Jody Emel, was an unwavering source of intellectual and emotional support. She has ceaselessly compelled me to find and emphasize the relevance of the work by always asking her piercing question: So what? My dissertation committee members—Tony Bebbington, James McCarthy, and Jim Glassman—have equally driven me to sharpen my analysis with their incisive feedback. Other faculty members at Clark were important sources of guidance, especially Dianne Rocheleau, Mark Davidson, and Jude Fernando. Perhaps the greatest attribute of the Graduate School is the tight-knit community of doctoral students who prioritized community building over competition. In particular, Bill Kutz, John Lauermann, Adriene Johnson, Pheakkdey Nguon, Katherine Foo, Mark O'Keefe, Kelly Kay, Kevin Surprise, and Chris Knudson helped advance my project in critical ways.

After earning my doctorate, I was fortunate to hold two fellowships at Kyoto University, first with the Center for Southeast Asian Studies (CSEAS) and then with the Hakubi Center for Advanced Research. These institutions graciously provided me with complete freedom to publish from my dissertation and initiate the process of writing this book. I am particularly indebted to Noboru Ishikawa for hosting me at CSEAS and providing indispensable feedback and career advice. I am also appreciative of the inputs I received from Kono Yasuyuki, Nate Badenoch, and Yoko Hayami. Nishaant Choksi was a frequent reviewer of early chapters of the manuscript, urging me to question the received wisdom of my ideas in ways that have profoundly shaped the arguments I eventually arrived at.

Upon moving to the Department of Geography at the National University of Singapore (NUS), I was fortunate to work among a formidable group of geographers, anthropologists, and scholars of Southeast Asia. Neil Coe was a particularly influential mentor, providing invaluable advice in the development of the manuscript and its role in my professional trajectory, as well as detailed comments on the proposal and several chapters. Nathan Green generously reviewed draft chapters and helped me to hone in on the central theoretical framing of the book. Several others at or visiting NUS kindly provided valuable feedback on the introductory chapter: Nikita Sud, Paul Gellert, and Ting Hui Lau. Members of the Politics, Economies and Space (PEAS) research group provided rigorous feedback on my book proposal and drafts of related papers in workshop sessions, otherwise known as the "PEAS treatment." Special thanks are due to James Sidaway, Chih Yuan Woon, Shaun Teo, Carl Grundy-Warr, Henry Yeung, and Shaun Lin for their inputs. As part of a Mainland Southeast Asia reading group, Jamie Gillen, Gerard Sasges, Simon Creak, Erik Harms, and Anna Koscheeva were willing to adjust their reading schedules to give notes on several of the manuscript chapters. Many others have been an important part of the intellectual milieu within which this project was formed, particularly Vatthana Pholsena, Jonathan Rigg, Rob Cole, and Elliott Prasse-Freeman.

Over the past decade, I have had the chance to present my work at various fora where the engagements with panelists, discussants, and audience members have helped me to shape my ideas, and thus I would like to recognize the important role they played. These included seminars given at the University of Wisconsin–Madison (the Friday Forum at the Center for Southeast Asian Studies and the Yi-Fu Lecture Series at the Department of Geography), Kyoto University (the Japan-ASEAN Seminar at CSEAS, the Hakubi Seminar at the Hakubi Center for Advanced Research, and a seminar at the Graduate School of Asian and African Area Studies), and the University of Hawai'i at Mānoa (cohosted by the Department of Geography and Center for Southeast Asian Studies). I have also received valuable feedback on presentations given at the Workshop on Large-Scale Land Transactions at the University of Michigan, the Land Grabbing: Perspectives from East and Southeast Asia Conference at Chiang Mai University, the European Association for Southeast Asian Studies Conference in Berlin, and the American Association of Geographers Conferences in Chicago and San Francisco.

I have great appreciation for the editorial guidance provided by the University of Hawai'i Press, particularly the support from Executive Editor Masako Ikeda, Managing Editor Gianna Marsella, and copy editor Eileen Chetti in bringing this project to fruition. Three anonymous readers gave reviews that would make any author envious. They were critical yet constructive and generous, detailed yet engaged with the overarching concepts. The final product is immeasurably better as a result. Additionally, I would like to thank the editorial team at Impress Creative and Editorial in Penang: Gareth Richards and Eryn Tan. Their sharp eyes have made a professional book out of my text.

Finally, I would be remiss not to recognize the essential sources of funding that enabled me to carry out fieldwork. These include the US National Science Foundation's Doctoral Dissertation Research Improvement Award (Grant 1333391), the US Department of Education's Fulbright-Hays Doctoral Dissertation Research Abroad Fellowship, the National Geographic Society's Young Explorer Grant, and a grant from the BRICS Initiative for Critical Agrarian Studies.

Abbreviations and Acronyms

AEPF	Asia Europe People's Forum
BRI	Belt and Road Initiative
DONRE	Department of Natural Resources and Environment
FAO	Food and Agriculture Organization
GERUCO	Vietnam General Rubber Corporation
INGO	international nongovernmental organization
Lao PDR	Lao People's Democratic Republic
LFA	Land and Forest Allocation
MONRE	Ministry of Natural Resources and Environment
MPI	Ministry of Planning and Investment
NEMM	New Economic Management Mechanism
NGO	nongovernmental organization
NTFP	non-timber forest product
NVA	North Vietnamese Army
PONRE	Provincial Department of Natural Resources and Environment
Quasa	Quasa-Geruco Joint Stock Company
SEZ	special economic zone
SOE	state-owned enterprise
Sun Paper	Shandong Sun Paper Company Limited
TFAP	Tropical Forestry Action Plan
VLRC	Vietnam-Laos Rubber Joint Stock Company
VRG	Vietnam Rubber Group

Glossary of Non-English Terms

ai nong	siblings
bai saneur	official letter of complaint or proposal
ban	village
bot ban theuk	note of record
chao meuang	fiefdom ruler, mayor
chintanakan mai	new thinking
chit chai	will, resolve
din ban chap chong, din chap chong	reserved land
hai	swidden
hit, hit khong bapeni	traditions
huang ham	prohibit
khan na	bund
khwam samakkhi	solidarity
konglon	village security officer
Lao Loum	lowland Lao
Lao Soung	upland Lao
Lao Theung	midland Lao
lot thai na	hand tractor
mak chong	malva nut (*Scaphium affine*)
meuang	fiefdom, town, political center
mop	give
na	paddy
nai	leader
nai ban	village head, chief
neua thi	area
nop	greeting with hands pressed together
oudomsomboun	prosperous

pa dong, pa dong dip	dense forest
pa khok	dry dipterocarp forest
pa xa	cemetery forest
paeng	divide
pao wang	empty
paxaxon	citizen, people
paxaxon pen chao, lat khoum khong	the people own the land, the state manages it
phi mahaesak	spirit forest
pok pak haksa	protect
saethakit thammasat	natural economy
sahai	comrade
san	lady palm (*Rhapis excelsa*)
sasana phi	belief in spirits, animism
siang paxaxon	voice of the people
souan	gardens
tam	low
thang hai thang suan	clear an area for swidden and gardens
tuang kheun	protest
vixakan	technical staff member

Note to the Reader

Scholars of Laos often remark that a standardized system of romanizing the Lao alphabet does not exist. This is true in the sense that there is no national system of transliteration. However, this does not mean that no systems have been developed or commonly used, even if not formally accepted. The French developed a romanization system that has been the most influential in determining place names as well as how Lao people spell their names with roman (Latin) letters, despite some inconsistencies. This system was further standardized by the US Board on Geographic Names and the Permanent Committee on Geographical Names for British Official Use in a 1966 agreement (BGN/PCGN 1966). The system has been used by the Lao government but never endorsed as a national system.

The Lao Ministry of Health (MOH) has recently sought to develop its own standards of romanization and, in 2020, adopted a modified version of the BGN/PCGN 1966. (See the explanation and justification for the romanization system at the MOH website: https://laoconverter.info/development.html. A tool for romanizing Lao words is also available.) While this system has not been endorsed by the government as a whole, it is more commonly used and standardized than any other and thus forms the basis for the spelling of most Lao words in this book. Exceptions are made in several instances. Place names follow the most common spellings, which differ from the MOH-modified system. For example, I follow the common spelling of the Lao capital as Vientiane rather than Viangchan, which is closer to the actual pronunciation. Additionally, I follow Lao people's chosen spelling in writing their names in roman letters.

Names of all individuals discussed in the text have been changed to pseudonyms, apart from those of public figures. I have done this to protect the identity of my interlocutors and provide them with a measure of security considering the sensitivity of the issues we discussed.

Frequently, they openly and frankly shared their experiences and perspectives under the condition that their identity would not be linked to the information they provided. Additionally, I have also given villages pseudonyms to make it harder to identify them and their residents. Inevitably, it is impossible to remove all information that could potentially be used to triangulate the identity of specific people and places. However, the efforts taken have made it exceedingly difficult and unlikely.

I conducted most of the interviews for this project in Lao and paid for them to be transcribed. When interviewing Brou villagers, research assistants conducted the interviews solely in Brou without translation to Lao to enable the interviewees to express themselves more freely, especially if government officials were nearby. I then paid the research assistants to translate and transcribe the interviews into Lao. I worked with Lao-language transcripts when analyzing the data and then translated interviews into English when preparing quotes for use in the manuscript. I frequently asked Lao speakers familiar with land and resource issues to check and edit my translations. Inevitably, meaning and nuance have been lost in the process, especially when translating from Brou to Lao and then English. However, when translating from Lao to English, I have sought to stay as close to the original meaning as possible while also ensuring readability.

Due to significant depreciation of the Lao kip over the last several years, I have used the exchange rate prevalent during the fieldwork period (2013–2015) in which US$1 equals 8,000 kip.

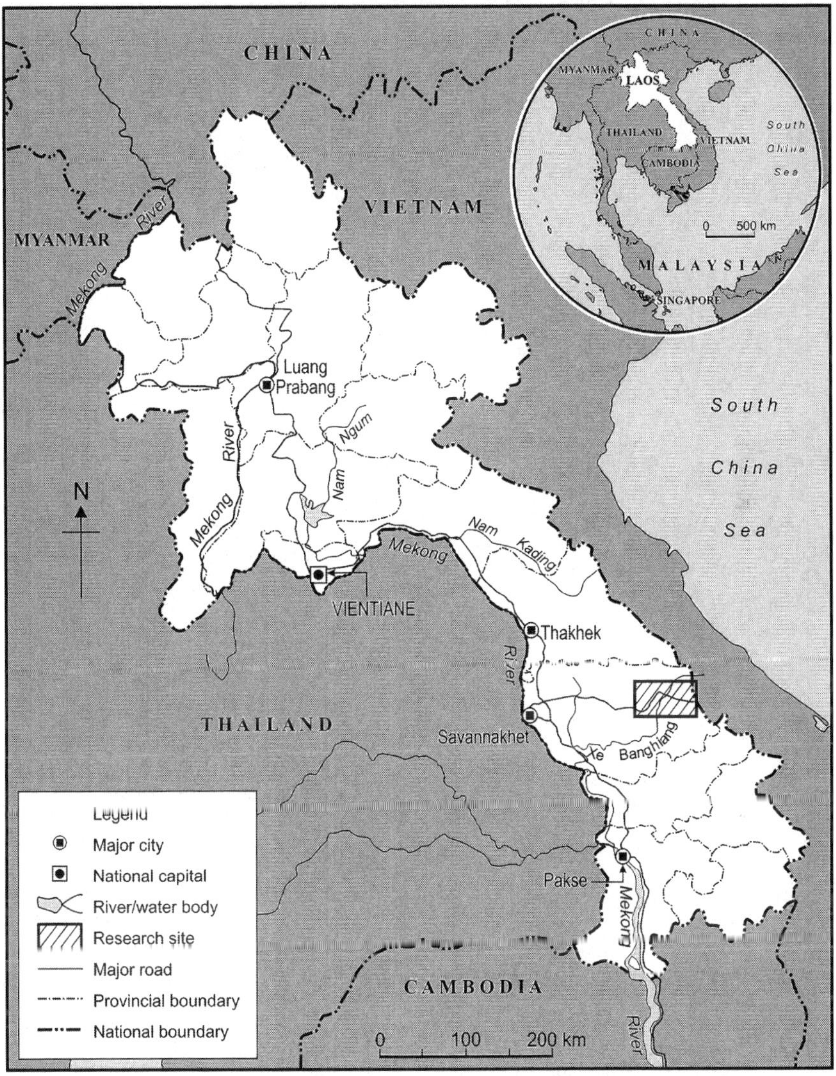

Map 1. Location of research site in Laos. Map by Lee Li Kheng.

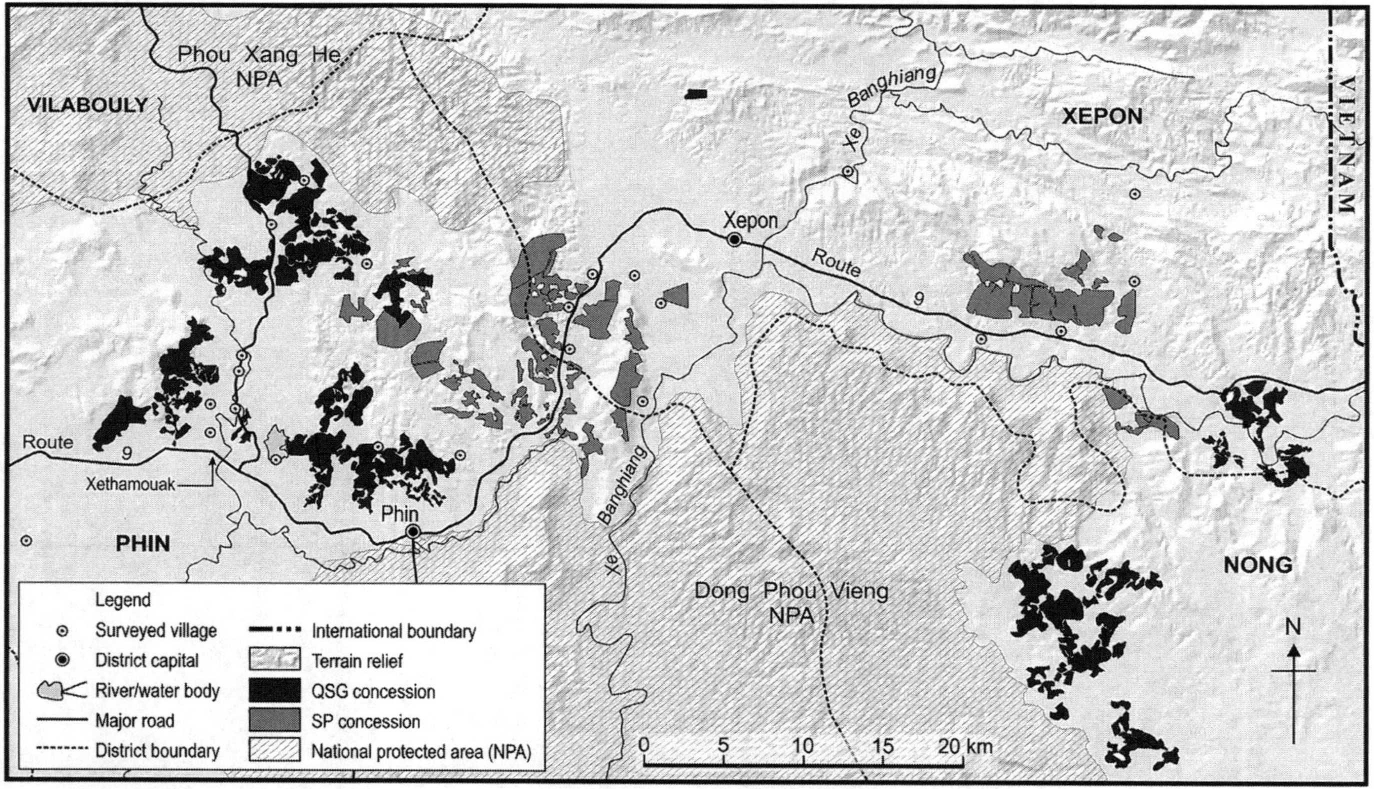

Map 2. Concession areas and surveyed villages in eastern Savannakhet province. Map by Lee Li Kheng.

Introduction

As I wrapped up an interview at the village head's house in Ban Xaylom—a small ethnic minority Brou village in southern Laos—the village authorities indicated that discussing the theft of their lands in the abstract was not sufficient.[1] We needed to see the eucalyptus and acacia trees that a Chinese company had planted on the village's land in their pulpy flesh. With the village head (*nai ban*) and guard (*konglon*) on one motorbike and a Brou research assistant and I following on another, we headed north through their paddy fields, up to the edge of a vast expanse of trees planted in even rows, a scene depicted on the cover of this book.[2] As we rode through the plantation, the village guard pointed to several different sites among the trees, the bases of which were surrounded with earth blackened by herbicides. He repeatedly explained, "This is our land, that's our land," invoking a hidden layer of former land uses: paddy fields—including his own—and adjacent plots of sloped vegetable gardens that had disappeared. They were solely preserved in the villagers' collective memory of the history of land uses and ownership at this site.

Ban Xaylom lies at the foothills of the Annamite Cordillera, which separates Laos from Vietnam in eastern Savannakhet province. The Lao government granted a portion of the village land to Shandong Sun Paper Company Limited (Sun Paper), a private Chinese pulp and paper company. This grant, known as a state land concession, allowed Sun Paper to lease and utilize government land for fifty years in return for an annual fee and tax payments. Several years prior to our plantation tour, provincial and district government officials had paid a visit to the village to request land. When villagers refused multiple times, the officials eventually ignored them and gave the company the green light to begin clearing vegetation to prepare the land for planting. Anticipating resistance, district officials instructed police officers and soldiers to escort the bulldozer operators as they leveled rice fields, grazing lands, bush fallows, and primary forests. Despite their initial defiance, villagers ultimately felt they were in an impossible situation that constricted their ability to act. In their words, "We were afraid of the soldiers and police officers hitting us. If they wanted to arrest us, they could do what they wanted."[3] Furthermore, "The orders for the plantation come from above [from the central government], but we are low [*tam*], so we were scared to do anything."[4]

The establishment of the pulp and paper plantation had a marked effect on villagers' lives. They had been dispossessed of the sloped lands on which they had long practiced swidden cultivation, a rich method of agroforestry with an extended history across Laos and upland Southeast Asia more generally, including among Brou peoples. Swidden systems rotate crop cultivation among multiple plots for periods of up to twenty years. The plantation would leave villagers with a single plot, thus rendering their swidden system inoperable by preventing them from leaving land fallow to restore its fertility. The company cleared some villagers' paddy fields and dumped debris onto the lands of others or into nearby streams, which blocked the flow of water necessary for irrigation. With reduced rice production and difficulties finding edible forest products like bamboo shoots and wild vegetables, villagers found themselves relying more on food purchased from the market. However, they had a limited amount of cash to make these purchases, as the company had not fulfilled its promise to compensate them for their lands. The villagers declined to take up wage labor on the plantation, which they still viewed as their land, and thus the company hired migrant laborers from northern Laos. In reflecting on how the project had affected their lives, village leaders poignantly captured the devastating loss of access to productive resources: "If you follow what the party and the state said, there is development. But now we have nothing to use for development."[5]

Ban Xaylom is an exemplary case of land grabbing: the coercive, violent, rapid, opaque, and unjust dispossession of peasants, forest dwellers, pastoralists, and other marginalized land users that has been witnessed across the postcolonial world over the past two decades to make way for plantations, mines, hydropower dams, and special economic zones (SEZs).[6] There are many cases of villages like Ban Xaylom in eastern Savannakhet that lost land to Sun Paper as well as other plantation companies. It fits into narratives that Laos has become a hot spot within the global land rush, especially in Southeast Asia, alongside Cambodia, Myanmar, Indonesia, and the Philippines.[7] And it seemingly demonstrates the ease with which foreign investors seize land in impoverished, peripheral countries with little resistance, perceived to be due to top-down, weak, and corrupt political systems.

Yet only several kilometers up the road, and neighboring Ban Xaylom, Sun Paper had a completely different experience when seeking to acquire land in Ban Phailom. Similar in size to Ban Xaylom, Ban Phailom is populated by Phu Thai peoples, an ethnic group that dominates the local government, and village elites had close governmental ties. It is a wealthier village with better developed infrastructure than most, including a separate village office, a temple, a small market, and roadside shops and restaurants. When consulted by district officials, Phailom village leaders contended that they did not have any land available for the plantation, and district officials advised the company to look elsewhere. They confidently claimed that if the village did not formally concede their land by signing a contract or agreement, then it could not be acquired. At one point, Sun Paper cleared land in a neighboring village and encroached on Ban Phailom's land, clearing secondary forest. Village leaders complained to the company, and the land that had been cleared but not yet planted was returned to Ban Phailom. Ultimately, they were spared the destructive socio-ecological transformations of their lands and surrounding environs to which Ban Xaylom had been subjected.

Ban Phailom was not the only village to refuse or resist the encroachment of Sun Paper's plantations. Other villages directly refused to concede their land, confidently ignoring the political pressures bearing down on them from local government officials. In some cases, they complained to government offices about the company's mistakes or infractions, making claims that were ultimately heard and acted upon. Some limited incursions into their lands by planting crops in their fallow fields to show that they met state criteria of productive use and hence were unavailable for the concession project. In contrast, others camped out in their fields with hunting rifles to stop bulldozers in their tracks. In some cases, they made complaints to district, provincial, and central-level government agencies, which listened to their claims. Ultimately, Sun Paper was able to clear and plant only half of the 7,324 hectares of land that the government had granted them across two districts of Savannakhet.

Comparing cases like Ban Xaylom and Ban Phailom demonstrates that resistance and reactions to land dispossessing investments are treated in diverse ways. Such differentiation is the central puzzle that this book investigates: why some groups of people are robbed of their customary agricultural fields and forests—their territories and lifeworlds—while others are spared this ruinous outcome. These differences operate within and across villages, but also across territories and regions, such as the wealthier lowlands in contrast to poorer uplands. They are also shaped by the type of company targeting village lands. These uneven geographies of dispossession can be confounding, and they are critical to unpack in order to understand the spatial patterns of who retains, loses, and gains control over land among intensifying flows of transnational capital into rural environments. They are closely tied to contradictory state objectives of land use and ownership: whether and how land should be constructed for capitalist investment and accumulation or retained for peasant productivity. Throughout the book I examine this process as *(dis)possession* to capture the dialectical relationship between possession and dispossession. When it comes to land, one group's loss is another's gain, a tension that is at the heart of changing forms of land control, capturing how they are dialectically related. The resolution of this contradiction shapes the geographies of landownership.

This book unravels the webs of social relations that land is entangled within and that shape what it can be used for and by whom. I focus on the social qualities of land that investors encounter when they establish their projects and how they seek to work with state power holders to reshape those social relations to their advantage. From afar, the rural lands of Laos may appear to be up for grabs. The Lao government and its multilateral development donors have often presented the countryside as an open resource frontier: the population is sparse, lease rates are low, and there is plenty of state land awaiting an infusion of capital.[8] Yet this could not be further from the truth, a reality that many companies realize when their projects hit the ground, or at least attempt to. Fundamentally, this is because land is not simply an entity that can be transacted between two parties, such as the Lao state and a foreign company. Instead, it comprises a complex set of social and ecological relations—a dense sociality that would-be land investors must work through.

Uneven Geographies of (Dis)possession

Activists and critical scholars have characterized the phenomenon of global land grabbing as a massive redistribution of land away from marginalized land users of the Global South to a diverse class of transnational capitalists.[9] In particular, the release of the report *Seized: The 2008 Landgrab for Food and Financial Security,* by the Spanish international nongovernmental organization (INGO) GRAIN, put land grabbing in the spotlight, which in turn generated considerable media, activist, and scholarly attention.[10] Researchers have linked the interest of international investors in land to a set of intersecting processes.[11] The 2007–2008 food crisis saw the price of food spike, along with the value of land associated with it, and similar dynamics could be seen in other nonfood commodities. Additionally, the 2008 global financial crisis created a demand for alternative, secure investments. Scholars have framed this form of land grabbing as a "foreignization of space," a form of "security mercantilism" that produces "massive structural holes in the tissue of national sovereignty."[12]

It is not surprising then that land grabbing has generated serious concern, which continues to endure more than a decade later.[13] Cases like Ban Xaylom have been reported from across the Global South, from Cambodia and Ethiopia to Brazil and Eastern Europe.[14] The aggregate extent of land being acquired is especially alarming. Globally, it has been estimated that 33 million hectares of land deals were concluded between 2000 and 2020, encompassing an area larger than the size of Norway.[15] In Laos, 1 million hectares of land were granted for mining and plantation projects between 2000 and 2016, equivalent to 4 percent of the national territory.[16] Many of these concessions, granted for periods of up to fifty years, have been to investors from the country's more politically and economically powerful neighbors, such as Thailand, Vietnam, and China.[17] This generated concern among foreign and domestic observers that the government was selling off its land and that its territorial sovereignty was being compromised.

To explain what constitutes a process of land grabbing, scholars have turned to the concept of *dispossession.* A critical intellectual lineage of the term comes from the historical materialism of Karl Marx and his analyses of the enclosure movement in fifteenth- and sixteenth-century England, which he saw as a precursor to the development of industrial capitalism. At the end of volume 1 of *Capital,* Marx writes about the theory of "so-called primitive accumulation" as a critique of Adam Smith's view that inequalities in the social accumulation of wealth preceding capitalism result from differential capacities and efforts of individuals to amass wealth and capital over time. Instead, Marx argues that these differences resulted from coercive and violent processes in which wealth was taken from some groups and given to others, a history of expropriation "written in the annals of mankind in letters of blood and fire."[18] The displacement of peasants and serfs from feudal and common lands left them without any means of production, "freeing" them to move to burgeoning cities to sell their labor power in factories and creating class bifurcation between the proletariat and bourgeoisie. A vital element of this process in rural areas was the enclosure of common lands, transforming them into private property and facilitating the emergence of agrarian capitalism.

Marxist political economists have argued that primitive accumulation, enclosure, and privatization are not simply historical processes that enabled the development of capitalism.[19] Instead, they are ongoing and essential elements of contemporary capitalist accumulation in that they remove barriers to the expansion and intensification of capitalist social relations. Land grabbing is testimony to the importance of coercive land transfers for the expansion of capitalism into new sites of accumulation, and it draws connections to the violence of (neo)colonial dispossession across much of the non-European world. David Harvey proposes the concept of *accumulation by dispossession* to capture the ongoing nature of primitive accumulation, which, in contrast to *accumulation by exploitation,* produces wealth not by extracting value from labor but by acquiring resources and assets cheaply or even freely. He argues that this is a process essential for restoring profitability and resolving crises of capital overaccumulation under advanced capitalism.

Such theories have been influential for analyzing contemporary processes of land grabbing because they show how dispossession has been an essential element of the expansion and intensification of capitalism across the Global South, linking the changing social relations of property associated with enclosure and privatization to neoliberal economic globalization. However, theorizations of contemporary processes of primitive accumulation are limited in that they tend to present dispossession, enclosure, and privatization as foregone conclusions, functional to global capitalism, that will eventually dominate noncapitalist spaces. Such narratives overlook the complexities and limits accompanying the capitalization of resources like land, embedded in longer histories and struggles to restrict the ease of transferring it to private actors. In other words, just because dispossession is *supposed* to occur does not mean that it *will.*

A closer look at land grabbing—at a global scale and in Laos—reveals that much less land has been dispossessed than the numbers seem to convey. Globally, it is estimated that a maximum of 73 percent of reported land deals have gone into production, although this figure could be as low as 30 percent.[20] In Laos, just over half of the 1 million hectares granted for plantations and mines has been developed.[21] As other researchers argue, these data suggest that the narrative of "global land grabbing" has focused on the spectacular land deals announced in the media rather than on the more complex, messy, and contested process of actually transferring land to investors.[22] Land granted does not equal land acquired and developed.

The limited materialization of land deals raises questions about the degree to which "global land grabbing" is a coherent phenomenon. Some argue that the macroscale drivers of land grabbing are important but do little to explain the localized logics of land investment in particular places.[23] Scholarship on land grabbing in Southeast Asia has shown how elements of this narrative are relevant to but do not neatly align with the actual processes of investment and dispossession occurring in the region.[24] In Cambodia and Laos, regional political-economic changes, such as market liberalization in previously closed-off economies, may be more influential than global macroeconomic forces. In Indonesia and Malaysia, investments are driven by global and regional market dynamics, particularly in the palm oil industry. However, the timeline of land investment there started in the 1980s, much earlier than identified in global land-grabbing narratives.

Most important, though, companies often struggle to secure and control access to large portions of the land they are granted.[25] There is much that stands between capitalists and the earth, including peasants and Indigenous peoples who have been using the land for generations if not millennia. Although land is inequitably owned worldwide, it is much more widely distributed than most other resources, like timber or precious minerals. There are many land users and owners with whom potential investors must contend.[26] Additionally, a significant body of research demonstrates that land grabs have generated wide-ranging resistance across the world, or what has been referred to as "political reactions from below."[27] Many countries, such as Brazil, have imposed restrictions on foreign landownership due to concerns about the threat it poses to territorial sovereignty.[28] Land grabs have generated nationwide protests, such as when the government of Madagascar was overthrown after granting 1.3 million hectares of land to the Korean company Daewoo Logistics to grow maize.[29] Land investments have also often led to localized forms of resistance, such as protests against the enclosure, dispossession, and filling in of Boeung Kak Lake in Phnom Penh, Cambodia.[30]

What forces shape these uneven geographies of dispossession that constitute the global land grab? It is essential to investigate the extra-economic forces necessary for dispossession—the role played by the law, the state, and violence in divorcing people from their lands.[31] Marx recognizes that the state played a critical role in facilitating the forceful expropriation of peasants and serfs from the lands they depended upon for sustenance and income. For Michael Levien, dispossession is enacted by "coercion-wielding entities," such as the state or other politically powerful actors.[32] At sites of contemporary land grabbing, the state is not necessarily a victim of powerful transnational corporations and foreign governments seeking land. In fact, it often invites such investments and facilitates the dispossession needed to provide land to investors.[33] Statutory laws were used to legalize the theft of land from the poor, Indigenous peoples, and other subjects during the colonial period—a process that continues to this day.[34] The process of legalization turns claims of land into rights to land and can be used to enforce dispossession in the long run.[35]

Nevertheless, extra-economic processes of dispossession can be contested. As dispossession is not only a political-economic process driven by the laws of capital, it should also be studied as a field of contestation shaped by social forces such as class struggle as well as ethnonationalism and Indigenous autonomy. Derek Hall and colleagues contend that the power to exclude someone from accessing land is a double-edged sword.[36] While exclusion from land is typically seen as the domain of the rich and powerful, poor and marginalized land users must engage in some form of exclusion if they are to keep others off their land. State regulations, for example, can be used to legally support land expropriation in some cases *and* contest the legality of land acquisitions in others.[37] Similarly, the ideological legitimation afforded by granting unproductive "degraded" lands or "wastelands" to investors for ostensibly more productive investment can enable the dispossession of peasant land.[38] Yet these discursive categories can be contested when peasants show that the land has been put to uses that the state views as productive, whether by planting permanent tree crops or demonstrating that taxes have been paid for years on end.[39]

When dispossession does occur, it is often socially and spatially uneven, affecting some groups of people and territories more than others.[40] To understand the heterogeneity of dispossession, it should be viewed not only as a political-economic process and function of global capitalist expansion but also as a fundamentally *political* and *social* process requiring the use of extra-economic tools. It involves investigating the social relations at play before, during, and after attempts to transfer land from the poor and marginalized to the wealthy and powerful.

Socializing Land

To investigate the uneven geographies of (dis)possession—why some groups of people lose access to land while others do not—it is important to account for the social struggles and forces that direct access and control over land in different ways. Toward this end, I propose the concept of *socializing land,* defined as the ongoing process of enmeshing land into complex, contradictory, and dynamic social relations that shape how it is used, accessed, controlled, and owned.[41] I use the concept to investigate how the social relations of land are oriented toward different purposes, especially the contrasting orientations of land for small-scale, peasant semi-subsistence production versus land for large-scale capitalist accumulation by agribusiness investors or other resource investors. The socialization of land in different directions is a field of struggle that is central to (dis)possession in the global land rush.

The concept of socializing land entails an ontology of land as fundamentally social. In capitalist property systems, land is treated as a "thing" or an independent entity, an asset that can be exchanged.[42] This is a misunderstanding of what land is that misses out on the complex social and ecological connections that are associated with any one plot of land. Little of the earth, especially the land desirable for investment, is empty of social qualities established by human communities. Furthermore, human ties and connections to land emerge and evolve over time, whether in a piecemeal fashion as farmers expand their agricultural frontiers, in disruptive periods due to war, conquest, and colonization, or in revolutionary transformations such as national land redistribution. Relations to land are therefore multiple, layered, intersecting, and sedimented over time.

The sociality of land is linked with the potent concept in critical scholarship on land, agrarian studies, and political ecology that there is a social life to land (and nature, more broadly).[43] All natural resources have both material and social dimensions that shape how they are transformed into commodities.[44] Land is not only a material entity characterized by features such as its topography, soil fertility, and locational fixity that affects its use value to different groups of people.[45] Human communities maintain diverse social, cultural, and spiritual connections to land that give it life. Landscapes are shaped by complex histories of how people foraged and hunted on, cultivated, settled, built structures on, transformed, and laid claim to the land. The socialization of land can be understood as a process of continually integrating land into societies, polities, and communities, much the same way that individuals are socialized as they assimilate into society by internalizing its dominant values, beliefs, and norms.

Land is dynamic and lively. It is something that people have deep and multifaceted political, economic, cultural, and spiritual attachments to. Not only does land have a social life, but for many groups of people, especially Indigenous peoples and peasants, land *is life*. Their ancestral and customary lands are a fundamental component not only of their livelihoods but also of their lifeworld, identity, and being. However, as Nikita Sud argues, these relations to land are not static or fixed. As she demonstrates with cases across India, land is always in the making and constantly changing, even when acquired by the state or a developer and commodified as part of a project of capital accumulation.[46] For example, the case of Ban Xaylom demonstrates that even when villagers lost control of their land, they continued to retain memories and emotional connections to it, which could serve as a basis for future political demands and action. Tania Li suggests in her work on the expansion of cacao plantations in Sulawesi, Indonesia, that the commodification of land represents its "end" as a type of customary land system and forest frontier that can be shaped for different community means.[47] In this book, though, the sociality of land means that it never really has an end, even if the pace and type of change are dynamic over time. Relations to land always have the potential to change—dispossession and capitalization may be just one stage in the long and very social life of land.

Land is most often thought about in terms of property, without consideration of its broader and diverse forms of social relations. Even private property ought to be seen as a complex social relation rather than the ownership of a thing by an individual, recognized by the law.[48] However, property is only one dimension of the social relationships that people maintain with land. For Jesse Ribot and Nancy Peluso, access is an important relation to land and natural resources, defined as the ability rather than the right to benefit from things.[49] Hall and colleagues examine the other side of the coin: how people are excluded from accessing land due to the powers of regulation, the market, force, and legitimation.[50] And Christian Lund focuses on how possession—holding on to and making claims to land—is distinct from, but an essential element of, legalizing land as property or long-term rights to land.[51]

The concept of socializing land works with and builds upon these broader conceptions of how people relate to land that include combinations of access/exclusion, possession/dispossession, and property. It offers a broad approach for thinking about them in relation to one another by focusing on the social relations to land that change over time and operate unevenly across space. However, I seek to go further to understand how and why social relations to land differ and change for varying purposes, leading to different outcomes. Appreciating the dense sociality of land is essential but not sufficient for understanding the different forms that it takes, which could range from being equitable and communal to being unequal, exploitative, and private. I therefore explore several different orientations of socializing land—the purposes and interests those social relations to land serve. The first two are the most important for this book and define the axes of struggle over land in Laos: socializing land for the peasantry versus for capital. The third concerns full social ownership over land, which I will touch on only briefly, as it has not materialized in this form in Laos or hardly anywhere else.

Socializing land for the peasantry addresses the various social relations, customs, and rules that are in place to ensure that rural peoples can access, control, and even own the land that is essential for their agrarian livelihoods. Land can be socialized for the peasantry through organic, incremental processes in which land use and ownership develop through the expansion of an agricultural frontier, resulting in new forms of agricultural production. Or it could be the result of long-standing spiritual and cultural practices of Indigenous peoples that define how land is used by different groups within a community. It could also occur through political projects, such as national land allocations or land reforms that redistribute land and ensure access to it by a broad section of the peasantry. The common thread is that social ties, relations, and connections to land are established that support peasant use and control. Even landless people often have historical ties and connections to land or may seek to access and relate to land through informal arrangements or more radical land occupations.

However, the socialization of land for the peasantry can be precarious. It is often threatened and thus must be protected. If there is a social life to land, then it is a life worth defending. The ties to land that the peasantry develop over time or that are instituted through policy and reform are a mode of social embeddedness of land that can limit, or at least make more contentious, processes of dispossession. This idea is based on the work of Karl Polanyi and has been instrumental for scholarship on the limits that land grabbing has faced over the past decade and a half.[52] For Polanyi, the economy was historically embedded in society, subject to its rules, norms, and customs. The expansion of the market economy in the nineteenth century was part of a project to reverse this equation so that society would be subject to and dependent on the market in order to disembed economic relations from social relations. Polanyi argues that some elements, like labor, land, and money, were not real commodities but fictitious because they were not originally produced for exchange. Treating them as commodities on the market would lead to their destruction. The expansion of the market into these realms eventually led to countermovements to prevent the social and ecological destruction that would ensue. Countermovements sought to re-embed the economy into society by creating new rules and regulations, such as labor laws, to limit its worst impulses. As a result, the economy would never truly be disembedded from society.

Countermovements aimed at protecting the embeddedness of land within society or re-embedding it are evident in the examples referenced earlier of communities resisting local land dispossession, demonstrations and political campaigns against governments that have facilitated land-grabbing regimes, and regulations by national governments to limit how foreign investors access land. These struggles are not inherently against the commodification or privatization of land, as peasants tend to support their own private ownership of land. Instead, they are against the construction of land as a private commodity that can be alienated from the community and owned by outsiders, especially when such a change in possession is enforced coercively.

There are, nonetheless, limits to a Polanyian conception of social embeddedness in that it leads to the assumption that countermovements against the commodification of land will inevitably emerge and serve to defend against it or re-embed land within society or a community after the fact. The reality is that resistance to land commodification, especially if associated with dispossession, is incredibly uneven and there are plenty of instances in which people do lose their land to investment projects and little is done in response, whether imposing new regulations, restituting land rights, or compensating for lost assets. Political reactions to land grabbing and associated dispossession and privatization have ranged from resistance to adverse incorporation and acquiescence, demonstrating a heterogeneity of responses from different segments of society under various forms of political pressure.[53] Hence, it is essential to think through the social dimensions of land when its peasant ties are not defended but instead unraveled or overpowered as new forms of commodified land use and ownership emerge.

To analyze the sociality of land in processes of dispossession and commodification, I outline the idea of socializing land for capital, which concerns when and how the social relations of land are structured to enable capitalist investment, control, and accumulation, or to render land "investible."[54] This is a seemingly paradoxical notion as capitalist use of land is typically associated with its *private* ownership. While land may be assigned private ownership by a single entity, I argue here that it is important to focus on the ways that its social character changes through this process to support private ownership. There are two important aspects of changing social dynamics and relations in support of capital: first, the social dynamics that enable dispossession and changing control over land to take place; and second, the new social forms of production and ownership that are created. The key point is that while land may be treated as private property, such as in plantation estate schemes, such property still comprises and is embedded in a complex and dynamic social context and takes on new social forms of production.

While the sociality of land is critically important for its defense, social land relations can also play a part in the process by which control over land shifts. One problem with a Polanyian analysis is that it is based on a simplified account of the social relations that characterize the double movement that pervades the transformation of land before, during, and after projects to privatize and commodify it. The notion of society is presented as a homogenous field from which land is fictitiously disembedded. This disregards the highly unequal class, racial, ethnic, and gendered relations within society and over land that enable the commodification of land to take place. The disembedding of the market occurs within preexisting social structures. Not all segments of society are against the commodification of land or support a countermovement to re-embed it—many have supported and benefited from and continue to support and benefit from the commodification of land as private property. Informed by Marx's dialectical materialism, it is useful to focus on contradictory social relations within political-economic transformations and how they are linked in ways that are mutually interdependent but undermining.[55] From such a perspective, social relations of land are inherently contradictory, whether articulated by class, race, ethnicity, or gender.

It is within the context of these unequal and contradictory social relations that land transformations, such as commodification, take place and are resisted. The English land enclosures that Marx writes about, for example, were not imposed upon society from the outside but operated from within a highly unequal feudal society in which lords had the power to drive peasants off the land. Protests and riots against enclosure came from dispossessed peasants rather than the whole of society. Similarly, the global land rush is dependent on a whole host of actors that have promoted commodification for the purposes of economic development. These not only include the World Bank and transnational investment firms but also host governments that grant land and local elites that facilitate deals to secure political and economic advantages.[56] There are complex social processes at work that underlie efforts to construct control and ownership of land in the service of capital rather than the peasantry.

Not only are social dynamics at work in constructing land as an asset for capital, but they continue to play a role after land has already been granted to private investors. While Polanyi sees the inherent embeddedness of the economy as a quality that led to attempts to re-embed it through regulation, he is more ambivalent regarding the social qualities of market economies when they are treated as if they are disembedded from society, as in neoliberal political-economic contexts.[57] Similarly, he has little to say about the social qualities of landownership when it is treated as a privately owned commodity, apart from the attempts to limit the destructive effects of such processes. While spatially and temporally uneven, the global historical march of land privatization across nearly every rural and urban context makes it essential to ask what role social relations continue to play in private property systems.

Instead of viewing the marketization of land as simply an attempt to disembed land from its social ties, it can be seen as a transformation of the social relations of land. The privatization of land does not turn it into a completely alienated entity devoid of social attachments but instead changes the relationships that different groups of people have to it. As social theorists of property have long argued, private property is not only about the ownership of a thing by an individual, as recognized by the law, but instead it is a complex social relation.[58] Property can be understood as "an organized set of relations between people in regards to a valued resource."[59] These social relations do not disappear when land is treated as property—land does not suddenly become asocial. In Polanyian terms, it could be said that when land is privatized, while it may become disembedded from a former set of social relations (such as the communal use of pastureland), it also becomes re-embedded in a new set of social relations (such as community recognition of individual landownership), backed by state power. Land grabbing does not rid land of its sociality but changes its composition—who has what claims, connections, ties, and access to the land.

In many cases, ownership is not completely private. In Laos, as well as in many other contexts of land grabbing, foreign and domestic investors do not buy land outright but access it through long-term state land leases and concessions (typically more than thirty years). In other words, the state remains the ultimate owner of the land and the transformation taking place is one from peasant communal and household use and ownership of land to state ownership of land. In the Lao case, the government may have claimed that the land had always belonged to the state, but such ownership had not been realized prior to the land concession. As will be explored in much greater depth in chapter 2, this is a new relationship of landownership between people and the state, in which the former do not have direct possession of the land, but they are still indirectly part of the ownership of land as members of the nation, even if this effectively means that they have lost control.

The socialization of land also occurs in the production process, in which the social form of production on the land becomes more collectively organized. No longer are peasants individual producers on small plots of land. Rather, the land has been aggregated into large plantation plots where they work together on the land, in a new class position as wage laborers. I draw inspiration for this notion from Marx's analysis of how the social relations of the production process under capitalism become increasingly complex, leading to new forms of socialized labor:

> As soon as this metamorphosis has sufficiently decomposed the old society throughout its depth and breadth, as soon as the workers have been turned into proletarians, and their means of labour into capital, as soon as the capitalist mode of production stands on its own feet, *the further socialization of labour and the further transformation of the soil and other means of production into socially exploited and therefore communal means of production takes on a new form.* What is now to be expropriated is not the self-employed worker, but the capitalist who exploits a large number of workers.[60]

Marx's focus here is largely on the social forms of labor organization, but the same notion could be extended to how such social forms of production relate to land on plantations. The use of land has become collectivized, but by and for capital: land plots are aggregated and people work on them in groups, but the product and profits belong to the company.

The third meaning of socializing land is one that I do not explore in great depth in this book because it is not a reality in Laos (and in most places): fully socialized ownership and control over land. This is the idea that land remains aggregated in larger blocks but is collectively owned and democratically managed by groups of people within society. This may be the case at the scale of the nation-state, village, settlement, or some other social form. Just as Marx saw the proletariat overthrowing capitalist production and socializing the factory—collectively owned and managed by workers—the same process could potentially happen for plantations, as unlikely as that may seem. They could be collectively owned and managed by a group of people, such as by villages that were previously dispossessed of their land or nationalized by the state. Just as education and medicine have been socialized in many countries to ensure universal access, the same could be applied to land. This is, of course, an aspirational and political goal, but in the Lao case it is not totally unfeasible. After a concession ends, the state could decide not to recontract with the company but set up some other arrangement. However, since this outcome is so far from taking place in any way, it is mentioned here simply as a future possibility. Nonetheless, it is worthy of further exploration and will be returned to briefly in the conclusion.

There are many different ways in which land can be socialized. The two main orientations addressed in this book—for the peasantry and for capital—are by no means a binary or a linear progression. They are two different directions toward which the social relations of land can move. They can be operating at the same time and in the same place, existing in tension with each other. The socialization of land should therefore be seen as a field of struggle or contestation over which disputes of use, ownership, access, and control are fought. They can be thought of as a struggle over political hegemony, concerning which type of socializing land becomes dominant. For Antonio Gramsci, hegemony exists when dominant classes use combinations of coercion and consent to present their interests as being in the interests of all, a logic that becomes "common sense."[61] Land investments can be viewed as hegemonic projects in the making and we can trace the relations between actors that enable or counter them. For example, when governments grant land deals, they seek to present them as in the interests of the nation and all people, bringing about progress and development. However, they are dependent on dispossession, highlighting their contradictory relationship with peasant users of targeted lands. The state is in the position of having the coercive power to dispossess and displace while simultaneously being accountable to the people's interests upon which its political support rests. I now turn to how these two key orientations of socializing land have played out in Laos, which sets the context for the book.

Capitalizing Land in Late Socialist Laos

The concept of socializing land can be applied to a variety of political-economic contexts where there are tensions concerning how rules, norms, and social relations shape the use, control, and ownership of land—for purposes of capital accumulation versus everyday use by peasant farmers as well as forest dwellers, pastoralists, and residents. The concept is inspired by and particularly useful for thinking through conflicts over land in socialist and post socialist contexts, the latter including many countries that have experimented with socialist forms of land reform or even nationalist projects of state control over land. Many of the postcolonial countries that have been targeted in the global land rush have a history of socialist or nationalist land use, which has afforded the state significant control over land. It is apt to analyze how the socialization of land by the state has led to tensions concerning whether and how it should be allocated to peasant communities or land investors.[62]

Laos is particularly revealing as a case study concerning how the socialization of land produces tensions of access and allocation. The history of socialist politics in the Lao People's Democratic Republic (Lao PDR) since its founding in 1975 has been an important element of policies that allocate land to the peasantry in relatively equitable ways. On the other hand, these policies have enabled the state to exert substantial control over land, which it has used to attract foreign land and resource investors as the country began to liberalize economically in the mid-1980s. These investments have accelerated rapidly from the early 2000s onward. This has set the stage between two visions and orientations of state control over land—for the peasantry or for capital—which have animated land struggles over the past two decades.

The socialist revolution that ended in 1975 saw a significant change in the approach to property and agriculture when the Lao People's Revolutionary Party took over the country at the end of the Second Indochina War (commonly called the Vietnam War or American War) and established the Lao PDR. Based on the principles of Marxism-Leninism, the Lao People's Revolutionary Party pursued the development of a socialist economy "to advance, step by step, to socialism without going through the stage of capitalist development."[63] Private businesses were nationalized or replaced by state-owned enterprises (SOEs) and cooperatives. Controls were placed on entrepreneurial investment, commodity prices, and domestic trade, and Thailand intermittently embargoed cross-border trade. Most members of the entrepreneurial and professional classes fled the country.

To increase agricultural production, adhere to the principles of socialism, and maintain political security across the countryside, the government began a campaign of agrarian collectivization in 1978. Reflecting the country's socialist ideals, a 1978 resolution of the politburo stated, "We must turn private relations of production into collective relations of production . . . so as to serve the people's lives and the socialist industrialization of our country better."[64] Participation in the cooperatives was voluntary, although many joined out of fear of the repercussions they would face if they refused. The cooperatives were nominally democratic, were run by elected officials from within villages, and were relatively small, typically between twenty and seventy households within a single village. Additionally, they varied in form and the degree to which they represented what the government envisioned for socialist agriculture—the genuine aggregation of land and agricultural inputs within the community, cooperative working arrangements, and equal distribution of the outputs (and, of course, increased productivity and the sale of part of the harvest to the state). While a few cooperatives came close to this ideal, many only externally appeared to be a cooperative while internally they were still organized as smallholder peasant production as before. In other words, they had formally pooled their land and assets but effectively maintained control over their household plots. Historically, land access in Laos was relatively equal and not significantly characterized by relationships between landlords and peasants. The collectivization program therefore did not constitute a major redistribution of landholdings.

Problems with cooperatives were apparent during their first year of implementation in 1978 and especially the following year. Grant Evans has written extensively about the many reasons for this, the most important being that they were not more productive than private peasant production and did not offer benefits for most households who entered them.[65] Furthermore, their management was rife with conflicts, particularly related to organizing labor inputs and distributing the fruits of such labor among the members. As participation was semi-voluntary, households could leave the cooperative when it was not working for them, which led to a rapid decline in participation early on. As a result, the government abandoned the collectivization campaign in 1979. The number of cooperatives nationwide decreased significantly, but cooperatives continued to operate throughout most of the 1980s until they were officially discontinued in 1988.

Due to problems with agricultural collectivization and the poor performance of the centralized socialist economic system more broadly, the revolutionary leader and then prime minister, Kaysone Phomvihane, announced in 1979 that the country would begin taking its first steps toward a form of "market socialism."[66] In 1986, these sentiments were framed as *chintanakan mai,* or "new thinking," and crystallized in official policy with the development of the New Economic Management Mechanism (NEMM).[67] The policy abolished price controls, lifted internal barriers to trade, and allowed SOEs to access international markets while requiring them to be efficient, accountable, and profitable. The NEMM prompted further transformations of the economy in the late 1980s and through the 1990s. Market incentives for SOEs were particularly impactful on state-owned forestry enterprises, leading to a logging boom in the late 1980s and early 1990s.[68] Privatization of SOEs was pursued, reducing the number from six hundred in 1986 to twenty-four in 2001, retaining those most strategic for the government.

In reflecting on the government's move to liberalize the economy, Evans notes that "socialism has come and gone in Laos."[69] However, the reality is much more complicated. As Holly High argues, Laos is still a socialist country, in political, economic, and cultural terms.[70] Unlike in Russia and Eastern European countries with the regime changes and market-based economic overhauls of the 1990s, it would not do justice to the Lao political economy to refer to it as "post-socialist." Not only does Laos still retain a socialist political structure, but it is also ideologically committed to the long-term construction of a socialist society, as stipulated in the 1991 constitution.[71] This ideological project, combined with the legacies of the more strictly socialist period, means that the state still plays a vital role in managing and regulating the economy according to socialist-inspired ideals, which has profoundly shaped how capitalist accumulation has materialized. For the purposes of this book, the continued role of socialism in Laos has had profound impacts on how land is socialized. On the one hand, it has ensured state distribution, recognition, and protection of peasant lands. On the other, it has enabled the state to assert control over most of the country's land and grant it as land concessions to investors.

These tensions can be seen in the legal developments that began in the 1990s that supported the socialization of land for both the peasantry and capital. The constitution set the stage for creating new laws that began a transition from a country governed by decree to what the government has more recently referred to as a "rule of law state," in which the country is managed by a consistent and comprehensive legal framework. These new laws began to define land use and ownership.[72] Following socialist traditions, policies and legislation were put in place for formalizing the allocation of land to farmers, based on the principle of providing land for the tiller.[73] In the early 1990s, in conjunction with international aid organizations, the government began a program of Land and Forest Allocation (LFA) that was formalized as a national policy in 1996. The program aimed to delineate the boundaries between villages and zone village land use into different categories of residential, agricultural, and forestry lands.

The LFA program also granted some households temporary land-use certificates, which were intended to be precursors to land titles. When the land had been productively used for three consecutive years, the certificates could be converted into titles, but this mostly did not occur. Land titling programs, initiated by the World Bank and AusAID, began in 1997 but were largely limited to urban and peri-urban areas and the major cities' agricultural plains. In consequence, the two programs of LFA and land titling, although intended to converge, never did so. Large areas of the country remain untitled, estimated by the government to equal half of all land plots in the country, and are largely in cities, towns, and surrounding agricultural plains.[74] Additionally, the LFA program was unevenly implemented, often conducted only in areas where INGOs or development projects were operating.

The LFA program was biased against upland swidden cultivation, pejoratively referred to as "slash-and-burn" agriculture. Along with programs that resettled upland peoples in the lowlands, one of the aims of LFA was to stabilize and eventually eliminate swidden cultivation, in line with the government's objectives outlined at a forestry conference in 1989. It did so by creating a false divide between agricultural and forest land, considering that swidden systems combine agricultural, fallow, and forest land as one. It increased the amount of village land classified as forest and reduced the amount of land available for swidden agriculture. It also limited the amount of land that each household could use to three plots, thus severely curtailing the extent of swidden cultivation systems and creating incentives for swidden land to operate as more of a private household system than a communal one.[75]

In contrast to these government programs that sought to ensure land access for farmers, although in unequal and regressive ways for upland peoples, the government also began instituting policies for providing land to investors. In 1992, a decree was passed that allowed the granting of land concessions to domestic and foreign investors for commercial use on state land.[76] In other words, it was the first step toward socializing land for capital. Although the first state land concession was granted in 1991, most were granted after the Land Law was amended in 2003, which created a land-granting and allocation mechanism.[77] In concert with a development strategy focused on resource extraction—mining and hydropower development designed to make Laos the "battery of Asia"—the government heavily promoted economic land concessions.[78] In 2006, the government announced the policy of Turning Land into Capital, a development strategy for exchanging land and natural resources for revenue, infrastructure, jobs, and economic growth.[79] By 2009, 1.1 million hectares of land concessions had been granted to, although not necessarily developed by, domestic and foreign investors for agribusiness, tree plantation, mining, real estate, manufacturing, and infrastructure projects.[80]

It has often been presumed that the country's land is under the control, if not ownership, of the state. However, state land has emerged relatively recently as a category of landownership. Furthermore, state land often overlaps with territories that have long histories of customary land use. As a result, the granting of state land concessions raises questions about where the boundaries between state, village, and household land are drawn. It also demonstrates the multiple, overlapping, and contradictory ways land has been socialized in Laos. In late socialist Laos, the goal of a socialist society is still alive as a political project, and the state retains its socialist political structure. Yet the economy has mixed various forms of state, collective, and private control. Access to and control over land reflects these contradictory directions of the economy. On the one hand, the country's socialist history—a peasant-based revolution, a history of collectivization, and public control over land vested in the state—has a legacy that keeps land within the hands of society, the community, or the public, rather than being granted to private investors. This is further reinforced by long-standing histories of customary land use and management. On the other hand, it is because of these histories that land has been pooled as a social resource that can be controlled by the state and allocated to domestic and foreign investors. These contradictions of socializing land are explored in depth in this book in order to elucidate the social relations that shape how different groups of actors control access to land.

Methods

To investigate the contradictory dynamics of (dis)possession in Laos, I conducted a comparative and multi-sited ethnography of two plantation companies and their interactions with a range of government agencies and villages across eastern Savannakhet in southern Laos (see maps 1 and 2). The research was conducted between June 2013 and February 2015 with a brief follow-up visit in July 2022. The project was set up to uncover the complex interactions among plantation companies, government officials, village authorities, and peasant households across a variegated landscape that shape for whom land is socialized. The research was conducted under challenging political conditions that required close engagement with the state, which was a source of frustration but also provided insights into the critical role of the state in shaping how struggles over land play out. Data were collected using a combination of participant observation, focus groups, semi-structured interviews, government data collection, and participatory mapping.

Eastern Savannakhet presented an ideal landscape for studying the conflicted and uneven development of plantation concessions. It is situated within a broader region of central and southern Laos where some of the largest land concessions have been granted. This part of the country is much less mountainous than the north and has better road infrastructure, thus making it a more viable area to establish plantations in large, contiguous blocks of land that are easier to access. The largest concessions for rubber, especially by Vietnamese companies, and for pulpwood plantations have been across central and southern Laos. Furthermore, more land has been granted as concessions in Savannakhet (228,568 hectares) than in any other province.[81] Yet only a third of this area has been developed, likely reflecting the conflicts that many companies face when acquiring land.

The geography of eastern Savannakhet is also an ideal target for the government's concession-granting strategy. The easternmost districts of Phin, Xepon, and Nong are the three poorest districts of the province, populated mostly by the ethnic minority Brou peoples. The government hopes to develop these areas through foreign investments that would supposedly lead to new infrastructural development and jobs for rural communities. Additionally, many of the low-lying areas of the province in the western portion are part of a large plain of paddy rice production, which the government views as important to national food security. In contrast, the landscape of the eastern districts is more undulating and upland as it moves closer to the Annamite Cordillera. Swidden rice fields and fallow systems are more common in this area, and there has been little land titling. These are precisely the types of landscapes that the government seeks to eliminate because of their perceived association with deforestation and poverty, and monoculture plantations appear to be the ideal replacement.

In reality, the landscapes of eastern Savannakhet are much more complicated than the state imagines them to be, which can be problematic for land investments. This can be seen in map 2, which represents how the land granted to but not always developed by companies fits into the region's broader geographies. The area where they can be developed is relatively constrained between national parks to the north and the south. The companies have an incentive to develop their projects close to the road for ease of transportation, but such areas are flat and low-lying with a higher percentage of paddy land that the government does not want converted. Farther away from the road are the sloped, swidden territories that the government aims to turn into resource extractive and productive landscapes, but even these areas comprise a mix of topography and land uses in which the boundaries between lowland paddy and upland swidden fields are blurred.

Finally, this is an area with a complicated geopolitical history that influences contemporary land development. Bordering Vietnam, eastern Savannakhet was part of the historic Ho Chi Minh Trail that North Vietnam used to transport goods and weapons to South Vietnam during the Second Indochina War. It was heavily bombed by the US Air Force during the secret war in Laos, which is evident in the craters across the region and the bomb casings that are used to decorate shops, homes, and government offices.[82] During the war, many villagers fled to the forest and caves to hide from the bombing. The villages in this area were almost exclusively aligned with the communist Pathet Lao and North Vietnamese armies. Like many other areas bordering Vietnam, there is a strong Vietnamese presence in the area that can be conducive to Vietnamese investments and restrictive for non-Vietnamese companies, like Sun Paper, a dynamic addressed in chapter 1.

A key element of my comparative approach was to select two companies that had different experiences in acquiring land, reflecting different capacities to shape social relations of land in their favor. As discussed in the opening paragraphs of this introduction, one of those was Sun Paper, which was able to acquire only half the land it was granted—much less than it initially sought from the government. The other company was Quasa-Geruco Joint Stock Company (Quasa, as villagers referred to it, pronounced *kwah-zah*), a Vietnamese state-owned rubber enterprise and subsidiary of the Vietnam Rubber Group (VRG). Quasa had cleared and planted all the land granted to it, and much more quickly than Sun Paper. Both companies were operating in the same districts of Savannakhet and thus engaging with the same provincial and district offices—some government officials were assigned to work with both companies. Additionally, China and Vietnam are the two largest investors in plantations in Laos and two of the country's most significant allies, thus raising important questions about the ways geopolitical relationships shape how projects are developed—a topic also covered in chapter 1.

Another comparative element of the project was to examine different types of political reactions to the threat of land dispossession across villages, ranging from acquiescence to defiant resistance. Considering a lack of available data on these differences, I conducted preliminary focus groups across twenty-three potential villages to narrow down the number of cases to eleven villages, four affected by Quasa, six by Sun Paper, and one by both companies. These eleven villages are listed in table 1, along with some of their essential characteristics. Since I was investigating multiple companies and villages, I took a multi-sited and comparative ethnographic approach to studying struggles over access to land to understand the interactions and relations among a variety of actors across different degrees and outcomes of resistance versus dispossession. While this limited the depth of understanding of a single village that comes from spending a significant amount of time there, it was essential for tracing connections among actors and across sites that otherwise would not have been possible.

The methodologies employed in this project were also shaped by the challenges of conducting research in Laos due to suspicion of foreign researchers and the sensitivity of the topic of land concessions.[83] To overcome these limits, I engaged closely with the government. I was embedded within the Ministry of Natural Resources and Environment (MONRE), as it was one of the few institutions that could provide political cover for my project. Conducting this research through the government was often challenging and frustrating. It took six months to receive research approval, and district officials often delayed the start of my field trips. However, it was also incredibly fruitful once it was in full swing. Not only was I able to access a trove of government and company documents related to the two companies' land concessions, but I was also able to participate in and observe the interactions among state officials, company representatives, nongovernmental organization (NGO) staff, and villagers. This ranged from observations of government working cultures and practices at different administrative levels to taking account of the tenor of conversations when government officials and company representatives met. I witnessed the discomfort that government officials created when they escorted us to the field and how villagers relaxed and opened up when they were not present. I also noticed, though,

Table 1. Referenced villages and key dynamics that shaped their dispossession

Village and district name	Investing company and its relation with local government	Ethnicity	Landscape	Type of village relationship with government	Dynamics of intra-community solidarity	Outcome of dispossession shaped by resistance
Nammak, Phin	Quasa, strong	Brou	Mostly upland swidden, some lowland paddy	None	Internal disagreement, lack of solidarity	Significant loss of land, no resistance
Phoulao, Phin	Quasa, strong	Brou	Mostly upland swidden, some lowland paddy	None	Internal solidarity	Significant loss of land but limited by resistance
Salang, Phin	Quasa, strong; Sun Paper, weak	Brou	Mostly upland swidden, some lowland paddy	None	Lack of solidarity, elite capture	Significant loss of land, no resistance
Kaengchee, Phin	Quasa, strong	Brou	Mostly lowland paddy, some swidden	High-level connection with the vice president	Internal solidarity	Some loss of land, limited by resistance
Sokleek, Phin	Quasa, strong	Brou	Mostly upland swidden, some lowland paddy	None	Internal solidarity, highly strategic action	Limited loss of land due to strategic resistance
Kaengvang, Xepon	Sun Paper, strong during initial period	Brou	Mostly upland swidden, little lowland paddy	None	Internal disagreement, lack of solidarity	Significant loss of land, little resistance
Xaylom, Xepon	Sun Paper, strong during initial period	Brou	Mostly upland swidden, little lowland paddy	None	Internal solidarity	Significant loss of land, state-repressed resistance

(Continued)

Table 1. (Continued)

Village and district name	Investing company and its relation with local government	Ethnicity	Landscape	Type of village relationship with government	Dynamics of intra-community solidarity	Outcome of dispossession shaped by resistance
Na Khouay, Xepon	Sun Paper, strong during initial period	Brou	Mostly lowland paddy, very little swidden, small total area	None	Internal solidarity	No loss of land, outright refusal
Chalan, Xepon	Sun Paper, strong during initial period	Brou	Mostly lowland paddy, some upland swidden	None	Breakdown of solidarity	Some loss of land, initial resistance but eventual acceptance
Phailom, Xepon	Sun Paper, weak	Phu Thai	Mostly lowland paddy, small total area	Ethnic-based links with district government	Internal solidarity	No loss of land, outright refusal
Saphang, Phin	Sun Paper, weak	Brou	Mix of lowland paddy, lowland swidden, and reserved lands	Veteran-based links with the National Assembly	Internal solidarity, highly strategic action	Some loss of land, limited by resistance

how villagers often took advantage of the presence of government officials to air their grievances, demonstrating the two-way nature of village–state relationships. I could therefore appreciate the contradictory dynamics for both villagers and companies when seeking to work through the state to defend or acquire control over land.

Organization of the Book

Each chapter of the book addresses a different element of socializing land in Laos, which shapes whether and how community ties to land are defended against dispossession or the state takes control over land and allocates it to capital. The chapters capture the different forms of relationships between actors that influence the ultimate outcome of land control, ranging from the geopolitically inflected relations between investors and the state to the internal relations of a village (between village authorities and households). They also address different political narratives and connections that affect how land is controlled, such as state narratives of "productive" land use and the political connections that villagers have with state officials. Each chapter progressively peels back the layers of the problematic of (dis)possession, moving from high-level interactions and abstract narratives to the intimate connections among farmers and specific plots of land. They uncover different contradictory relations between actors and processes to paint a comprehensive picture of how control over land is produced.

Chapter 1 demonstrates how the political relations between foreign investors and the state affect how state power, especially coercive force, is applied to separate people from their lands and socialize land for capital. Quasa's geopolitically influenced ties with the Lao state at multiple administrative levels were much more potent than Sun Paper's, and thus district officials placed a considerable amount of pressure on villagers to force them to concede their land. Lacking such political ties and often unwilling to develop them, Sun Paper frequently encountered village resistance that the state was reluctant to repress. As a result, villages targeted by Sun Paper were more likely to be able to defend their social ties to land.

In chapters 2 and 3, I address the ideologies and narratives of property and nature that contextualize struggles over how land is socialized. Chapter 2 focuses on how ownership of land is produced in Laos, particularly the way the notion of "state land" is used to justify land concessions and dispossession. I show how this concept is not as stable as it seems at first. The meaning of state land is contestable and so are the relationships that the peasantry has with it. Much land in Laos falls into a gray area where there are shared relationships of ownership between the people and the state. State land is thus a category that perfectly demonstrates how land can be socialized for the peasantry or for capital—many struggles over land are shaped by this ambiguity.

Chapter 3 examines how the politicization of villagers' land and environmental uses plays an important role in determining whether it is presented as available for capital or protected for peasant use. Influenced by the socialist histories of land covered previously, the state prioritizes lowland ecologies of current or potential paddy rice production for peasant production, and thus their acquisition is more easily resisted by rural communities. In contrast, upland ecologies of swidden rice fields and fallows are targeted by the state for replacement with industrial tree plantations, and it is much harder for villagers to resist their acquisition. However, the boundaries between upland and lowland ecologies are not always clear, and the direction in which they are socialized is hotly contested.

While the first three chapters examine the structural relations, ideologies, and policies that shape the potential for resistance, chapter 4 highlights the political strategies and relations that villagers use to resist, make their claims to land heard, and retain village control over land. This is conceptualized as "resisting with the state," which captures how villagers' resistance is targeted toward the state but operates within the orbit of state power. They navigate the boundaries between outward, antigovernment resistance that generates repression and acquiescence to government rules and bureaucracies in which their claims would remain unheard. In other words, when villages protest the acquisition of their lands, they use legal strategies, such as submitting official complaints to the district government or even to the National Assembly. To make sure these complaints are heard, they mobilize different forms of personal, kinship, ethnic, or veteran connections to avoid getting stuck in the bureaucracy and ignored by obstinate officials.

Chapter 5 focuses on social and political relations internal to the village that affect the potential for villagers to mobilize against dispossession of land for capital. I examine the contradictory role of "solidarity" in shaping village action. It is a term with strong socialist associations that the government intends to mobilize to produce harmony among villages and grassroots participation in government projects and policy. However, an overabundance of solidarity can also generate resistance to government projects when they go against a village's interests. The chapter reflects on what it means for land to be socialized within the village, depending upon the types of social relations among villagers that have formed over time. It engages with the problematized concept of "community" and what it means for coherence in a village to be produced, changed, and shaped before, in response to, and after extractive investments are made.

The book concludes by reflecting on the intersections of the contexts, narratives, relations, and strategies covered in producing uneven processes of (dis)possession and associated agrarian change. The conclusion considers the implications of these processes for the futures of rural environments and livelihoods in southern Laos and the future of land investments and plantation expansion. I assess what these changes might mean for the social relations of land access and ownership in the future and what it might mean to socialize land in ways that are more meaningful and beneficial for rural peoples.

Chapter 1

Landing Plantation Capital

In October 2013, prior to receiving authorization from the Lao government for my independent research, I joined a team of MONRE officials on a Swiss-funded aid project to evaluate the "quality of land investments" in Laos. It was fortunate that the evaluation included Quasa, among other companies operating in Phin district of eastern Savannakhet, and thus granted me preliminary research access. Our counterpart from the Department of Natural Resources and Environment (DONRE, the district administrative level of MONRE), Ai Soukanh, arranged an interview at the company's headquarters in the capital of Phin, which is a small town situated on Route 9 that runs across the province from Thailand to Vietnam. Sitting under the gaze of a bust of Ho Chi Minh, with government and company staff on opposing sides of a long wooden table, we interrogated the social, economic, and environmental impacts of the company's rubber plantation. Quasa's translator spoke Vietnamese and Lao with native fluency, as an "overseas Vietnamese" (*viet kieu*) who was born and raised in Laos.

Quasa blended in with the political life of this border region that neighbors the company's home country. Its headquarters was in an old government building a stone's throw away from the new district government compound, and many of its staff initially resided in the former district government office on the other side of the road until it was later converted into a new office for DONRE (figure 1.1). When government buildings were decorated with colorful flags and congratulatory banners during the Lao People's Revolutionary Party's annual meetings, Quasa followed suit on the walls of its compound. A massive billboard filled with images of the company's plantation stood at the roadside, proudly celebrating the company's contributions to the socioeconomic advancement of the district.

Since the Lao government's approval of Quasa's project in 2007, the company's staff had developed and maintained close ties with district

Figure 1.1. The old cabinet office of the Phin district government where Quasa staff initially resided. Photograph by Miles Kenney-Lazar.

government officials who had helped them securely control and plant the land granted to them by the central government. In their interactions, Ai Soukanh and Quasa staff treated each other like old friends. This was hardly surprising when I learned that the company had paid for Ai Soukanh's daughter to study in Vietnam to become a manager at the company's latex-processing facility, which was then under construction in Phin. At the end of our interview, the company director shook each participant's right hand while placing gifts in their left hand—envelopes adorned with the company logo, each containing 200,000 Lao kip (about US$25). Although providing participants of an official meeting with a per diem payment is common practice in Vietnam and Laos, I commiserated with a Lao member of the Swiss research project about our inadvertent acceptance of cash from the company we were investigating. Overhearing our conversation, a MONRE technical staff member (*vixakan*) casually interjected, "It's nothing. I get money from companies all the time."

The same MONRE staff member had suggested that we interview Quasa representatives in the morning so that they would be inclined to treat us to lunch afterward. After a meal and several rounds of beer at one of the few restaurants in the remote town, the Quasa staff took us on a tour of the rubber plantations and a training center for tapping latex.

They had ample time to promote the benefits of their project and gloss over the serious social and environmental problems that had been revealed during the interview. An intense day of company–government engagement began to reveal the strategies Quasa had employed to aggressively expropriate, clear, and plant trees on all 8,650 hectares granted to the company only six years after signing a land concession contract with the central government in 2006. Quasa had developed what the chief of Phin district once described to village leaders as a "sea of rubber" (*thale yangphala*), alluding to the large expanses of contiguous, uniform, monocropped trees, the tops of which sway in the breeze like waves (figure 1.2). By early 2015, Quasa began tapping 300 hectares of trees and clearing a site to construct a rubber latex-processing facility.

The following month, accompanied by MONRE and DONRE officials, I visited Sun Paper's Lao country office in Xepon district, which neighbors Phin to the east. Located sixteen kilometers from the district capital and six kilometers from the nearest paved road, the office sits on the third floor of what was then a newly built complex of empty dormitory and office buildings next to the site where it planned to build a pulp- and paper-processing factory. Separated from the political life of the district and the social life of nearby villages, our interaction felt isolated and disconnected from the Lao countryside. The conversation was often

Figure 1.2. Quasa's "sea of rubber." Photograph by Miles Kenney-Lazar.

stilted and awkward as the company translator, who had taken on the Lao name Manichanh during her language studies at the National University of Laos, shuttled our questions and answers in and out of Mandarin, showing her proficiency but not ease with the Lao language. The DONRE official had arranged the interview easily enough, but he seemed unfamiliar with the company staff. Our interactions were rigid as Sun Paper's country director and land manager repeatedly aired their primary grievance plaguing their plantation project: "There isn't land, there isn't enough area."

Although construction had begun on Sun Paper's pulp and paper factory, the company was at a loss as to how it would eventually supply the factory with enough raw material to run at full capacity. Sun Paper's staff estimated that doing so would require 100,000 hectares of pulpwood (*Eucalyptus* and *Acacia* species) plantations. Although the central government had initially given Sun Paper the rights to acquire up to 39,000 hectares of land, surveys conducted at the provincial level showed that such a large amount was unavailable. As a result, the company's concession contract was limited to a mere 7,324 hectares. In 2015, five years after the contract signing, Sun Paper had planted only 3,228 hectares with trees, less than half of what they were granted and just over 3 percent of the estimated plantation area needed for the mill to be efficient and profitable.

Such accounts of a Chinese company's struggles, especially when compared with the triumphs of a Vietnamese enterprise, hardly match the sensationalist narratives of China's ascendance across Southeast Asia and the ability of Chinese investors to acquire land. Laos, along with Cambodia, is often described as a close friend of Beijing.[1] The development of SEZs on the Lao–Chinese border has been framed as a form of "soft extraterritoriality," extending the Chinese state southward into Laos, a country seemingly ceding its sovereignty.[2] An *Al Jazeera* documentary even claimed that Laos is "fast becoming a Chinese province, an unofficial colony."[3] Anxieties over the dominance of China in Laos have been heightened by the construction of the Lao–China railway, which extends from Boten at the border with China to Vientiane, the national capital of Laos, and is part of China's Belt and Road Initiative (BRI).[4]

An essential element of the narrative of "global land grabbing" has been the seeming ease with which transnational corporations have been able to buy or lease land across the Global South. It appears to reflect the neocolonial power imbalances between core and peripheries of the global political economy that shape the dependence of resource-rich countries of the Global South on capital-rich countries of the Global North. One of the key differences in the land rush since 2008 has been the rise of Global South investors, such as those from China and India. However, research on land grabbing has complicated this narrative by demonstrating that host states are not necessarily victims of a global political-economic order but play a complex role in attracting, managing, regulating, and sometimes even contesting such projects. Land investments must be understood in terms of how they operate through the state as a complex configuration of processes, people, and relationships.[5]

Host states can play contradictory roles in affecting access to land, transforming the social relations of land to fit the investing needs of capital. It is therefore crucial to investigate how transnational capital interfaces with the state. Socializing land for capital requires the cooperation and support of various political actors that wield power in relation to land, such as domestic elites in Mozambique[6] or ethnic armed organizations in Myanmar.[7] State sovereignty is not only a characteristic of states that becomes eroded by regionalizing and globalizing capital. Instead, global resource capitalists, such as mining corporations, are dependent on national territorial sovereignty as a means of securing access to land and the resources contained above and below it vis-à-vis local claimants.[8] State sovereignty provides coercive power and shapes the property systems that global capital needs to access land and resources locally. Thus, when transnational capitalists have weak relations with land-controlling states, they may be unable to mobilize such powers. Furthermore, the state can impede or even cancel foreign land investments altogether. Ultimately, land might remain within the social domain of the communities that have historically used it.

In this chapter, I argue that Quasa's and Sun Paper's experiences in accessing land are reflective of their varying capacities to work with the Lao state to socialize land for capital. This concerns their ability to overcome the socialization of land for the peasantry—the social and political constraints placed on the alienation of land from farming communities. Rural people have deep local bonds and ties to land that have developed over time and that they will not allow to be severed easily. These relations to land have been historically bolstered by the state, which has the mandate of protecting and improving the lives of its citizens. However, the state also has a policy of granting land to foreign investors and thus has a responsibility to secure land for them. In other words, the state is pursuing contradictory objectives and plays a critical intermediary role between plantation capital, the land essential for their projects, and a land-using and occupying peasantry. The relationships that plantation companies develop with the state—across institutions and administrative levels—are crucially important in determining whose landed interests the state serves. Ultimately, when a project like Quasa's "succeeds," it leads to devastating losses for local communities, while the comparative "failure" of Sun Paper's investment mitigates some of these losses, enabling more land to be held on to by rural communities.

Embedding Capital in a Fragmented State

In the early twentieth century, French colonial dreams of transforming Laos into a resource landscape of Indochina were dashed, notwithstanding 2 hectares of rubber plantation in Champassak province and a tin mine in Khammouane province.[9] In the south, coffee plantations on the Bolaven Plateau were the most successful resource industry, amounting to almost 10,000 hectares and producing up to five thousand tons at their peak in the 1930s.[10] Almost a century later, though, Laos has finally been transformed into a resource-extractive economy producing a wide range of agro-industrial, forestry, mineral, and energy commodities. Not only have 1 million hectares of land been granted for plantation and mining concessions but seventy-eight hydroelectric dams were operational in Laos as of 2021. Additionally, billions of dollars of timber have been sold (most timber exports go unreported, so the exact amount logged and sold is unknown).[11] Road infrastructure across the country has been upgraded to facilitate the export of these commodities and cross-regional trade as part of the Asian Development Bank's plan to develop an integrated Greater Mekong Subregion as a "natural economic area." China's BRI has further accelerated infrastructural and economic integration, particularly with the completion of the Boten–Vientiane railway in December 2021.

In part, this transformation has been achieved through the construction of Laos as a "resource frontier." As Keith Barney demonstrates, this narrative has been established by multilateral development banks, exploratory mining firms, and the Lao state itself, generating a "representation of Lao territorial space as an available, untapped space, which has remained out of the reach of international capital."[12] Eastern Savannakhet is the epitome of a resource frontier in Laos. This area has been a prominent site of logging since the 1980s, like many parts of southeastern Laos. Its proximity to the Vietnamese border and its rich forest resources have made it a target for timber harvesting by logging SOEs and

Vietnamese companies. Villages affected by Quasa's and Sun Paper's plantation projects had seen the forests within their village boundaries logged decades earlier with approval from the state. While government officials and traders in the district became wealthy from logging—some of the interiors of houses I visited in the district were covered with hardwood panels—villagers reported a severe loss of forest resources with little to no material benefits for them in return. Sawmills were established throughout this region. In the 1990s, some of the villages surveyed provided a portion of their land to a logging SOE to build a sawmill, which hardly bothered them because land held hardly any economic value at the time, and there was little conception of formal land rights and ownership. Seeing the spoils of logging accrue to SOEs and the government but not them, villagers became involved in logging themselves as the companies hired them to harvest timber, often illegally. This became standard practice across eastern Savannakhet. As Sarinda Singh reports, the alleviation of poverty in the uplands of this region has been driven mainly by villagers' engagement in illegal logging.[13]

This area is also home to the Sepon gold and copper mine, one of the country's largest mining operations. The mine is in Vilabouly district to the north of Phin and Xepon districts and was opened in 2003. The turnoff to the mine is several kilometers west of the capital of Xepon. Large trucks carrying mining equipment in, and gold and copper out, traverse Route 9 to and from Thailand to the west. When I first arrived in Phin in October 2013, the state of the district capital's infrastructure betrayed that it was at the heart of a resource-extractive landscape. Looking east from the small, nondescript guesthouse where we stayed, we could see that Route 9 was pockmarked with potholes, large and small. At various intervals, the road had buckled, creating spontaneous speed bumps. At other stretches, the pavement seemed to have been stripped off completely (figure 1.3). This was not a bad road—it had been reconstructed several times. The potholes and impromptu speed bumps, though, were the result of repeated pressure placed on the road by heavy mining and logging trucks that rode through town day and night. Each time they crashed into the uneven asphalt, they kicked up clouds of dust that coated the shops and houses by the roadside, even leaving a fine layer of dust on the furniture inside the rooms of the guesthouse where I stayed.

A foundational component of the resource frontier framework is that there is land open for investment. Laos's low population density compared with neighboring countries has been used to promote the idea that

Figure 1.3. Route 9 running through the capital of Phin district. Photograph by Miles Kenney-Lazar.

the lands and resources of the countryside can be easily acquired and extracted. Juliet Lu and Oliver Schönweger show how Chinese plantation companies have bought into the narrative of "empty land." For instance, the director of Sun Paper told Lu and Schönweger, "They [central government officials] really know how to talk, they said all of the land was high quality and available. It was a big leader who said this, so we really believed it."[14] Yet spending a short amount of time in the Lao countryside reveals that it is far from empty. Instead, it is full of people, histories, land uses, and politics. Critical scholars have long contended that frontiers do not naturally exist but are produced, including the discursive and material removal of long-standing human-territorial relationships.[15] Anna Tsing highlights how capitalism makes frontiers as "particular kinds of edges where the expansive nature of extraction comes into its own" and that frontiers are "able to disengage nature from local ecologies and livelihoods, 'freeing up' natural resources."[16] Similarly, in the case of the Lao uplands, Barney writes that "the freely available frontier land of the development programmer's imagination must be created; produced where it did not exist before."[17]

Essential to the production of resource frontiers and economies, then, is not the appropriation of empty space but the *emptying* of such spaces by severing the ancestral ties between peoples and their lands and resources, and transforming property relations to support extraction by resource capital. As discussed in the introduction, such dispossession is driven by the coercion-backed consent produced by powerful entities, often the state. In the Lao case, only the state has the legitimate authority and monopoly over violence and coercion to take land and resources away from its people. Following Thomas Sikor and Christian Lund, legitimate authority is a type of power that includes at least a minimum of voluntary compliance and is bound up with the capacity of politico-legal institutions.[18] However, many forms of power are not legitimized and are exerted through coercion rather than consent. Importantly, the Lao state combines legitimate authority and not necessarily legitimate power, or coercion-backed consent in Antonio Gramsci's terms. So when the Lao government grants a land concession, foreign capitalists are entirely dependent on the state to throw its weight around to produce such land as an empty and available resource landscape. It is therefore vital to understand how capitalists interact with the state, especially in relation to the interests of other social classes, particularly the peasantry.

In classical Marxist theorizations, the state serves the interests of capital, as "the executive of the modern state is but a committee for managing the common affairs of the whole bourgeoisie."[19] However, solely viewing the state as a tool of capital has been critiqued as instrumentalist, ignoring the complex interactions of a variety of actors with the state.[20] Here, I employ a relational approach to understanding the interconnections between the state, capital, and civil society, derived from the work of Antonio Gramsci, Nicos Poulantzas, Bob Jessop, and the Murdoch School of political economy. In this Gramscian-inspired work, the state, as with cultural hegemony, does not inherently serve a particular function but is produced out of struggle and is a reflection of unequal relations among different classes within society. For Poulantzas, the state appears as a "*relationship of forces, or more precisely the material condensation of such a relationship among classes and class fractions.*"[21] Because of these contradictory relationships, the state retains some degree of autonomy from the capitalist class to manage the smooth functioning of capitalist society, which includes making concessions to the working class and other societal interests. Similarly for Jessop, the state is in the paradoxical position of being part of the society over which it has an overarching responsibility.[22] Furthermore, he views the state as an ensemble of institutions, organizations, and social relations, a power structure that is dialectically related to society's unequal power relations and a reflection of the "changing balance of forces in political and politically-relevant struggle."[23] Advancing these ideas, the Murdoch School of political economy, which emerged from scholarship on Southeast Asia, contends that "political outcomes are primarily determined by struggles between socio-political forces, especially social classes and class fractions, but also ethnic, religious, gendered and state-based groupings."[24]

Viewing the state as a set of social relations and a site of struggle among different classes helps to consider the interactions between transnational resource capital and domestic states, and thus how land is socialized for various objectives and to different actors. Particularly important is how transnational capital is embedded in the state; this is especially crucial for accessing biophysical resources that must be extracted from within the territories and governance structures of the nation-state.[25] For example, Ching Kwan Lee investigates the differences between the embeddedness of private international versus Chinese state-owned mining capital in the Zambian state.[26] Due to varying profit versus political motives, the former integrated itself more closely with the Zambian state than the latter, which required that it succumb to state and local interests and demands. Consequently, it was better able to achieve their long-term political-economic objectives. Similarly, Juliet Lu examines why provincial government officials in northern Laos have restricted the expansion of Chinese banana plantations but have not taken similar actions against Chinese rubber plantations.[27] While rubber investments were initiated by larger companies, including a powerful SOE, and were promoted and sanctioned by the state, banana investors were smaller, completely private companies that had not received state approval

Foreign investors in Laos face a range of problems in working with and through the state to acquire land. The Lao state has retained control over the mechanisms for establishing projects, especially the surveying of land and resources, negotiating with villages, and dealing with compensation and resettlement. This means that state approvals and involvement are required at every step along the way, and close coordination between resource capital and the state is essential for project development. The challenge, though, is that state authority over land is limited and fragmented in many ways that investors struggle to navigate in their attempts to acquire land.

Like any other, the Lao state presents itself as a coherent entity, one in which the central government asserts control over the affairs of the country, led by the party. However, its institutions and authority are fragmented across different agencies, factions, and levels of administration. Self-promoted as "one of the most politically stable countries in the region," the government seeks to impress upon foreign investors that there is a direct line of authority from the central government down to the village.[28] Investors are thereby reassured that projects approved at the national level will be implemented at local development sites. When investors apply for a land concession license, they are first granted a memorandum of understanding that gives them the rights to acquire up to a certain amount of land. However, the amount granted in the concession license depends on how much land is determined to be available through land surveying processes, which investors like Sun Paper did not understand at first.

While not stated overtly, Laos can be an attractive site for investors because it has retained a socialist political system in which the central state is perceived to have sovereign control over the country's lands, allowing it to allocate land to projects with little resistance. Yet, as Sun Paper's experience has shown, lower-level officials and villagers themselves have a much greater degree of de facto power than the central government might wish to admit. Central government officials estimate the potential amount of land available, which they sketch out on outdated topographic maps, without having a clear sense of the actual availability and suitability of that land at the local level. However, provincial and district officials play a critical role in determining how much land is available on the ground to be included in the concession certificate and eventually secured when developing the project. Hence there is a contradiction within the socialist state between the central state's granting of land and the local government's authority over how that land is allocated, which investors cannot always easily navigate.

Administrative power in Laos has long been decentralized. An essential aspect of the country's governance history has been the power struggle between the provinces and the central government—a form of "fragmented sovereignty."[29] Laos's rugged mountainous geography combined with poor infrastructure, decades of war, and a minuscule national budget meant that after the Lao PDR was established in 1975, provincial governments were often left on their own to finance their administrative costs.[30] Many provincial governments turned toward granting logging concessions, especially to Vietnamese enterprises, sometimes in exchange for road construction in ways that foreshadowed the Turning Land into Capital policy that seeks to exchange land and resources for financial capital and infrastructure. Since the formulation of this policy in 2006, the central government has sought to rein in control over land concessions. Many provincial governments were granting much larger amounts of land to investors than they were legally allowed to at the provincial level, which since 2009 has been limited to a maximum of 150 hectares on "degraded forestland."[31]

After the amount of land for a concession is approved and the time comes for land to be secured for the project by local-level officials, that is when the real problems of land availability become apparent. Provincial, district, and village authorities responsible for surveying and locating suitable land are the ones who clearly understand that the idea of "empty" land is essentially a myth, as Lu and Schönweger point out.[32] Yet they are still mandated to secure the land granted in the contract. They are also responsible for convincing and coercing villagers to part with their lands, and addressing the socio-environmental impacts and conflicts that result from the project. This can be challenging, as many have close relations with the people and lands in these areas. District-level officials often hail from or have family living in those areas, or have worked there for many years and developed close ties with rural communities. Village officials are also farmers who use the targeted lands daily for agricultural cultivation and foraging like their fellow residents. In return, local officials receive few of the financial benefits that flow to the central government, apart from meager per diems paid for the work they do in the field on behalf of the company.

Navigating this complex and fragmented governance landscape has been challenging for many companies that have suffered from various problems in recent years, such as decreasing commodity prices, conflicts with villagers and activists, incompetent management, and technical and environmental issues, which have prompted some to try to sell their concessions. Importantly, they have also been plagued by problems of government coordination, such as in the case of the Indian eucalyptus-planting company Aditya Birla, which was only able to secure land and plant trees on 15,000 hectares of a 50,000-hectare concession, divided into 800–900 plots of 2–80 hectares in seventy-nine villages, each of which it had to negotiate with government officials and villagers.[33] Over time, district government officials tired of working with Aditya Birla, expressing that they and the villages were not receiving enough benefits, and stopped helping the company acquire land. Lu and Schönweger's work on Chinese plantation companies in Laos shows similar experiences. These companies secured much less land than the government granted to them due to the unexpected complexities of working with local officials to find the mythical empty land of the produced frontier.[34]

Regional Geopolitics

The interactions between foreign capital and the Lao state are shaped not only by the fragmented nature of state sovereignty but also by the geopolitical relations that serve as the political infrastructure for new and increasing flows of investment into land. As the government liberalized its economy in the 1980s and 1990s, it sought to attract global investment and open itself to international capital. That being said, currently the largest investors in the country are from its neighbors: China, Vietnam, and Thailand. This partly reflects proximity and regional connectivity, and also the long-standing relationships between these countries and Laos. However, the qualities of geopolitical relationships differ and have important implications for how investments operate. Here I focus on the geopolitical relations that China and Vietnam have with Laos and how they influenced Quasa's and Sun Paper's projects.

Vietnamese investments and aid have not received the same media and scholarly attention as Chinese projects. However, they have been incredibly impactful and reflect a long historical relationship between Vietnam and Laos, manifested in economic and resource-based relationships on the ground. There appears to be a "Vietnamese pattern" of investments in which Vietnamese projects, especially for plantations, are developed more smoothly and quickly than others because of the close connections between the two countries.[35] This reflects a view commonly held by many that I encountered in my fieldwork—not only foreign commentators but also Lao government officials. Some of the government officials who accompanied me during my fieldwork expressed off the record that Vietnamese companies were able to marshal high-level political support that local officials could not regulate because of the close friendship between the two nations.

The Lao–Vietnamese alliance is long-standing, beginning with the creation of the Indochinese Communist Party and eventually developing into a wartime alliance between the Pathet Lao and the North Vietnamese Army (NVA) during the Second Indochina War from 1959 to 1975. During the war, the NVA provided massive military support to the Pathet Lao based in northeastern Laos to fight against the US-backed Royal Lao Army. The Pathet Lao supported the NVA to transport goods, machinery, and people to insurgents along the Ho Chi Minh Trail of eastern Laos to the National Liberation Front of South Vietnam, more popularly known as the Viet Cong. After the war ended and the Lao PDR was established in 1975, Vietnamese troops remained stationed in Laos, and Vietnamese advisers played an essential role in the Lao government. Vietnam and Laos formalized this governing relationship in 1977 by signing a Treaty of Friendship and Cooperation, which provided the legal basis to station Vietnamese troops in Laos and solidified the special relationship between the two countries.[36] The close ties between the communist parties of the two countries forged during the Indochina Wars continued to be tightened and strengthened in the postwar years, not only through the presence of troops and advisers. Lao party leaders went through political training in Vietnam, which continues to this day, and close political connections were established between neighboring provinces along the countries' shared border.

As Martin Stuart-Fox argues, the relationship between Laos and Vietnam has always been first and foremost political, as Vietnam sought to advance its political interests in Indochina and protect its long western border with Laos.[37] However, it also has a secondary economic dimension. Since the end of the war, the Lao government has granted generous resource concessions to Vietnamese SOEs, particularly for logging in the early years and for land-based investments later on, especially after Laos implemented market reforms in 1986 (following Vietnam's lead).[38] Land concessions to Vietnamese companies operate as a type of war reparation for Vietnam's sacrifices during the Second Indochina War that enabled the establishment of the Lao PDR.[39] Vietnamese resource investments in Laos are thus protected by the long-standing special geopolitical relationship between the two socialist states.

China's historical relationship with Laos has taken a much different path and offers insights regarding how Chinese investors engage with the country. The outsize role that China is currently playing in Laos has created the appearance that Chinese political-economic actors have immense power to operate within the country. But this ignores a fraught political history between the two nations that can complicate Chinese projects. China has become a dominant economic player in Laos over the past two decades as one of the most significant donors of development aid and the largest source of investment capital. The Lao government has signaled solid political support for the Chinese government, not only approving BRI projects but also avoiding getting involved in contentious Chinese developments in the South China Sea. Historically, though, these are relatively recent developments and obscure the limits of their earlier geopolitical relations, a tense conflict between Laos and China in the 1980s, and the shallowness of political connections.

Initially, there was socialist fraternity between the two nations. In the 1960s, the Chinese government provided aid to build roads in northern Laos.[40] The Chinese government also sought to align itself with the communist Pathet Lao. However, the Pathet Lao was more drawn into the revolutionary movement led by the Vietnamese Communist Party, in part because it was based more on a nationalist revolution than on a class-based one.[41] As a result, Lao and Vietnamese forces fought closely together during the Second Indochina War. After the war ended, relations between China and the Lao PDR deteriorated when Vietnam invaded Cambodia at the end of 1978 to overthrow the Chinese-backed Khmer Rouge, leading to a broader conflict between China and Vietnam as Laos supported Vietnam and denounced the Chinese. The Chinese engineers building roads in the north were withdrawn. China even supported insurgencies by anti-communist groups in Laos during the 1980s.[42]

Laos and China began restoring relations in the late 1980s. In 1987, efforts were made toward normalization, and gradual improvements were made year on year.[43] They were substantially upgraded in 1999 when China began providing significant development aid to Laos, including a sizable loan to help the country weather the Asian financial crisis. Since then, China has provided considerable assistance to Laos through infrastructure projects, cash grants, and low- or no-interest loans. Chinese economic aid has facilitated land and resource concessions to Chinese SOEs and private companies for hydropower, mining, and plantation projects.[44]

For Stuart-Fox, one of the key differences between Chinese and Vietnamese geopolitical approaches to the Lao government is their prioritization of political versus economic goals.[45] He argues that Vietnam prioritizes the political relationship between the two countries and thus focuses on maintaining close party-to-party ties, playing an advisory role in government administration and continuously memorializing the long-standing friendship and their struggles during the war. Economic opportunities that arise out of this close relationship are an added benefit. China, however, has developed political connections and given large amounts of aid for the primary purpose of gaining economic opportunities, such as access to resources and communication and transportation connections to the rest of Southeast Asia. Political benefits, such as Lao support for Chinese foreign policy on Taiwan or the South China Sea, are an added advantage.

The geopolitical relationships between Laos, China, and Vietnam play an essential role in shaping the political structure of land resource investments. However, there should be caution against assuming that the country of origin determines the trajectory of the project—there have been Vietnamese investments that collapsed[46] and Chinese projects that developed quickly.[47] Furthermore, the relationships that Vietnam and China have with Laos are not static and unconditional. Laos has defied Vietnamese interests by building dams on the mainstream Mekong River[48] and has granted special economic zones for casinos near the border with China that operate as a de facto extension of Chinese territory.[49] Nonetheless, such geopolitical relations are an important contextual aspect of foreign investments in Laos. The deep political connections that Vietnam has with Laos can be mobilized and taken advantage of by Vietnamese companies seeking state support for their projects at all levels. In contrast, Chinese aid has helped facilitate the approval of Chinese investments at the central level, but not always the political support necessary to develop such investments at local administrative levels. In other words, how geopolitical histories and relations shape transnational resource capital is essential, especially in how they affect their interactions with the territorial structures and relations of the socialist Lao state.

Quasa's "Sea of Rubber"

During fieldwork in Phin district, I spent a great deal of time with Ai Soukanh, a senior official in DONRE who had arranged the interview with Quasa noted earlier. Not only was I in his office frequently to figure out how to get research approval from the district government or to interview him, but we also often met for lunch or dinner when I was staying in the district town. At other times he would drive me around the district to visit different plantation sites in his beat-up minivan. A short, wiry man, he grew up in another district of western Savannakhet and previously was a teacher and studied finance, but eventually he ended up at DONRE to deal with financial issues related to land. He was given responsibility for a zone where Quasa's operations predominated and was thus tasked with both finding land for the company and addressing the conflicts that emerged when villagers' land was unjustly cleared. As a result, he often found himself in the middle of disputes between the company and villagers, which he believed were caused by both sides.

Despite Ai Soukanh's role in supporting Quasa and the financial support he received from its staff, he was frustrated with the company's practices. As he opened up about the flagrant legal, social, and environmental abuses that Quasa had committed, he revealed what it took for Quasa to plant its "sea of rubber." Although the exact process of land granting, surveying, mapping, allocation, and clearing was described differently by various officials and company staff, it certainly did not often follow this order, especially in Quasa's case. Ai Soukanh recounted how the company had acquired more than was allocated to it by clearing land outside the borders of the survey maps or in areas that had yet to be surveyed, which included villagers' agricultural fields. He lamented, "Why do they make mistakes by clearing swidden and paddy lands? . . . When we're with them, they do everything correctly. But when we come back, as we're not with them all the time, at nighttime they start clearing . . . they completely flatten the land." The company also bulldozed land up to the edges of paddy fields and streams instead of leaving a fifty-meter buffer as required by law, dumping soil and debris into fields and streams, damaging land, and clogging waterways. The company also cleared land in zones prohibited for agricultural use: staff admitted in an interview to illegally clearing 380 hectares of a production forest, a zone reserved by the government for timber harvesting, claiming they were unaware of its boundaries.

Ai Soukanh was most frustrated with his perceived inability to punish Quasa's abuses, even to fine or report the company, precisely because it is a Vietnamese company, and probably even more so because it is an SOE and thus an extension of the Vietnamese state. As with China, SOEs in Vietnam are often the most important and highly prioritized outward investors for the state.[50] Ai Soukanh especially wanted DONRE to fine Quasa for clearing land outside the border of its concession area, but he felt it was impossible because Vietnam and Laos are seen as "brothers"—with Vietnam often characterized as the elder. He further reflected on how challenging this was and how "the friendship between Laos and Vietnam can be difficult." Other government officials, including those from the central and provincial governments who joined my research trips at times, expressed similar sentiments that the Lao government had little control over Vietnamese companies compared to those from other countries. On the other hand, a central-level government official, who stated in an interview, "It's mostly the Vietnamese companies that have problems and don't follow the rules, regulations, and laws," said that local officials should be responsible for fining companies because "it's in their area."

Quasa's capacity to act with impunity in eastern Savannakhet is linked to the political cover that it benefited from as a Vietnamese SOE, regardless of whether this message was directly passed down from the central government to local officials or was inferred from the geopolitical relationship between the two countries. This is also connected to the status that Quasa benefited from as a subsidiary of the well-connected Vietnam Rubber Group (VRG). The origins of the VRG go back to the end of the Second Indochina War, in 1975, when the socialist Vietnamese government nationalized the rubber industry and created the Vietnam General Rubber Corporation (GERUCO), a conglomerate comprising many smaller rubber companies. In 2006, GERUCO was partially privatized when its name changed to the VRG and private ownership was introduced, although the Vietnamese state still retained majority ownership of the enterprise. The VRG, like GERUCO before it, is the largest rubber enterprise in Vietnam, owning 220,000 hectares of rubber plantations out of almost 970,000 hectares planted in the country.[51]

Since 2005, the VRG has expanded into Cambodia and Laos, where it intended to plant another 100,000 hectares. The political support and weight of the state-owned VRG were facilitated via high-level meetings and agreements between company representatives and senior Lao government officials that began in 2004.[52] Quasa was explicitly established as part of these expansion efforts. The other subsidiaries of the VRG in Laos, including the Vietnam-Laos Rubber Joint Stock Company (VLRC), which was granted a 10,000-hectare concession in Champassak province, have efficiently and effectively acquired land. VLRC's project infamously dispossessed villagers of 83 percent of their land in Bachiang district.[53]

The geopolitical context of the Lao–Vietnamese friendship and Quasa's position as a subsidiary of a powerful SOE with an authoritative agreement from the central government set the stage for its project and provided a degree of protection. Equally important, though, is how Quasa instantiated itself within the district government. While the VRG's entry into Laos was a state to state affair, Quasa's was built on province-to-province cooperation. Its odd-sounding name represents this arrangement: it is an amalgamation of the bordering provinces Quang Tri in Vietnam ("Qua") and Savannakhet in Laos ("sa"). In practice, though, Quasa did not engage much with the province and spent most of its time, effort, and money developing close relationships with the district governments. Quasa representatives knew such relationships were indispensable for allocating and expropriating land, ignoring company infractions, and resolving disputes with villagers in favor of the company. According to district officials, as a Vietnamese company from the neighboring province, Quasa had a unique understanding of this area and the land available from the war era, as it was part of the Ho Chi Minh Trail where Vietnamese troops operated. Regardless of the truth behind this claim, it certainly created the impression that Quasa could embed itself deeply in the territory of eastern Savannakhet.

Quasa developed close relations with the government, especially at the district level, through various forms of corruption, typical of patron–client relations in Laos.[54] At the national level, company staff explained that they paid officials from MONRE to write the company's environmental and social impact assessment report. It openly made such an admission because it felt the company's close engagement with MONRE strengthened rather than weakened its social-environmental credentials. At the district level, though, its activities were intended to develop close relationships with key actors and institutions. Such connections would be helpful in the future when it needed to call upon the district government to convince villagers to part with their land or accept meager compensation upon complaining about its loss. Quasa planted 14 hectares of rubber at no charge on the land of the former district governor, who was in office when the project began. Additionally, I learned that the experience of handing out cash in envelopes as a per diem payment to government officials was a common practice for Quasa. As Ai Soukanh explained, "When Quasa staff treat villagers or government officials to a meal, they give money to everyone afterward," at which point he made the motion of someone dealing out a deck of cards. Quasa employed the same strategies at the village level, frequently paying per diems to village heads. The company also assigned attractive, salaried plantation jobs, like guarding the plantation, to senior officials in the village.

Furthermore, the company developed close personal relationships with district officials and always maintained a tight line of communication with them. Ai Soukanh, for example, was a friend of several Quasa staff. Whenever I sought to set up interviews with Quasa, they repeatedly called him, suspiciously and aggressively questioning my motives, often trying to delay the interview or arrange to answer questions by email. Other district officials relayed that whenever Quasa ran into land conflicts, they would call up Ai Soukanh and other district contacts to solve them.

Quasa's status as a politically prioritized Vietnamese SOE that had developed a close relationship with the district government meant that district officials not only turned a blind eye to the company's abuses but also played an essential role in facilitating them. For example, the district government often allowed Quasa to clear land based on a rough estimation of the land allocated to it, drawn out on a topographic map, before conducting a detailed survey of the area. The land surveys were conducted only after the trees were already in the ground—I witnessed provincial teams surveying and mapping out plantations that were established several years earlier. Survey data collected from the provincial government in 2015 accounted for only 6,665 hectares or 77 percent of Quasa's plantations, showing that another 23 percent had yet to be mapped.

The district government also played a critical role in employing coercion-backed consent to force villagers to concede their land for the project and repress any resistance. In all the villages along the road leading north from Xethamouak toward the latex-processing plant, villagers told a similar story (see map 2). Quasa staff showed up in the villages with a posse of government officials from the central, provincial, and district levels who then organized a meeting with the villagers. They began by proclaiming all the benefits of development that the rubber project would bring to the village, essentially ending their poverty. They further exclaimed how the project was built upon the historical solidarity between the Vietnamese and Lao peoples and governments, and how crucial it was for the nation's development. Additionally, they asserted how Quasa would plant its trees on state land, and how all levels of the government had already approved it. In short, the village was placed under immense pressure to accept the project.

When villages were hesitant to comply with the project or outright refused, district officials quickly turned to the tools of coercion. The then district governor, who received a free rubber plantation from Quasa, visited villages to aggressively convince them to acquiesce. He asked for the names of those in the village who refused to concede land to bring them to the district government compound for questioning and education, which is a step shy of detention. It is also an ominous reminder of the reeducation camps that members of the opposing regime were taken to after the Pathet Lao seized power in 1975, including one located in a town nearby, Xethamouak.[55] A rumor spread that a villager in the area had been jailed briefly. Regardless of the rumor's veracity, it extended fear concerning what would happen to other villagers if they held out for too long. Ultimately, most, but not all, of these villages came to some forced agreement to concede land to Quasa in exchange for the in-kind compensation of basic infrastructure, such as roads, electric lines, village offices, or health dispensaries.

Sun Paper: "There Isn't Land"

By contrast, district officials in Phin and Xepon often seemed to regard Sun Paper's project as an oddity that they were not quite sure how to handle. The central government approved Sun Paper's investment in 2009 with great fanfare. The provincial and district governments were proud that their locale would host a state-of-the-art pulp- and paper-processing facility, the first of its kind in Laos, which they expected would create thousands of jobs for the area and spur economic development. The Xepon district governor even allowed Sun Paper to keep some valuable machinery for its planned factory on the lawn of the district government compound. It was later moved to another site when weeds sprouted and it became unsightly. Yet throughout the project's development, Sun Paper kept running into problems securing land for the eucalyptus and acacia plantations that would feed raw material to the paper mill. As the project ran on, the district government became increasingly unsure how to help the company—or was unwilling to do so.

Sun Paper's investment in Laos was critical for the Lao government because it reflected a strategy that resource-extractive countries often pursue: adding value to raw materials through secondary processing. Major plantation companies had been developing pulpwood plantations before Sun Paper, such as the Japanese giant Oji Paper, the Indian conglomerate Aditya Birla, and the Finnish multinational Stora Enso. But none of them had taken the risk of developing a processing plant, as they first sought to secure enough raw material to run it efficiently. Although it was the largest private paper company in China, Sun Paper had only been in the business of manufacturing and had never planted trees. So the company focused on what it knew best and planned to construct the paper mill first and then plant and secure the raw materials after, which a manager at Stora Enso thought was nonsensical. Initially, Sun Paper had even more ambitious plans: it sought to build a processing and export facility across the border in Vietnam, near the port of Dong Ha. However, the Vietnamese government ultimately nixed the project, potentially due to geopolitical concerns about Chinese investments in Vietnam, especially when it was to do with infrastructure.[56] Even so, Sun Paper planned to move forward with its investment in Laos, seeking to plant 100,000 hectares of pulpwood trees, which it estimated would be the amount needed to supply the mill. The Lao government allowed Sun Paper to acquire up to 39,000 hectares as a concession, and it would need to establish the rest through contract farming with smallholding farmers. Yet when a provincial team surveyed the land and realized how little land could feasibly be acquired for the company, the total concession amount was reduced to 7,324 hectares in the contract.

Nonetheless, the Lao government still prioritized the project, and after it was approved, the provincial and district governments put their full weight behind it. In some of the first villages where Sun Paper was allocated land, such as Ban Xaylom (discussed in the introduction), this meant exerting the ideological and coercive power of the state, including the use of military and police escorts as necessary. However, this mode of coercion-backed consent quickly began to fall apart as villagers increasingly asserted claims to the land allocated. The district government then became hesitant to back the company and contest such claims.

District officials attributed Sun Paper's land acquisition problems to a combination of two things: the complicated local claims to land that had not been addressed in the land surveys and Sun Paper's inability to quickly develop the lands allocated to it. Khampha, a senior official in the Xepon DONRE office, explained, "The company was slow to clear [the land] after it was approved . . . which allowed the villagers to produce on that land."[57] In comparison, Ai Soukanh liked to remark how quickly Quasa cleared the land after (and in some cases before) it had been approved—a point of simultaneous admiration and frustration. Khampha explained that this was due to problems with a lack of detailed land surveying and the lengthy period between surveying, approval, and then clearing of land:

> One thing that we've done wrong with the company concerns providing area [*neua thi*] for them. The provision of maps and documents with lease and concession rights to the company is not detailed yet, not clear. For example, in the areas we've allocated to Sun Paper, we've given them a map allocating 4,943 hectares [the amount of land granted to Sun Paper in Xepon]. Yet when going to clear and plant, they cannot follow this because the land survey of the area is not yet detailed or clear enough, and it takes a long time. For example, the day we went to do the survey, there were no villagers there. After the survey, one or two years later, the company got approval and came to clear everything. After they cleared, then villagers cleared land for swidden and gardens [*thang hai thang suan*]. Villagers say that no one came to produce. So the company and villagers are competing.[58]

This was all a wake-up call for Sun Paper, showing the company's representatives that the land that government officials had promised was never just "available" and "empty" on the ground. Any plot of land granted to Sun Paper could be contested, especially if the company delayed getting its trees into the ground.

It is worth noting that there was a range of different dynamics working against Sun Paper's project, particularly timing, location, and lack of experience. First, Sun Paper's project was approved and began to be implemented several years after Quasa's, which, as district officials explained, made it harder to allocate land to them. Both companies were operating after the government had placed a moratorium on land concessions in 2007. However, as central government officials explained, the moratorium only paused the approval of completely new land concessions, while projects that had already been initiated could continue.[59] Regardless of the direct impact of the moratorium, it did reflect a changing political attitude toward land concessions within the government, signaling that the era of granting enormous plots of land and doing whatever it takes to secure them was over.

Additionally, there was a burgeoning sentiment among government officials that there were no longer large tracts of empty land available. As quoted in a Radio Free Asia article on a land concession dispute in Sekong province, a senior official in the Ministry of Planning and Investment stated, "Land management is getting more complicated because most commercial plantations need large plots of land in one piece, but what we have is smaller plots scattered all over. It's becoming harder to get a large piece of land for investors."[60]

While government officials framed the transition over time as a decreasing availability of land, this reflects a changing social and political reality rather than the biophysical restraints of land. Erik, the manager of another pulpwood company operating in this region who was well-informed about Sun Paper's activities as it was a competitor in the area, remarked, "There isn't a lack of land in Laos, there's actually an abundance of underused land. The issue is whether or not farmers want to work with companies and allow them to use that land."[61] Another way of framing this point is that the issue is whether district officials are willing to put in the political work of convincing farmers to let companies use that land and forcing them to do so when they refuse. For the district government, the lack of available land over time meant that there was not enough land that could be easily claimed as state property without village resistance. Their opposition has hardened over time as villagers became increasingly aware of the impacts of land concessions: the economic value of land increased and their prospects of accessing land decreased.

Second, Sun Paper's project was arguably in the wrong location, one dominated by a Vietnamese presence of investors and migrants, and where the Vietnamese government is deeply concerned about the presence of Chinese companies near its border. Stuart-Fox argues that one of Vietnam's main political goals in its alliance with Laos is to ensure the security of the long land border between the two countries. Initially, Sun Paper sought to acquire land in Nong district, which borders Vietnam. Although Sun Paper spent US$16,000 surveying land there, it ultimately ended up with nothing to show for it. Several explanations were offered as to why, such as that the government planned to use the land for a new government office or that the land had been allocated to another plantation company. They all pointed to the government's reluctance to hand over land to the company in the face of competing land uses. However, provincial officials relayed the rumor that Vietnam lobbied Laos to prevent a Chinese company from acquiring land so close to the border. In a similar case, when the Vietnamese public corporation Hoang Anh Gia Lai considered selling half its rubber plantation in Attapeu province to a Chinese company when it was failing, the Vietnamese government became deeply concerned about a Chinese land investment so close to the border.[62]

The third dynamic concerns Sun Paper's lack of experience. Its Lao project was the first investment it had made abroad and its first time planting trees. Monitoring the company's activities closely, Erik was appalled to see that when Sun Paper first got started, it was planting its trees in rows going down the slope of hills rather than across them. This practice would invite erosion, a blunder that his boss would "kill him" for committing. (Erik later recognized that Sun Paper did improve its technique over time.) This also partly explains how differently Sun Paper approached the clearing process compared to Quasa. The former waited for the district government to provide a detailed survey and map of the land allocated to it and, as Ai Soukanh explained, "After the map is made already, they clear [land] following the map, they don't go beyond it."[63] Sun Paper was hampered by its stricter adherence to government rules and regulations, which ultimately hemmed in its project. In stark contrast, Quasa tended to clear land first and get it surveyed and mapped later.

Sun Paper's lack of experience permeated its project. Not only did its representatives have little understanding of the complexity of claims within areas of "available land," but they also had little understanding of how the government operated and thus how best to engage with it. Much of Sun Paper's behavior can be explained by its reluctance to engage in social and environmental abuses, illegal activities, or corruption that could damage its international reputation as a private company, especially as it had just begun to "go out," as the Chinese government had encouraged. Yet the company was also clearly unsure how to relate to the district government and villages. The company's representatives seemed to buy into the idea of the Lao government as a politically centralized state, meaning that once the central government approved a project, then the lower levels would fall in line and implement it on the central government's behalf. For Sun Paper, it was as if all that mattered was the contract it held rather than the multiple layers of human relations that would shape how that contract materialized. This is a reflection of the company's experiences in China, where approvals by higher-level government agencies are followed by lower-level officials.[64] Sun Paper's representatives were less familiar with the fragmentations of state authority in Laos, especially between different levels of government, and thus had a tendency to follow the steps set out for them by government officials, regardless of whether these led to a coherent path of acquiring land.

Erik was convinced that Sun Paper had engaged in corruption but primarily focused on paying off high-level government officials. This proved to be an ineffective approach in a place where power is de facto decentralized and local officials do most of the dirty work of dispossession. Ai Soukanh confirmed that Sun Paper did not provide gifts or perks, as the staff "don't take care of us like Quasa does." In the Lao cultural context, this lack of "care" meant that Sun Paper did not provide the same types of personal benefits as Quasa, whether in the form of padded envelopes, jobs, or meals. He noted that Sun Paper's lack of "care" was also problematic for gaining the support of villagers. He complained that Sun Paper "is stingy, they don't give anything to villagers or district officials beyond what is required by the regulations. They don't buy anything for the village head or other important village officials. For example, if the village head asks the company for a mobile phone to take pictures with, they wouldn't buy it, even if it was only 100,000 kip [US$12.50], but the Vietnamese would." Sun Paper was frank in recognizing this problem and that "the people aren't supportive because they didn't receive any benefits."

Sun Paper also operated at a distance from the district, ignoring the importance of developing close relationships, which caused resentment among district officials, the same officials working with Quasa. While district officials generally appreciated that Sun Paper followed the laws and rules closely, they also expressed how much easier it was to communicate and work with Quasa, including when problems arose. Not only was Sun Paper's distance geographical, considering the location of its office, but its staff also seemed reluctant to work closely with the district to develop their project. Rather than leading the charge in the search for land, they relied upon and waited for the district to find land for them and make deals with villages until they were required to find their own land. Additionally, Sun Paper often seemed meek, quiet, apologetic, and cautious in the way it engaged with the government. This was apparent in my interactions with company representatives—they were available to interview immediately, unlike Quasa staff. In the interview, Sun Paper staff were melancholic and almost embarrassed about their inability to acquire land. With government officials present during the interview, they politely brought up the challenges they had in finding land. Instead of making these complaints directly to the government, calling by phone like Quasa, they wrote an official letter to MONRE at the central level. In other words, they sought to deal with all their problems from the top down.

In the village, when Sun Paper representatives were operating on their own without district officials supporting them to acquire land, they often found it challenging to engage with villagers' claims across the landscape. Ban Salang is the only village where both Quasa and Sun Paper were granted land and thus offers a valuable comparison for their interactions with villagers. The village committee told both companies not to clear any land that villagers were using for production, whether upland swidden or lowland paddy. Quasa seemingly paid no attention to this, clearing land without regard to villagers' concerns, generating conflicts with villagers along the way. Sun Paper, however, was more accommodating. As village leaders recounted in a focus group, "the village head established a village committee to supervise and tell them which lands belong to individuals. We didn't speak strongly, but they would stop when they were about to clear individuals' land. . . . This company did not touch the lands of the people."[65]

Ultimately, Sun Paper ran up against the limits of dispossession due to decreasing support from the district government. As framed by Erik, "The problem that companies like Sun Paper have faced is that they use a top-down concession model. They may be able to force the government to give them some land, but eventually, the model is ineffective because of the strength of Lao farmers. . . . While the district can force villages to give up land, this approach only works for a while." While the district does the dirty work of dispossession, including the resulting conflicts and negative social and environmental change, it receives little financial benefit from the project apart from a per diem paid when officials travel to the field. The inability to locate land for the company may reflect the district dragging its feet, using its own "weapons of the weak" tactics, considering its marginality within the state power structure.[66]

As Sun Paper's relations with the district government and villages deteriorated, villagers' contestations of Sun Paper's claims on their land became more effective. As Sun Paper representatives faced increasing levels of resistance to their project and district officials tired of addressing the conflicts, the district and provincial governments required that Sun Paper negotiate its land deals with communities independently (see further details in chapter 5). If the company's representatives could agree with a community on how much land to lease and at what price, they could present it to the district and province for approval. Yet, without district officials present, the villages Sun Paper representatives approached on their own felt little pressure to concede their lands. Or else they asked for such high leasing rates that the deal became economically unattractive for the company. In other cases, Sun Paper began resorting to contract farming with individual households. The company would provide eucalyptus seedlings, farmers would plant and tend to the trees, and when harvesting, the company would pay farmers a percentage of the value of the wood. But few farmers signed up for these deals, as they questioned whether they would earn a decent income by working with a company they hardly trusted.

♦ ♦ ♦

The state power necessary for investors to dispossess peasants of their land and produce plantation estates is distributed across different levels of government and unevenly accessed by plantation companies. Control over land must be produced in relation to peasant claims and attachments to land to socialize it for capital. This entails developing the capacity to mobilize state powers of dispossession when necessary and create space to operate independently and extralegally with impunity. Investors build such capacity by developing close relationships with the state at multiple scales, especially at localized sites of resource commodity production where the messiness of dispossession takes place. They also do so by developing corrupt patron–client relations with village authorities. This shows their ability to integrate and mobilize relations of sovereignty.

What distinguishes Sun Paper's and Quasa's plantation projects from each other is how they were differentially able to shape the socialization of land in southern Laos. Although they had signed contracts to lease thousands of hectares privately, this land was granted to them by the Lao state. As the state plays a crucial role in socializing land, whether for the peasantry or capital, the companies' relations with the state were an important element affecting the development of their projects. Both companies had to work through the Lao state's complex political and social relations to land, particularly its scalar fragmentations between the central, district, and village loci of power over land. Furthermore, they had to engage with and work through farming communities' social ties and attachments to such lands—either strategically evading or ignoring them or mobilizing state power to dissolve and overpower them.

In many ways, Quasa captured state power over land, using district government power to force communities to concede their land and intimidate villagers who sought to resist. This also enabled the company to operate independently and clear land illegally without negative repercussions when it saw fit. Sun Paper, on the other hand, maintained an awkward engagement with state power relations. New to investing abroad and to Laos, it was unsure of the operation of political power in the Lao government, where to use and develop political capital, and how state control over land operates, particularly the need for it to be produced rather than be available for the taking. Sun Paper ran into numerous problems when acquiring and developing land, especially resistance from Lao communities who purposefully used and occupied lands in areas mapped out for Sun Paper.

Geographical and historical relations affect these differences. The contemporary remnants of relations developed via geopolitical, historical connections between Vietnam, China, and Laos play an important role in influencing the relations that companies can employ in developing their projects—in other words, shaping political landscapes. The country of origin does not determine the trajectory of the project. However, geopolitical relations are an important contextual factor molding the possibilities open to investors. Quasa significantly benefited from the high-level relationships set up by the state-owned VRG and the political discourse—repeated by government officials, company representatives, and villagers alike—that its project is a manifestation of Lao–Vietnamese friendship, building solidarity between the two countries. Sun Paper, in contrast, as a private Chinese company, did not have the same sorts of relationships to call upon or guide its project. Unlike Quasa, Sun Paper's representatives were not familiar with the Lao governmental structure, which is similar to that of Vietnam. Finally, it was operating in a region of Laos that Vietnam culturally and politically dominates, a region crisscrossed by the historic Ho Chi Minh Trail, which Vietnamese troops used to transport goods and weapons during the Indochina Wars.

How Quasa and Sun Paper strategically engaged with the state is as crucial as geopolitical relations. Quasa understood the importance of working with the complex, fragmented, and multiscalar social relations of land. The company's representatives developed close relationships at every administrative level of government, especially district officials and village leaders, thereby solidifying the linkages between various elements of an otherwise fragmented state to shore up the state's—and thus the company's—effective control over land. They established these relations with open-ended and extensive corruption and close working and personal relations with government officials. They set up a cooperative relationship in which the project's development was in the material and financial interests of both the company and the government. Unlike Sun Paper's representatives, they understood that their concession contract, survey maps, or even concession plot certificates did not guarantee access and control over land, which instead had to be produced through a combination of consent, coercion, and repression. Once these relations were established, Quasa representatives frequently operated independently and without regard to legal limits on their project, assured that they would not be penalized because of the favors that the district owed them and the political cover the Lao–Vietnamese friendship provided for them.

Sun Paper representatives, in contrast, assumed that centralized state control over land was a given, that the land they were awarded in their contract and survey maps was their property, which they had the right to use when and how they pleased. From their experiences in China, high-level projects should be implemented by the government in a centralized and top-down manner. Additionally, they were unaware of the complex social relations of the land that they had been granted, particularly peasant claims to it. They failed to recognize that despite the formal centralization of power over land in the socialist Lao PDR, district officials, village leaders, and peasant farming households govern rural lands and forests with a degree of de facto autonomy from upper levels of government that surprised Sun Paper. This included the importance of keeping the district on its side in land conflicts with villagers. In addition, Sun Paper's concession contract did not guarantee its control over land. While support from the central government afforded the company strong district-level backing at first, following orders passed down to it from above, district efforts to acquire land for Sun Paper tapered off in the face of village resistance and the company's hesitancy to develop its plantations immediately after land was allocated to it. This was compounded by the company's reluctance to "take care" of district officials and village leaders and the distance that it kept in communications with the district and villages.

How plantation companies interacted with and sought to alter the socialization of land via a fragmented Lao state to gain access to land and territory is conditioned by the always present possibility of resistance to their projects. It also structures the opportunities for that resistance to emerge effectively. While the practices and strategies of peasant resistance are the focus of later chapters, this chapter has demonstrated how they are affected by the political relations between plantation companies and the Lao state over land. When companies like Quasa establish these solid relations, the Lao government collectively acts on the plantation company's behalf to forcibly expropriate village agriculture and forestry lands with little meaningful economic development provided for the communities in return. When relations between companies and various administrative levels of the state break down, Lao peasants can exploit these fissures to amplify their claims to land. As Sun Paper representatives' relationships with district officials and village heads deteriorated in the early stages of the project, a variety of opportunities for resisting or outright refusing Sun Paper's attempts to acquire land emerged. Without the political support of the district government, Sun Paper no longer benefited from access to the authority necessary for separating the links between villagers and their agriculture and forest lands. As a result, resistance efforts could be aligned with the local state against the plantation company, which the following chapters explore in greater depth. In a context of competitive acquisition of land, a company's "success" is matched by destructive land dispossession for the peasantry, while a company's relative "failure" correlates with villagers' abilities to make effective land claims.

Chapter 2

State Land?

In 2012, the Phin district government allocated to Sun Paper a 423-hectare plot of land that lay within the boundaries of Ban Saphang, a long-established lowland Brou village. DONRE, the agency responsible for allocating land, aimed to transfer an area of dry dipterocarp forest (*pa khok*) that the Ministry of Agriculture and Forestry had classified as "degraded" and in need of revitalization via tree plantation investments. The targeted lands had not been officially zoned, registered, or titled. They appeared to DONRE and Sun Paper to be unused by villagers for agricultural production and thus available for an industrial monoculture plantation. Such lands met all the conditions for what the government considers "state land" and were ripe for a concession to plantation investors. Furthermore, DONRE staff asserted that Saphang villagers had provided their consent to accompanying district officials and company representatives to survey land for the plantation, identifying which lands belonged to villagers and which were open for plantation development.

Sun Paper's bulldozer operators were thus surprised when villagers confronted them as they began to clear trees and brush, demanding that they stop immediately. Villagers then petitioned the district government to halt the company's activities. When the district and then provincial governments failed to act, villagers lodged a grievance with the National Assembly, which prompted a visit from assembly members but not a resolution to the conflict. Villagers occupied their fields day in and day out, putting their bodies and farm machinery in the path of the bulldozers. A village police officer (an official position within the hierarchy of the Ministry of Public Security) even violently threatened company staff, recalling, "We've said everything to the company, so much that I can't remember anymore. We protected the land. We said that if you [the company] do that [clear our land], we will shoot you. So they marked off our land where I told them, otherwise they would have cleared everything. I really carried my gun to show them." The conflict came to a head when a company bulldozer crashed into a villager's hand tractor (*lot thai na*), which he had placed in front of his paddy land to protect it. Ultimately, the district government viewed the conflict as intractable and suggested Sun Paper move on to other areas to secure land, reflecting the diminishing political support the district government afforded to the company. Sun Paper was left with only about half the amount of land granted to it within the village boundaries.

This example is representative of how Sun Paper misunderstood the meaning and operation of property in Laos. As demonstrated in chapter 1, the company's representatives believed the Lao government's assurances that there were large swaths of empty, fertile state land that, once granted to them in the form of a concession, would become their property, ready to be cleared and planted whenever convenient for them. As such lands had not been formally registered to Lao villagers, Sun Paper's representatives were under the impression that the company maintained the only legitimate state-backed property claims to the concession territory. Furthermore, Sun Paper failed to recognize that the "state land" granted to it for fifty years did not already exist in practice, but instead had to be produced and negotiated vis-à-vis other land claimants. The land had to be socialized for them, for capital. Identifying the precise location of state land that can be allocated to investors, though, is a tricky issue, for both legal and spatial reasons.

It is commonly understood that the socialist state owns the nation's lands. However, ownership of land in Laos, both in law and in practice, is a much more complex affair among the various factions and administrative levels of the Lao state and its citizens. As a prominent official within the Ministry of Planning and Investment explained, "We haven't defined state land. There is still confusion as to which land is state land, which is village land."[1] With the liberalization of property ownership since the 1990s, state land must be defined in relation to other property categories and the claims of a wide range of people and communities. In other words, the boundaries between state, village, and private land are often murky, as has been the case across liberalizing socialist and post-socialist regimes.[2] They remain so until they are spatially delineated via acts of state territorialization to develop resource extraction and commodity production projects (among a variety of other state territorialization projects such as forest conservation, infrastructure development, and resettlement). As discussed in chapter 1, such land is anything but absent of social and legal claims, occupations, and uses, and thus ready for investment.

Instead, the lack of land formalization across the terrain of eastern Savannakhet and much of the rest of Laos renders it open for contestation, resistance, and conflict prior to its production as state land allocated for capital.

The problem of land grabbing in Laos, and throughout the Global South, is often attributed to a lack of private property in rural areas. An underlying narrative is that land and resource investors can engage in rapid, opaque, coercive, and unjust acts of appropriation, facilitated by socialist and other illiberal forms of the postcolonial state because rural people lack formal property rights and thus cannot protect their assets from expropriation.[3] As a consequence, the World Bank has recommended in a prominent report on land grabbing, or what they term "rising global interest in farmland," that "existing rights to land and associated natural resources are recognized and ideally demarcated to allow users to defend them against challenges and engage in voluntary transfers."[4] Land titling and land-use planning programs have become popular among bilateral donors, multilateral development agencies, and INGOs in countries like Laos. Such land tenure and property formalization exercises supposedly empower peasants to protect their lands from expropriation or gain financial compensation when they cannot.

Conversely, resource investors like Quasa and Sun Paper assume that state control over property guarantees their access to land. There is some truth to these perspectives. The Lao state does have significant power over land compared to rural communities, especially when it comes to resource investments. State control over rural land is an ongoing project of territorialization, expanding the state's spatial reach over rural landscapes vis-à-vis other actors. However, the lack of preexisting formal property relations means that claims to land by the state, investors, and villagers are all possible. The distinctive lines of registered property are yet to be drawn, and thus the process of mapping them out is one of contention. As Sun Paper managers have come to begrudgingly accept, Lao peasants' lack of formal documented claims to land does not mean that their claims can be ignored: "Villagers say 'this land is mine,' but they don't have a land title or a certificate of paid taxes. Yet we can't clear the land, all the same, so we still have a problem."[5]

While the previous chapter focused on how the embeddedness of plantation companies within a fragmented state shaped their ability to access land, this chapter highlights how the production of state property is a key site of contestation over land targeted for plantation expansion. Negotiations over the construction of property in advance of or during the implementation of state land concessions make the difference between dispossession and protection of peasant fields and forests. In other words, the operations of dynamic property regimes are instrumental in the socialization of land for the peasantry or for capital. The latter occurs when it is first transformed into "state land," a category of land that is still relatively new to Laos in practice and is essential for the creation of long-term land concessions to foreign corporations. Property—and its accompanying set of social relations—does not just exist out in the world but must be produced, carved out of territories, and maintained over time.[6] State land cannot simply be assumed to be the dominant form of property in the countryside in the absence of regularized, statutory property rights. Instead, it becomes one of several potential categories of land that can be produced along with customary regimes of village land use, management, and ownership.

State property is an essential category for socializing land in that it can be used for different ends—leased to foreign capital as concessions or allocated for village and household use via land-use zoning maps and certificates or even land titles. Furthermore, the act of producing such state property, part of a broader project of state territorialization, can be a challenging task. The process of manifesting new forms of property becomes an important site of contestation, shaping the boundaries and geographies of agro-industrial plantations vis-à-vis village and household territories of land use and occupation. Ambiguities of landownership can be taken advantage of by the state and resource investors, but also by Lao villagers. State authorities and plantation company staff can easily ignore local land uses that have not been mapped, surveyed, and cataloged. Yet, when villagers claim that their lands—including those reserved for future use—have been cleared or threatened by the plantation project, government and company staff are heavily reliant on local knowledge of customary property relations in the absence of formal land-use and ownership records. Without a codified property regime in place, access to and control over land and resources become dictated more by relations of power and authority than by law, including customary histories of land use and management, state ideologies of a national landowning community, and state recognition of village authority.

An Open Terrain of Contestation

Before rubber and pulpwood plantations were established in the late 2000s via state land concessions, the rural lands of eastern Savannakhet had yet to be officially registered as formal property for the most part, despite land-use planning and land titling programs in other parts of the country. In other words, these rural lands were beyond the reach of some of the most important formal projects of state territorialization. Since the pronouncement of the NEMM in 1986, which put the country on a path of market liberalization, significant legal reforms have been pursued that have facilitated the creation of private property systems.[7] In the late 1990s and early 2000s, the World Bank developed a land titling project with the Lao government. Ultimately, though, it only covered urban and peri-urban areas and some paddy areas in the large plains of the countryside, altogether avoiding the uplands that constitute most of the country's land area. In upland areas, many international development organizations worked with the Lao government on land-use planning exercises to zone out agricultural and forest areas and allocate land to households. The government would provide them with temporary land-use certificates to be converted into land titles later. Largely dependent on international donor funding, such exercises were conducted on an ad hoc basis according to the locations of development projects, which happened not to include significant areas of eastern Savannakhet, especially outside the towns and immediately surrounding paddy areas.[8]

According to the 2003 Land Law and related regulations on land registration, land-use plans, certificates, and eventually titles should have been produced in this region via land surveying, a review of historical land claims and inheritance, and adjudication of disputes. Instead, it occurred through a forceful carving out of village territories as "state land" to be immediately transferred to companies as long-term concessions. Government officials proclaimed that "unused" areas within village boundaries (that is, land not used by individual households) suddenly belonged to the state. Soon after, the companies were informed where such lands were approximately located. They arrived with bulldozers to begin clearing land, and eventually these new properties took shape in the form of neat rows of monoculture rubber, eucalyptus, and acacia trees divided into grids by straight roads. This can be seen clearly in the aerial imagery in figure 2.1, which shows the planned grid of the plantation abutting the layered, overlapping mosaic landscape of village residential, agricultural, and forest lands.

Some of these issues were supposed to be rectified by a land mapping program conducted by MONRE in 2013. However, this activity took place after most of the plantations were already established. Further, the program was carried out so quickly, and with so little input from

Figure 2.1. Aerial imagery of Quasa's young rubber plantations, next to a village residential, agricultural, and forested landscape. Source: National Geographic Department, Prime Minister's Office, Lao PDR. Reproduced with permission.

villagers, that they were unaware it had even occurred. Nor did they see the final maps produced, which sat untouched in a district government office. The state had demarcated only the borders between villages, but even these were negotiated among villages based on long-standing uses and claims to land. Yet a lack of formal property did not mean that the lands within village boundaries were a blank canvas to be painted with industrial tree plantations, as Sun Paper assumed. Instead, it operated as a space of negotiation, where various claims among villagers, state agents, and company representatives concerning how land should be used played out.

That claims over land and space extend far beyond the realm of formal statutory property in the form of land-use certificates and titles reflects how property is a complex social relation.[9] Property is shaped by a wide variety of historically rooted and dynamic power relations among key societal actors, which are not only concerned with the law. However, land formalization programs in the Global South are driven by a much more simplistic version of property promoted by the World Bank and other bilateral donors. Such conceptions are built on the ideas of the influential development economist Hernando de Soto, who argues that underdevelopment and failures of capitalism outside the West occur because the assets of the poor are not legibly represented with titles and deeds. They cannot therefore be leveraged as collateral to attract credit and be used as capital.[10] For de Soto, property, as a title, can release the innate capital-generating potential of the developing world's assets to generate wealth for the poor. It is, in short, a "magic bullet" for poverty eradication.

One of the principal problems with this line of argumentation is its fetishization of the title. The World Bank, its client states, and a range of other development organizations have placed an immense amount of faith in the title to generate wealth and protect the assets of the poor from unjust expropriation. This perspective fails to see that secure access to land is about much more than a formalized title. It has long been recognized that de facto land tenure security can exist outside land regularization because of the dense social ties among members of a land-using community.[11] As a social relationship, property mediates relations between people with respect to the biophysical, material world—in this case, the agricultural and forest lands in southern Laos. The ability to gain, maintain, and use property rights depends on a constellation of social relations that lie outside the domain of a land title, such as the broader legal system and environment, cultural practices of land use, and dynamics of power and patronage between people and the state, among many others. Understanding how people assert and maintain control over their assets requires a distinction between *property* and *access*. While property is typically understood as a "bundle of rights" or "the *right* to benefit from things," access can be understood as "the *ability* to benefit from things" or a "bundle of powers."[12] Property is concerned with socially and legally recognized rights that enable people to benefit from land, forests, and housing structures, but access focuses on whether they have the power to do so. In other words, access relates to a much broader set of social relationships that shape whether people benefit from land and resources, regardless of whether their rights to do so are socially and legally recognized.

In distinguishing between property and access and seeing how they relate to each other, and in the absence of formal property to support rural Laotians' claims to land, there are many other relations that comprise their property and access to land and resources. What they lack in legal rights, they maintain in rights that are de facto socially recognized within and among communities and by the local government. Furthermore, there are many other relations that constitute their ability or power to use, manage, and occupy rural lands and resources. For Thomas Sikor and Christian Lund, questions of property and access are intimately bound up with questions of power and authority.[13] Access claims to land

and natural resources are secured when recognized as legitimate by a politico-legal institution. The process of recognizing such claims as property works to imbue these institutions with a recognition of their authority. However, in the absence of formalized claims to land and resources recognized by the authorities, as in the case of land claims in many parts of rural Laos, access claims become subject to a broader set of power relations with varying degrees of competing legitimacy. Such claims lack the territorial authority of property formally recognized and enforced by multiple administrative levels of the state.

In the context of southern Laos, the idea that there exists state land that can be transferred to foreign investors is challenged in ways similar to claims by peasants that they have customary rights to certain agricultural and forest lands. There is a lack of formally established property legitimized by politico-legal authority in both cases. The attempt to produce state land as a new form of property in such areas requires that the land be carved out of the existing landscape by emphasizing centralized state management of land. As a result, the state must seek to create these new forms of property, not by relying entirely on legitimized state authority but by enacting other forms of state power. These range from coercive threats to development promises to heavy-handed negotiations with villagers, or the "power of informality."[14] Similarly, customary claims to land made by villagers are outside any sort of formal property system and thus are not recognized as legitimate by any form of authority. Their claims to land access must be protected by engaging in other mechanisms of power, such as mobilizing state ideologies of land to the tiller and emphasizing their credentials as veterans and model citizens. Most important for this discussion, villagers contest the boundaries of plantation property through their deep knowledge of their customary systems of land uses and tenure arrangements, which government officials know little of. Furthermore, they materially challenge the establishment of new property lines by bulldozers with signs, bodies, and guns, as in the case of Ban Saphang described earlier.

These are precisely the social and power relations with which Quasa and Sun Paper had to contend. The central government approved their plantation projects, and initial maps of the projects were drawn out before a detailed survey of village land was conducted. These projects were created under the assumption that state land could be carved out of rural territories based on abstract maps without consulting people on the ground. Yet this all changed when the project moved down to the district level. Company managers quickly learned that maps drawn for them by the central government in their concession contracts did not correspond with an area of state land that already existed. Such maps were drawn without any survey at the local level of the land-use patterns and customary ownership claims of local populations. In securing such land for the plantations, however, the district government and the company had to negotiate these uses and claims.

Producing "State Land"

Legally, the final product of conceding "state land" to Quasa and Sun Paper was creating a "state land-use certificate" (figure 2.2). After a host of other legal documentation that comprises state land concession projects—memorandums of understanding, economic and technical feasibility studies, environmental and social impact assessments, and concession contracts, among others—the concession certificate legally guarantees a company's right to use a specific plot of land. The document notes the village where the plot is located, the size of the plot, and its precise location, marked by numbered points linked to GPS coordinates listed on the back of the document. The authenticity of the documents is marked by a legal code number in the upper right-hand corner, and the official red stamps and signatures of the director of the Provincial Department of Natural Resources and Environment (PONRE) and the head of the land allocation and development division. Each certificate is only for a specific plot of land as part of the larger concession area. As a result, each company has hundreds of these certificates, the original copies of which are kept in PONRE's office in the provincial capital. Although these certificates are not typically available to the public, through my work with and the approval of MONRE and the relationships I cultivated with provincial and district officials over time, I was permitted to take pictures of all the certificates available for Phin and Xepon districts.

To someone unfamiliar with the process by which they were created, the certificates may appear as a clear, professional bureaucratic account of the area of state land awarded to plantation companies as concessions. Not only do they account for the precise location of a state land concession plot, but they also show how it is related to other surrounding land uses.[15] Yet this document belies a complex relation of "state land" and its messy production by state agents, company staff, and villagers. A closer examination of how such land-use certificates were produced shows that the category of "state land" is not so straightforward.

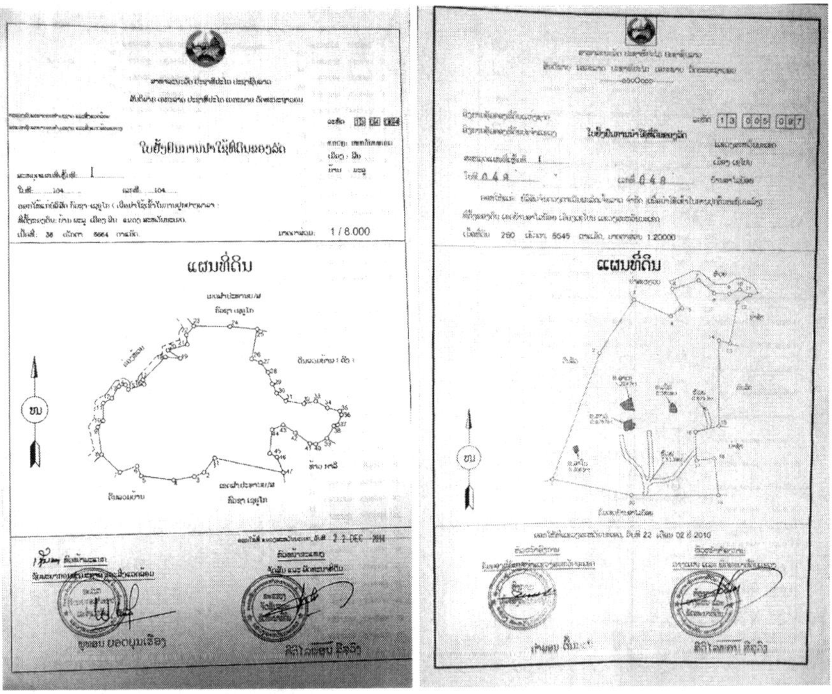

Figure 2.2. State land concession certificates awarded to Quasa and Sun Paper. Photograph by Miles Kenney-Lazar.

In each document, various land uses, and ownership by non-state landowners, are identified in adjacent areas.

In the Quasa certificate (on the left in figure 2.2), apart from other connected concession areas to the north, the south, and a stream to the northwest, there is a label indicating collective village land to the southwest and the northeast, and a villager's private land to the southeast. In the Sun Paper certificate (on the right in figure 2.2), the landscape is more detailed and complex, including areas within the polygon that have been excised. This difference reflects the degrees to which Quasa can more easily produce unobstructed plantation territories than Sun Paper, as discussed in chapter 1. Surrounding the Sun Paper concession area are other plots of state land, a conservation forest, village land, and cemetery forest areas. Within the concession plot are areas demarcated as streams; companies are legally prevented from clearing land within fifty meters of streams. There are also individual plots of households, ranging in size from 0.3 to 1.2 hectares. Thus, these maps already hint at how state land is situated within a complex landscape of other forms of preexisting relations to land, out of which state land must be carved and within which it must be situated. These include struggles to define areas as state land and those that would remain under village or household control.

The complexity of land relations that preexisted the production of state land concessions and that continue to persist alongside them indicates that the production of state land is a messy and fraught process, and therefore one that is open to contestation. State land concession certificates create the impression that a detailed survey has been conducted to distinguish between state and non-state land uses before plantations are established. The company can then use these to precisely clear the land that has been rightfully allocated to it without infringing upon village land uses. However, this is typically not the order in which such events occur. Instead, the processes of land granting, allocation, consultation with villagers, mapping, and clearing land are imbricated, occurring simultaneously or even in reverse order. In many cases, the land concession certificates are created after the land has already been cleared and trees have been planted. Rather than representing a careful prearranged discussion with villagers over land use and ownership that outlines the boundaries between land suitable or not for the concession, such maps reflect the struggles and contestations over land that occurred beforehand.

During one of my earliest visits to the field, a government research assistant from MONRE and I had planned on only conducting interviews with district officials and company representatives, but we encountered a team of PONRE land surveyors and took the chance to join their field trip. Although they were surveying land for Quasa's concession to produce the types of concession certificate maps discussed earlier, the trees had been planted more than seven years previously. Instead of planning out the plantation areas, they were solidifying the legal authority of Quasa's claims to the land. It became apparent how important this was when we reached the site of contention—Ban Kaengchee had a long-standing grievance that the company had cleared beyond the area allocated to it, up to the borders of and including village rice fields. Because the villagers had brought up these complaints to the district government time and again, the government decided to conduct a more detailed survey to outline the current boundary between the plantation and household lands (see figure 2.3). This allowed the district government to establish it as a state concession area by creating a formal certificate endorsed by the village chief.

Figure 2.3. Government officials, company representatives, and village authorities discuss and survey (top) the boundary between the plantation and villagers' land (bottom). Photographs by Miles Kenney-Lazar.

Standing at the site of contention among district and provincial officials, the village chief, and Quasa staff, our presence exacerbated an already tense political situation. We had traveled there with a district land official who oversaw land issues in this zone. When we encountered several employees of Quasa at the field site, we had no interaction with them, despite occasionally stealing glances at one another. I was hesitant to ask the village chief any questions in such a politically charged situation. As I discussed this with the accompanying MONRE official, he suddenly started asking the village chief what he thought of the plantation. Not surprisingly, the conversation quickly became awkward and the village chief looked unsure of what to do. Not only was he surrounded by district and company staff, but he had also been paid a daily stipend of 50,000 kip (about US$6.25) to participate. At first, he reflected on how all the freshwater fish and crabs had disappeared after the plantation was established. Then, upon wondering how freely he should speak, he asked a district official who was listening in whether it would be a problem to talk to us, and he was assured it would not. He then said he was happy with the project and that his village had not experienced any problems with the company, contrary to the conflict that had brought us all together at this site in the first place.

On a later field trip, I held a focus group discussion in Ban Kaengchee, attended by village authorities without any government officials present. This discussion was conducted in the Brou language with the help of a Brou research assistant who had been working with an INGO on land issues and community development in Ban Kaengchee for several years. A different story emerged from the village chief and his compatriots there, compared to what the chief had said at the land survey site. A group of villagers said that although they had agreed to concede 250 hectares of village land, they had only done so under two conditions. First, the company must pay for the extension of electric lines to the village and construct a new road and a bridge. Second, the company must not clear any private agricultural lands nor bulldoze within thirty meters of such lands or streams. Quasa violated both conditions and acquired far more land than most of the village agreed upon, up to 1,000 hectares according to what district officials told villagers. They felt deceived, more so by the local government than by Quasa, reflecting how "the Vietnamese [Quasa] aren't from here, so we can't blame them too much, but our district officials were the ones that told them to do this, they're the ones that authorized this."

The process of allocating land in Ban Kaengchee mirrored events in other villages slated for the Quasa project. After an agreement had been met for the village to give land to the company, the discussion turned to how much land and where it would be located. However, location was always discussed in vague and general terms rather than in the precise coordinates of the concession certificates produced years later. For example, the village committee in Ban Sokleek acquiesced, after much agitation, to concede a small portion of village land to the company, consenting to the concession of 50 hectares on "three hills" near the southern border of the village. Meanwhile, Ban Phoulao authorities explained that they eventually acquiesced to the concession of 492 hectares "over there," pointing to the western portion of the village territory during an interview. In these cases and more, villagers never saw maps of the planned or allocated areas to the companies, nor did they participate in any land surveys. They simply agreed, under heavy coercion, to concede a vaguely defined portion of village land, with the assurance that their agricultural fields would not be cleared. Their involvement in shaping the specific boundaries of the plantation plots came later when they saw that this arrangement had been violated and their fields were being encroached upon.

Even though most villages had only a vague understanding of where the plantation would be developed prior to the clearance of land, maps of land allocated to the company did exist before consultations were held with the village. The Quasa and Sun Paper plantation projects were mapped by consulting preexisting land-use maps and conducting rough land surveys. A provincial official referred to this as a "5 percent survey" because such surveys only capture about 5 percent of the relevant information on the ground regarding land use and ownership—the other 95 percent is established later when land is being cleared and trees are being planted. The focus of these surveys is finding land that is suitable for the company. First, the government and the company single out a generally suitable location: an area with fertile land not too far from the road but without a heavy population density, typically in impoverished upland areas inhabited by ethnic minority groups. Then officials from the Ministry of Agriculture and Forestry identify different types of land use on the ground and begin to cut out any areas of high-value or conservation forest and agricultural fields, both paddy and swidden. They assess the quality of the forest and the value of the trees and aim to pinpoint "degraded" lands, which are often swidden fallow lands, secondary forests, or other forest areas with low density, as is typical for plantation development in Laos.[16] Through this process, in negotiation with villagers and company staff, the government begins to carve out spaces on the map and on the ground that can eventually be produced as "state land." However, producing state land is further exacerbated by questions over the complex and blurry distinctions between the state and village.

The Conundrum of State–Village Land

"The people own the land, the state manages it" (*paxaxon pen chao, lat khoum khong* in Lao) was a common refrain among many villagers. It was raised in the context of discussions concerning how land was being allocated to agro-industrial plantation projects, specifically whether it was villagers' or state land being granted. District government officials even repeated it from time to time. Media reports typically assert that all the land in Laos belongs to the socialist state and thus can be sold at will to foreign investors, and that the state only allows villagers to temporarily use the land until the government takes back this right.[17] Yet this phrase indicates a much more complex relationship of control and ownership at play over land.

The complex process of producing "state land" demonstrates its inherent openness as a legal category. The 2003 Land Law is the most conservative legal definition of the relationship between the government, Lao citizens, and land. Even so, it states, "Land of the Lao PDR is under the ownership of the national community as prescribed in Article 17 of the Constitution in which the State is charged with the centralized and uniform management [of land] throughout the country and with the allocation [of land] to individuals, families and economic organisations for use, lease or concession."[18] It does not state that the government owns the country's land, but only that it manages it on behalf of the "national community," or the people, who are the actual owners. And in the referenced Article 17 of the Constitution, a legal document that overrides all others, citizens are afforded even greater land rights: "The State protects the property rights (such as the rights of possession, use, usufruct and disposition) and the inheritance rights of organisations and individuals. Land is a national heritage, and the State ensures the rights to use, transfer and inherit in accordance with the laws."[19] The state does not hold exclusive rights to all land throughout the country and has the mandate to protect the property of its citizens.

Legal property relations in Laos were unclear for twelve years after the founding of the Lao PDR.[20] As the government was planning a collectivization project after the revolution, they may not have wanted peasants to think that their land would be confiscated. Only in 1988 did Kaysone Phomvihane, the former president of Laos, give a clear indication of the legal status of land: "Under our new system, the entire land is the common property of the entire society with the state as the representative. . . . The state recognizes the legal rights of farmers' families to use the land they possess for cultivation purposes."[21] This sentiment set the stage for how the 1991 constitution and later land laws would frame state land and private property. It also perfectly captures the idea of socialized land, as the land is protected as a shared resource, but control over it rests with the state, which can manipulate what it is used for or how common interest is defined.

In addition to property law, the village is afforded a significant amount of authority to manage its affairs, as prescribed by the 2003 Law on Local Administration (discussed in greater depth in chapter 5). Perhaps more importantly, however, villages are not just communities or groups of people living together, sharing a common area—they are the lowest administrative level of the Lao government. Many villages throughout the country have been resettled, voluntarily or coercively, and smaller villages of different ethnicities have been combined. The village in Laos is a modern construct and an important component of the state apparatus. Almost every element of the Lao government and the party reaches down to the village level. The village is not only run by a democratically elected village head and the head's deputy, who both receive a small government salary; village governance also includes a committee comprising a police officer, land officer, forester, women's union leader, and party secretary. The village, in all its heterogeneity and contradictions, does not exist outside of or in opposition to the government but is one of its crucially important components. Therefore, distinctions concerning state versus village land do not concern a binary between separate entities but an internal relationship within the Lao state between different levels of authority and questions concerning which has the right to make certain decisions regarding land use. While the village lies at the bottom of the government's formal hierarchy of power, which starts from the top with the central government, it maintains a certain degree of its decision-making rights. In other words, although the district receives orders from above, it can also contest them when they do not match their interests in land and resource use and livelihood development strategies.

De facto use of land demonstrates even further the ambiguities of state–village landownership. In the absence of land titling, land-use zoning programs, and land concessions, villagers are left to their own devices to manage their lands according to customary practices. For example, despite government policies to stabilize and eventually eradicate swidden cultivation throughout the country, villagers of eastern Savannakhet have primarily practiced swidden cultivation without interference from the government, depending on the amount of land available within their village borders. Brou peoples have been practicing swidden cultivation for centuries and have only adopted paddy cultivation in the last several decades. Swidden-cultivating communities have complex forms of customary land management and tenure. Although swiddeners historically left land fallow for many years, they remembered which lands had previously been cultivated and had systems for determining when the time was right to cultivate them again. In some parts of the country, the government has sought to take a more active approach toward reducing swidden cultivation through land-use planning programs. Still, villagers often ignore or intentionally misunderstand these plans so that they can continue their agricultural practices, a classic example of everyday resistance commonly seen throughout Southeast Asia.[22]

In recounting how the investment projects were presented to them, villagers demonstrated the way their discussions and negotiations with district officials oscillated between recognition of village authority and an attempt to override such authority with centralized, top-down state power. In some instances, district officials respected village rights to decide whether to allocate land, how much to give, where it would be located, and what they would get in return, thus recognizing village authority over its territory. In others, this seemed to be a ruse intended to get villagers to concede land willingly. When they refused, government officials demanded that the land be transferred to the company because upper levels of government had already approved it and the land belonged to the state, thus leaving villagers without any choice.

Under extreme pressure, most residents of Ban Phoulao agreed to allow Quasa to develop 492 hectares of village land in exchange for the extension of electric lines to the village and yearly maintenance of the dirt road to the village. Not surprisingly, however, Quasa failed to deliver on its construction promises, even after clearing and planting on all the lands. When the company later requested another plot of land to expand the plantation, the village immediately refused without conditions, effectively ending plantation expansion within their village territory. A group of Phoulao villagers spoke during a focus group about the complex, shared relationship over land between villages and the Lao government in a nuanced way that policy discussions on land tenure and ownership in Laos rarely evoke. They noted, "It's village land; it also belongs to the state. But we live here, we protect it. We are the owners," reflecting the distinction between the state as manager of the land and the people as owners. The role of Phoulao villagers in this relationship had been violated by the government's aggressive claims to state land within the village territory.

Several Kaengchee villagers expressed a similar sentiment during a focus group meeting, reflecting on their disappointment that their authority over their village territory had been betrayed by the government, who were in cahoots with the company: "We didn't sell the land, we divided it [*paeng*] to the state to develop, but we don't see any development. If you're going to follow principles, the state is the manager, but the villagers are the owners. The state gave [*mop*] the land to the villagers, so why is it acting like this?" Villagers recognized the complexities and ambiguities that comprise relationships of property in Laos. During a focus group in Ban Salang, village leaders expressed their deep frustration with how their village's land claims were completely disregarded by government officials, who assumed the land belonged to the state:

> When they started clearing land, I asked them how much of the village area they would preserve. The provincial official responded, "*Aow!* This is state land. . . ." He responded this way, it wasn't nice. I asked "Oh! You say that it's state land? If it's state land, why did the state have to come to promote this work? Why doesn't the state clear it immediately? So why do you say that it's state land? How many people does the state have? . . . The village covers the village, the district covers the district, the province covers the province [*ban koum ban, meuang koum meuang, khwaeng koum khwaeng*]. So how does this work? . . . Who is the state?" . . . I know that the documents that come from the central level are good [*khak*] but individuals use the land. It doesn't fit the government's plan. This is not the way to help!

While these comments are wide-ranging, they demonstrate how much the village resents government officials' lack of respect for their role in owning and managing land, even if as part of a co-owning relationship with the state. The leader poignantly captures how confusion regarding the precise relationship between the village and other levels of government in managing land has undermined their land claims and led to expropriation.

Tenure without Title

Dominant development discourses on property, land formalization, and land tenure contend that the loss of village land to plantation investments results from a lack of formal property throughout the area that villagers can use to support their land claims.[23] Yet, as the previous discussion shows, a lack of property does not mean a lack of attention to land claims or an ability to secure some form of land tenure. Surveys of land suitability for Quasa's plantations in the Ban Kaengchee area specifically avoided areas of paddy land, for example. Government officials promised that the company would not clear up to the edge of individual agricultural lands, even if the company did not follow these intentions. In the absence of formal property, government officials and even company staff had to pay attention to how property solely comprises social relationships in regard to land, space, and resources that are not mediated by the law. In other words, they had to pay attention to customary landownership, which took on a remarkable degree of power in the absence of formal property.

Both company staff and government officials found the lack of systematic, formal property ownership a confounding problem. This was reflective of James Scott's argument that the state seeks to make resources and territories legible to be more easily taxed, governed, and even appropriated.[24] A lack of zoning or cadastral maps made it difficult for the state and the companies to determine which lands might be available for acquisition and which lands were under use or management by villagers. While some plots of land, like paddy fields, are clearly under production and ownership, other types, such as forest land reserved for future agricultural cultivation, are much less noticeable. In other words, land is oftentimes not legible to the state, a necessary step for creating state property on behalf of resource capitalists. Sun Paper representatives found the lack of formalized property particularly bedeviling in their search for land. They were under the impression that state land had already been reserved for the company as a type of formal property. Yet every time a plot of land was allocated to them by the district, it led to conflicts over which areas were already under use or reserved for future use by villages, none of which were based on any sort of land documentation. Expressing their frustration, they frankly confessed, "Ultimately, we can't find land, we can't get land. We've summarized the reasons why. The first is that the people's land use is not clear. The second is that the people don't support us because they don't receive benefits."

Discussions with Phin district officials showed that they were experiencing many of the same difficulties. When I asked one official about the challenges of finding land for the company, he responded, "Oh, it's very difficult. It's a hardship because we haven't allocated land systematically. . . . Any land could be villagers' land." It was a common sentiment among government officials and company staff that there was something nefarious about these undocumented claims to land. A provincial official who was a liaison for me in Savannakhet liked to explain the complexities of land claims and allocation to me in illuminating ways, in terms of both how such processes work and a governmental perspective on villagers' actions. In an interview with Khampha from the Xepon DONRE office, this provincial official jumped in to explain that "when the company comes, villagers claim they will use the land that they haven't used for many years, it's not right." This was in response to a comment from the district official: "If we listen to the voice of the people [*siang paxaxon*], then companies cannot get land and implement their projects." In a later one-on-one encounter, the provincial official made a remark that reflected false and harmful stereotypes of ethnic minorities as dishonest and unreliable. He claimed that "ethnic minorities have an attitude of frequently changing their decisions. They might agree to give land to the project in the morning but then refuse to give it in the evening," though he did admit that they might agree at first out of fear. Nonetheless, for government officials, a lack of formal property lent a certain degree of power to villagers to call the shots over who owned and used what land, constraining where the plantation could be located.

Ban Saphang villagers' attempts to maintain control over their land, introduced in the opening passages of this chapter, matched district government officials' fears that villagers held too much power over customary claims of landownership in the absence of formal property. According to district officials and the Sun Paper manager, villagers had fully agreed to concede 423 hectares for the project and had even participated in the survey of village land to identify unused areas that could be conceded to the company. To prove this to me, on a computer in the DONRE office they showed me a land survey drawing they had created in a cracked version of the design program AutoCAD (figure 2.4). This was an initial step in the creation of a state land-use certificate, in this case not yet produced even though Sun Paper had already planted eucalyptus and acacia trees on part of the land allocated. The drawing shows a polygon of state land in the middle, oddly shaped because it was the land that remained from the earlier, imprecise "5 percent survey" once villagers' plots of land had been excised from it. The area of state land was cut into by villagers' household agricultural plots, the identification of their names demonstrating that a detailed survey of local-level land use and ownership information had been carried out.

As a consequence, when the majority of Saphang villagers objected to and sought to prevent Sun Paper's clearance of their lands, district officials were annoyed and claimed that villagers had gone back on their word. These villagers, however, felt that they were the ones who had been wronged and tricked. They conceded that they had participated in the land survey, but that they had not understood its purpose, perhaps reflective of how villagers often do not conceptualize their land or property in such an abstract Cartesian manner. They believed that district officials simply wanted to zone out village land, potentially paving the way for

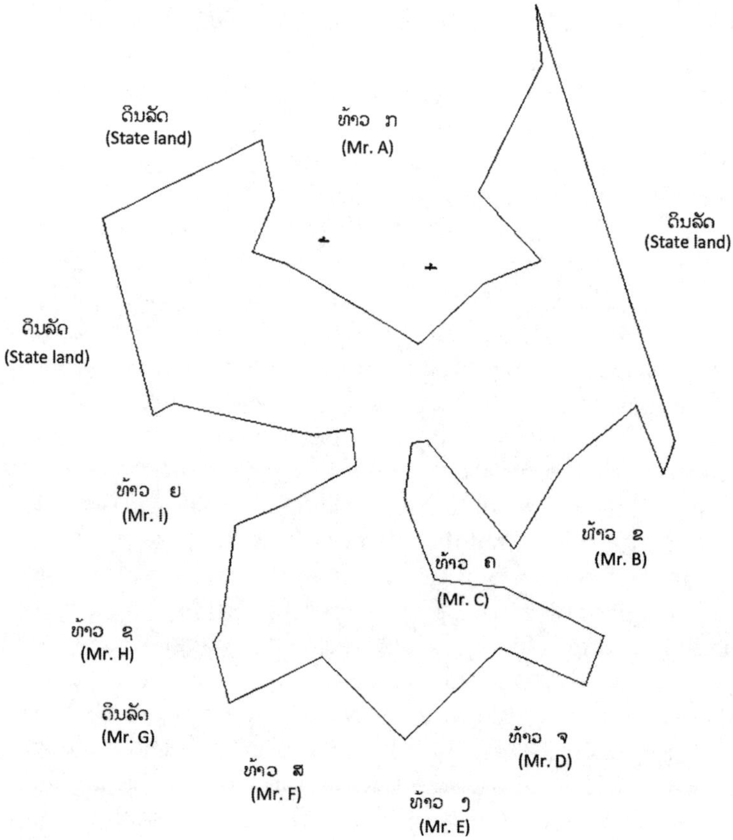

Figure 2.4. Drawing of state and village land surveyed. Source: DONRE, Phin district. Reproduced with permission.

the formalization of villagers' claims to land. So they participated in the survey and pointed out which lands belonged to whom, both lands that were currently in use and those reserved for future use (*din chap chong*). A PONRE official explained to me that one of the problems with Sun Paper's approach was that they tried to survey lands quickly, often involving only a PONRE staff member and the village chief. In the end, though, they lost time because of all the land conflicts their rushed approach created. Saphang village leaders maintained that they had never consented to concede any land to Sun Paper and had consistently refused the district government's proposals. Village leaders recalled that at one point their discussions became heated, and a district officer responded to villagers' refusal by stating, "That's fine if you disagree, but this land is part of a state target already. It's going to be taken already. Whatever happens, so be it, villagers disagree, but I'm still going to take it."

Frustrated with the district government, Saphang villagers sought another pathway for their dispute to be taken seriously. Several members of the village leadership had fought in the army during the Second Indochina War against the Lao royalists and Americans. They had developed close connections with comrade veterans, one of whom was now well placed as a government official within the Savannakhet provincial branch of the National Assembly. This type of political advantage is useful for lodging complaints with the government and ensuring that they are heard (this is covered more directly in chapter 4). Using this connection, they successfully lodged a complaint with the National Assembly and brought assembly members to visit their village and evaluate the dispute. Although villagers killed a cow so that the visiting National Assembly officials could eat well, the case was ultimately not resolved in the villagers' favor. National Assembly officials reaffirmed that Sun Paper had the right to develop land that villagers were not using based on the concession agreement and recommended that villagers work as laborers on the plantation.

Villagers also understood from district government officials that land not clearly identified as belonging to villagers would be defined as state land and cleared by the company. Villagers noted, "After the land survey had been completed, the company and district government informed us that apart from the land that the village had reserved [*din ban chap chong*], the remaining empty land belonged to the state." With these messages from district and National Assembly officials, it quickly became clear to villagers that their best option for protecting their lands would be to find ways to mark them out as lands that had already been divided up among themselves for current and future use. At first, they posted signs on lands reserved for future use, but Chinese bulldozer operators ignored them, in part because they could not read the Lao-language signs. Eventually, villagers started camping out in their fields, taking turns to make sure that someone from the village was always there to defend their lands from being cleared. The hand tractor that bulldozers ran into was itself a form of identification intended to mark off the boundaries of villagers' lands.

The lack of formal property, making villagers' lands illegible to the state agency, and officials' reliance upon villagers' customary claims to land meant that villagers maintained an advantage throughout the negotiations and contestations over their lands. The systematization of information about land and property often bolsters state control rather than engendering more inclusive forms of participation in property markets.[25]

In other words, when there is a lack of knowledge about land relations, it can be to the disadvantage of the state instead of local land users. Despite the heavy-handed, top-down political coercion Saphang villagers faced, they were always in control of critically important information concerning which lands belonged to villagers and which had not yet been allocated. The category of reserved land (*din chap chong*) aided them in this strategy because they could effectively claim any areas of land that had not yet been developed and remained forested as land that had already been allocated for future use and was necessary for future agricultural expansion in the village.

♦ ♦ ♦

Property plays a critically important role in mediating contestations over the land dispossession inherent in the creation of state land concessions for agro-industrial plantation development by foreign investors. The focus in this discussion has been on the role of "state land," which must be produced for it to be available to investors. Yet precise definitions of state versus village and household land are often unclear on the ground—even after land surveys are conducted—and thus highly contested. At the same time, state control over land is fundamental for allocating land to villages and households for their use. Without some degree of state support, customary land uses and claims would not carry any weight. This is closely linked to the central argument of this book—that land can be socialized for different purposes, particularly toward the interests of capital versus the peasantry. The discussion here elaborates upon that argument by demonstrating the critically important role of property, especially state land, in the socialization of land toward different ends. The expansion of state control over land is part of a process of transforming property relations, which can be used to support capitalist land investments or long-standing customary peasant claims, and thus this process is hotly contested.

In contrast to common conceptions of socialist property systems in which the state owns all land in the country, this chapter has shown how state ownership over land is not predefined. Instead, it is produced through the process of granting and allocating state land concessions to foreign investors. State land is carved out of a territory that has yet to be divided into clearly defined formal land uses and ownership. On the one hand, this creates an opportunity for the state to mold the landscape into the type of investment territory that resource capitalists seek. On the other, it presents an illegible landscape that state agents and company staff must contend with. They have to pay attention to the land claims that villagers make, as there is no other available source of information about customary land claims. As a consequence, the state land that is constructed and allocated to companies as land concession certificates is the result of several rounds of contestation and negotiation.

The production of state land is a perfect example of a process that is contested in terms of how land is socialized for the interests of different classes. Most obviously, state land is a fundamental category that allows foreign investors to access land in Laos. Foreign entities are not legally permitted to purchase land in the country, and leasing large blocks of state land is much cheaper and easier than negotiating with multitudes of small, private landowners. State land concessions are a hybrid type of property that demonstrate how land grabbing is not simply a process of land privatization. Social processes are at play in transforming land into a state asset that can be used by private capital. Peasant landownership and use claims are ignored or violently erased to create new forms of property, mapping out, marking off, planting with trees, and creating new concession certificates to show that the land is a state project aligned with the interests of resource capital.

Yet state land is not inevitably for capital. In both political and legal terms, although land in Laos is managed by the state, it belongs to the people. The state has always been in the position of ensuring that people have access to land—this has been a major part of the party-state's ideological project since the peasant revolution. The state does restrict what land people can use and how they can use it, such as by resettling people from upland to lowland areas or by limiting swidden cultivation practices. However, it also fundamentally provides people with the right to access, use, and eventually own land. This can be done formally, such as through land and forest allocation programs that define the types of land rural people can use and for what purposes or through allocating land-use certificates and land titles based on historical land uses. Even informally, where land titling or zoning have not taken place, the state can support rural peoples' cultivation of land according to customary practices provided they do not contravene the law. These land-use practices can be recognized in a variety of ways, including village claims of current and future land uses or land tax receipts. The production of state land is therefore not inherently for capital but can also be constructed for the peasantry.

The contradictory and divergent uses of state land are consistent with a view of property as a complex set of social relations, and its production and transformation are regularly contested. Development institutions make the case that the best way to combat unjust land expropriation is through widespread land titling programs. While the effectiveness of titling for protecting land rights in contexts of intensive land capitalization has been extensively critiqued, this chapter has shown that the capacity to protect land rights and access is not absent without a title.[26] This is because the relationship between people and land, or land tenure, is about much more than titles. It includes a variety of social relationships, such as the complex and blurry relationship between "people" and "the state" in "owning" and "managing" the land. Similarly, it includes the customary relationships that people have with land and the state's desire to recognize legitimate and long-standing land uses, but also to identify unused and unavailable land that can be granted to companies. Most important are the unequal power relations between investors and villagers, which are heavily tilted toward the former and favor their interests in struggles over land, with or without titles.

Considering and investigating the social relations between people and land that shape how land is allocated is also about much more than property. It additionally includes the socio-ecological relations between villages and their surrounding environments and how they are politicized within the Lao governmental context. In some cases, these practices are viewed as modern, productive, ecologically sustainable, and in line with state objectives. In other cases, they are characterized as backward, unproductive, and ecologically destructive. As the next chapter demonstrates, land-use practices characterized with the latter terms are more likely to be targeted for allocation to investors, although the difference between these categorizations is frequently disputed.

Chapter 3

Socializing Nature

Singkham, a Brou research assistant, and I visited Ban Kaengvang, a small village straddling Route 9 in Xepon district, in June 2014. It was one of the first villages where land was allocated to Sun Paper and where the company established its seedling nursery. Singkham was a close friend of one of the villagers we interviewed, who was eager to help out with our research project and took us on a tour of the village lands to give us a better sense of the landscape discussed in the interviews. Taking a dirt side road to the west of Route 9, we climbed slowly into the hills, flanked on both sides by a mix of forests, bush fallow, and cleared swidden. Eventually, we parked our motorbike, walked a short way into the woods, and came across a wide clearing of a steep slope, where about a hectare of trees and brush had been recently cut and burned. The blackened stumps of some of the larger trees could still be seen, interspersed across the field. A group of women was sitting at the bottom of the hill, sifting through broom grass they had just collected from the area. In the middle of the hill was a cluster of villagers making holes with dibble sticks and placing rice seeds in them (figure 3.1).

While swidden cultivation, pejoratively referred to as slash-and-burn agriculture, is a common practice across Laos, it is rare to see such steep slopes in eastern Savannakhet completely cleared of trees. My suspicion that something different had occurred was confirmed when our informant explained that the previous year the hill had been covered with a fifty-year-old forest—some said it had never been cleared at all. Furthermore, it did not lie within the boundaries of Ban Kaengvang but belonged to a neighboring village, Ban Khaen, which lay just over the border in Phin district. Although Khaen villagers were hesitant to allow the clearance of this dense forest (*pa dong dip*), they eventually gave permission after Kaengvang villagers agreed to sacrifice a pig—a village tradition (*hit*)—to pay respects to and request permission from the spirits

Figure 3.1. Villagers plant swidden rice on a cleared hillside. Photograph by Miles Kenney-Lazar.

of the forest to clear it. Although Kaengvang villagers were allowed to use the land that year, Khaen villagers asked them to return the land the following year.

In contrast to stereotypes of slash-and-burn agriculture as an integral element of a downward spiral of poverty and environmental destruction, Kaengvang villagers did not clear the primary forest of their own volition but because they were left with no other option. The new tenant of this swidden field had previously held 3 hectares of swidden land closer to the village that he had been cultivating over many years in a rotational cycle—far more sustainable than the clearance of new forest. However, the government allocated this land to Sun Paper and the company cleared it of brush and fallow and planted it with eucalyptus trees. The swidden farmer remarked that if he had been financially compensated, he could have bought land elsewhere, but without any money, he was desperate and asked to clear land in Ban Khaen. Villagers also reported that Sun Paper had already logged all the big and valuable trees from this forest two to three years before, meaning that it was hardly pristine.

About eleven kilometers north by road, Ban Chalan villagers were similarly dispossessed of their land to make way for Sun Paper's processing factory, yet through a different process that illustrates the diverse ways in which ecologies are socialized and politicized. Ban Chalan, along with Ban Na Khouay, lies in a small lowland valley of paddies (fields of wet rice cultivation, or *na* in Lao) and patches of bush fallow and forest, just a few kilometers southeast of Route 9, hemmed in by hills to the northeast and southwest and the Xe Banghiang River to the east. Through discussions with the district government, this area was selected as the location for Sun Paper's pulp and paper factory, the crown jewel of the company's investment. Sun Paper initially sought 400 hectares of land for the factory and to develop pulpwood plantations that would cover the area of the Na Khouay and Chalan villages.

With a significant amount of villagers' paddy in the area, the district government was compelled to first consult with the villagers and landowners. Na Khouay villagers outright refused to concede land to the project, and the site was moved exclusively within Chalan territory and reduced to 152 hectares. Starting in 2011, government officials and company representatives repeatedly asked to acquire land for the project, yet Ban Chalan leaders and landowners refused each time. By the fourth time Sun Paper visited the village, its representatives were armed with a list of all households that owned land within the planned concession area and a compensation price for each landowner. The rates, 25–30 million kip per hectare (about US$3,125–US$3,750), were much higher than had been discussed initially. Seeing such high figures and fearing receiving nothing at all if they continued to refuse, the villagers decided to accept the compensation and the expropriation of their land. They continued to plant rice on the acquired lands, cultivating until the construction began (figure 3.2).

These accounts of the Kaengvang and Chalan villages' differential experiences with land acquisition, particularly the processes of consultation and compensation, reflect patterns of how plantation and processing facility development have occurred across Phin and Xepon districts. In villages with mountainous, sloping, and upland terrain, where swidden (*hai*) cultivation agricultural systems predominate, the land was conceded and allocated to plantation capital without considering villagers' land-use and tenure histories. Often, they were coerced into accepting the project, leading to dispossession and socio-environmental transformation. In contrast, for villages lying in lowland valleys, where land is predominantly used for paddy production or can be converted to paddy in the future, consent to concede land was sought by the government, even though villagers were under significant pressure and aimed not to appear antagonistic

Figure 3.2. Rice planted on land allocated for the Sun Paper factory, with eucalyptus trees planted in the background. Photograph by Miles Kenney-Lazar.

to government policy. Some successfully refused, negotiating the boundaries and size of the land allocated, like Ban Saphang (discussed in chapter 2). Others drove up the price of compensation, like Ban Chalan.

These dynamics mirror the differential political ecologies of lowlands and uplands across the country.[1] The lowlands have been typically treated by the government as sites of potential—for agricultural development, urban expansion, and economic modernization. The uplands, in contrast, are often viewed as sites of backwardness that need to be emptied of people so that they can become spaces of forest conservation and resource extraction frontiers.[2] A vital element of this differential treatment is the ecological relationships between people and their environment through their agricultural practices in uplands and lowlands, especially how these practices are politicized by the Lao state within the context of a changing political economy. Most of the land area in Laos is sloped and mountainous, meaning that only a small portion is suitable for paddy development. As the government views paddy as more productive than swidden agriculture, it has become a prized agricultural resource and one that the government hesitates to convert to other land uses such as industrial and urban development. Swidden, in comparison, is a practice that the government has long sought to eliminate because of its supposed environmental destruction, lack of productivity, and association with poverty. As a result, swidden landscapes have become a key target for replacement by agro-industrial plantations.

This chapter examines how different ecologies are targeted for investment and how the degree of consultation, contestation, and compensation over the transfer of lands reflects how nature is socialized. As argued throughout the book, land can be socialized for different purposes, toward the interests of the peasantry versus those of capital. An important element is how the socio-ecologies of different types of land shape their socialization. The social relations of rural natures can serve to protect them for peasant and Indigenous access and use or they can be transformed by the state for capital to facilitate resource extraction.

As with land, rural peoples develop deep ties with various natures over time—with the surrounding rivers, forests, minerals, vegetation, and animals that are indispensable to their lives. Indigenous peoples have deep spiritual connections with such natures and many believe they are inhabited by spirits. In comparison with land, though, their rights to these types of natures are not often recognized by the state, and the state often socializes them for capitalist resource extraction when they are valuable, such as tapping the energy potential of rivers for hydropower.

Rural ecologies are also closely related to and imbricated with land. Across different types of land and land uses, diverse forms of ecologies and social relations influence how land is socialized. Across different landed natures and socio-ecological relations, how land is socialized by and for peasants differs from how it is socialized for capital. Socio-ecological relations that match the state's drive toward socialist economic modernization in the form of peasant goods—principally paddies and other permanent cash crops and their potential expansion—are harder to wrest away from farmers and transfer to investors, even when they are untitled (as demonstrated in chapter 2). In contrast, the state seeks to replace some forms of socio-ecological relations, especially those that are part of upland swidden systems, by allocating them to foreign investors. These distinctions influence how the impacts of land investment projects are socially distributed across the landscape—which socio-ecologies are sacrificed or spared, and the degree of compensation through cash or infrastructure. However, the zoning of rural landscapes into those socialized for the peasantry versus capital are not always cleanly separated, which creates opportunities for contesting land allocation plans. It can be further complicated by unwieldy biophysical materialities of different ecologies that can present challenges to capitalized investment.

Legacies of Socialist Natures

When interviewing government officials, my research assistants and I sought to exude a polite demeanor, deferring to interviewees' authority, which their position afforded. While we asked them about sensitive and controversial topics, we phrased questions diplomatically to put them at ease and keep the conversation moving. Yet toward the end of the research project, I had become frustrated with the way district officials had assisted Quasa and Sun Paper to violently dispossess villagers of their land. In an interview with Khampha at the Xepon DONRE office, I finally blurted out what was on my mind without filtering it as I usually did. Why had they allowed Sun Paper to clear land in villages such as Ban Xaylom that had explicitly refused to concede their land and had even complained to the district about the project? Although generally very calm, Khampha also began to lose some of his composure in response to my interrogating question, as I had exposed an uncomfortable truth and created an uneasy situation. In an earlier interview, he had claimed that the village was always involved in the land survey before land allocation, which ensured that villagers' household lands would not be allocated to the company. By referencing a specific case, he now explained why there were many instances when this did not happen.

Khampha straightened up and wondered aloud how he could phrase his answer in a way that would "help me understand," meaning that he felt my perspective needed to be straightened out. First, he noted that the district had little choice in the matter due to the top-down pressure they faced. If they did not help the company clear land as delineated on the map created by the provincial level, they would have problems with the provincial and central levels. Second, he explained that a record of land allocation had already been made in Ban Xaylom, and all the villagers had signed it, although he added that villagers did not have the right to approve the clearing of land in any case. Plus, for him, "Some villagers always talk and complain, there's no unity among them—some agree, some do not." In other words, their lack of solidarity demonstrated that they could not legitimately make collective decisions as a village (see chapter 5). Third, and finally, Khampha admitted that agro-industrial plantations were a strategy for replacing swidden landscapes:

> Villagers want to cut deep forests for swidden so that there won't be many weeds when they plant rice. We want to prevent them from cutting the forest, and we want to make their lives more comfortable. . . . The government policy is that the purpose of investments is to reduce poverty by creating jobs for the people. Villagers don't know or are not interested in developing their land, they just want to continue their lives like before. They want to clear the forest that has big trees. . . . We don't want investment on all their land, only land that is empty, not used in any way.

Khampha associated swidden with environmental destruction and a lack of industry, reflecting a typical condescending attitude of government officials toward upland peoples and their relationships to the environment, especially as ethnic minorities. Swidden is framed as an inferior cultivation system, equivalent to an "emptiness" in the landscape to be filled with something else. In contrast, government-sanctioned land investments would provide villagers with the motivation to be industrious that they independently lacked.

Such perspectives are not unique to Lao government officials. Rather, they are grounded in and influenced by longer colonial histories of the treatment of nature–society relationships across Southeast Asia. Throughout the region, colonial governments treated swidden cultivation by upland peoples, who are commonly Indigenous or ethnic minorities, as a wasteful use of resources.[3] Nancy Peluso and Peter Vandergeest write about the emergence of the "political forest" during this period, with examples from Indonesia, Malaysia, and Thailand.[4] Forest reserves were created on paper that did not necessarily replicate actual forested areas. Still, they reflected the political desire to create colonial spaces of resource control for the purpose of both conservation and extraction. In colonial Burma, for example, the category of "waste lands" was created, as it was in other British colonies; these were lands that could not be categorized as urban or agricultural to be titled or forest to be enclosed as reserves.[5] Today, these categories influence land laws in Myanmar that compartmentalize much of the country as "vacant, fallow, and virgin." These colonial strategies were part of what James Scott refers to as the taming of nature, simplifying complex ecologies in ways that make them legible to the state for intervention, whether by creating forest reserves or new sites of plantation investments.[6] French colonial forestry management in Indochina explicitly restricted the activities of upland ethnic minority peoples, especially their swidden agricultural practices and the use of fire, and instead favored state-sanctioned logging operations.[7]

As the polities of Southeast Asia began to be liberated from colonial rule after the Second World War, postcolonial governments dominated by majority lowland peoples adopted many of the same colonial policies and categories of forestry and land use, particularly regarding upland ethnic minority peoples practicing slash-and-burn agriculture. As Vandergeest and Peluso show, the continuation of the colonial forestry project was promoted across the region by the Food and Agriculture Organization (FAO) of the United Nations. Southeast Asian states effectively created their own "empires of forestry," completing and extending the production of political forests and linking colonial with contemporary practices of forest management.[8] They promoted policies of forest management, use, and exploitation that were in line with postcolonial goals of national economic development and growth. As a consequence, forest reserves were to be used for the benefit of the nation, which meant that they should be managed for the harvesting of timber, while local use—especially swidden cultivation, which was viewed as backward and destructive—was to be prevented or limited. The FAO promoted a regime that maintained a strict division between agricultural and forest areas, which practically eliminated spaces for swidden cultivation, as it is a practice of agroforestry. As Vandergeest and Peluso note, "rather than being regarded a form of agriculture that manipulated multiple parts of the landscape under different maturities and mixes of vegetative cover, FAO practice urged that swidden agriculture be viewed as 'agriculture out of place'—i.e., as taking place in a forest rather than in a proper field."[9]

The FAO played a dominant role in postcolonial forestry networks in the 1950s and 1960s among independent states of Southeast Asia. However, the power of its legacy carried on throughout the following decades. Particularly influential was its coordination of the Tropical Forestry Action Plan (TFAP), which was proposed in 1985 and intended to act as a framework to arrest tropical deforestation. Echoing a neo-Malthusian logic, the TFAP explicitly blamed deforestation on poverty and population growth in what was then known as the Third World. As the introduction to the plan states, "It is now generally recognized that the main cause of the destruction and degradation of the tropical forests is the poverty of the people who live in and around them and their dependence on the forest lands for their basic needs."[10] A range of different solutions was espoused to transform forest-using peoples' agricultural and forestry practices and create land-use and forestry management plans. One such solution was the replacement of swidden cultivation with permanent cropping systems.

As the Lao economy began to liberalize in the 1980s and the country continued to open to international economic aid, the FAO-coordinated TFAP became increasingly influential. With the support of several major development donors, the TFAP for Laos was completed in 1990. Consistent with the global plan, one of its main aims was to eradicate swidden cultivation—which was argued to be causing deforestation and forest degradation—and to develop commercial logging and fast-growing tree plantations.[11] As in other parts of Southeast Asia, the TFAP was well matched with national ideologies of modernization, development, and growth in Laos, although infused with a socialist bent. In 1989, just a year before, the first National Forestry Conference in Laos had been organized, where Kaysone Phomvihane stated that "forest destruction in the country has reached an alarming rate. It is the time to change from uncontrolled logging and destruction of forests to focus mainly on tree planting and forest protection."[12] The conference agenda highlighted the stabilization of shifting cultivation as an essential strategy for reducing deforestation and forest degradation.

While the Lao government subscribed to prominent colonial and modernist ideas that demonize swidden cultivation, they blended them with socialist ideas of modernization and progress, in many ways following examples set by neighboring and allied Vietnam.[13] Being a peasant society lacking in industrial production, Laos was not in an ideal position to make the jump to socialism. For Marx, socialism is a political-economic stage that societies pass into after going through advanced capitalism that develops the forces of production—such as technological advances—necessary to create a world of abundant social wealth. Not having experienced much in the way of capitalist development or industrialization, Laos needed to make a massive jump from what its leaders called its "natural economy" (*saethakit thammasat*) of subsistence production based on the raw use of available natural resources to an industrialized socialist economy.

The ideology associated with this kind of modernization can be seen in the symbols of the Lao PDR's national emblem: a hydropower dam, a paved road, a paddy, and a forest. Encircling the image is a cogwheel and stalks of crescent-shaped rice, representing increased industrial and agricultural production. Overall, the image demonstrates the government's perspective of nature as something to be tamed and simplified so that it can be harnessed for economic growth and productivity. The complex relations between people and nature throughout the countryside have no place in the nation's future. It is symbolic that the form of agricultural production highlighted is paddy in the lowlands, largely practiced by ethnic Lao groups as well as other ethnolinguistic groups within the broader Lao-Tai category, such as Tai Lue and Phu Thai peoples, historically referred to as Lao Loum (lowland Lao) by the government. In contrast, the only use of nature appropriate to the uplands in the image is preserving forests. Swidden rice has no role to play in this future, especially as the government aims to restore forested areas of the country back to 70 percent. This is reflected in government policy that is ultimately aimed at eliminating swidden cultivation, though recognizing the challenge of this has meant that swidden should be stabilized first—reduced in size and extent, limited to prescribed areas only.

While these policies are focused on agricultural and forestry practices of the uplands, it is not coincidental that they are the practices of ethnic minorities, especially those outside the politically and socially dominant Lao-Tai ethnolinguistic grouping, including minorities of the Mon-Khmer, Hmong-Mien, and Tibeto-Burman groupings, formerly referred to by the government as Lao Theung (midland Lao) or Lao Soung (upland Lao). The Lao party-state has consistently promoted an ideology of ethnic equality among the "multiethnic Lao people" that seeks to recognize and respect cultural diversity while also advancing the economic development of all groups. However, anti-swidden policies are one example of the government's biases in practice against ethnic minority cultural practices, considering the importance of swidden for their livelihoods and way of life.

To stabilize and eliminate swidden cultivation, the government has pursued a variety of different policies. First, it has depopulated sites of swidden cultivation by moving ethnic minorities from the uplands to the lowlands.[14] This has occurred in various waves and for different reasons. One has been to enhance state "security" over the uplands, where various ethnic groups fought for the Royal Lao government and the United States, and which the Lao government wants to keep a closer watch over. They also sought to eradicate opium poppy production in the uplands, practiced by some of these same groups. Another was to bring the rural population closer to government services, such as health clinics, hospitals, and schools. Transitioning villages to lowland paddy and other forms of "permanent" employment has been an essential motivation for the policy. A key aim has therefore been to sedentarize upland populations by restricting them to forms of agricultural production that do not shift around, as with swidden cultivation. However, many villages cannot be easily moved to lowland areas, especially in northern Laos, where there is little flat low-lying land available in small river valleys.

A second strategy has been to engage in land-use planning to stabilize swidden cultivation until a replacement can be developed. As covered in more detail in earlier chapters, since the 1990s, especially with support from foreign development agencies and INGOs, the land-use planning process has defined the borders between villages, zoned out village areas for different land uses (such as residential land, agricultural land, and conservation forest), and issued temporary land-use certificates (intended to be converted to permanent land titles later). While land-use planning aims are diverse—including regularization of land tenure, an increase in agricultural production, and forest protection—a critical intended effect was to reduce the area of land available for swidden cultivation. Land-use planning had the result of increasing the share of village land zoned as forest while decreasing land classified as agriculture. As with the TFAP, this problematic division of agriculture and forest land leaves no space for swidden fields that are left fallow, that turn into young bush fallow, and that eventually become a secondary forest if left long enough. Villagers were also instructed through the land-use planning process to use only three plots of land for swidden, thus reducing their cycles from up to ten to twenty years to only three, which has decreased productivity because of the lower quality of the soils and has also increased the labor needed for weeding.

Land use planning, however, has been implemented unevenly, and many areas, such as the villages in eastern Savannakhet targeted by the plantation companies, did not go through such a process and thus have not been under the same pressures of swidden stabilization and eradication. Nonetheless, the same anti-swidden objectives inform how local officials approach villagers' land uses. Chapter 2 demonstrated how villagers' customary land-use claims can be effective even when official land zoning or registration has not taken place because there is a lack of knowledge concerning what land is being used or will be used productively and in line with government objectives. However, as discussed in further detail in this chapter, customary claims for upland swidden systems, especially fallow lands that are not under use, are much harder for villagers to justify than those for lowland areas that could potentially become paddies.

The third strategy of the government has been to replace swidden with other forms of more "permanent" and "productive" land uses suitable for the uplands, which is consistent with the Turning Land into Capital policy of increasing the value of landed production. Finding such replacements has not been easy, as many other agricultural systems are not as well suited to the uplands as swidden. Most effective has been the replacement of swidden with cash crops appropriate to the uplands, such as maize and rubber, which have come to increasingly cover the sloped hills of the uplands of northern Laos. In the case of tree crops, not only do they replace swidden cultivation, but they can also create the appearance of forested areas, and the Lao government now counts them as such in national statistics, even though their regular rows betray their human creation. In other cases, whole landscapes have been replaced with new investments, such as hydropower dams and reservoirs, and mines. This has led to investment-induced resettlement, thus bringing upland peoples to lowland areas, although often without the necessary land and natural resources to continue their agricultural lifestyles.[15]

Unequal Ecologies

In granting and allocating land to Sun Paper and Quasa, as with all concessions, landscapes, terrains, and ecologies—in short, geography—shaped the considerations of the Lao government. It has generally sought to grant concessions in more impoverished and remote areas of the country as part of its Turning Land into Capital strategy. It aims to mobilize concessions to eradicate poverty by creating new jobs and activity, and to develop infrastructure by establishing the roads and electric lines associated with the new investments. The government has even offered lower concession fees in districts classified as more remote. Phin, Xepon, and Nong districts were selected because they fit these criteria, classified as the three poorest districts of Savannakhet. Upland areas are more likely to be classified as poor, as the government's definition of poverty includes access to electricity, roads, piped water, and medical services, which are not as well developed in the uplands.[16] They are also outside the central zone of low-lying paddy production, which covers much of the rest of the province and is one of the most extensive plains of lowland agricultural production in the whole country. As you drive toward these districts on Route 9, the road's incline slowly increases as you reach the foothills of the Annamite Cordillera. It is also an area with less paddy and much more swidden field, fallow, and forest mosaics that fit the target zone of "empty" (*pao wang*) and "unproductive" land—Laos's politically constructed resource frontier. Many of these forests were heavily logged beginning in the 1980s and therefore are more readily classified as "degraded."

Yet there is significant variation of remoteness, terrain, ecology, and poverty within these districts. Although they are classified as remote, the areas near Route 9 and feeder roads are well connected to district markets, the provincial capital, and Thailand to the west or Vietnam to the east. Route 9 is a crucial piece of transportation infrastructure as part of the Asian Development Bank's East–West Economic Corridor to link Myanmar, Thailand, Laos, and Vietnam; by the end of my fieldwork it had been upgraded and repaired by the Japan International Cooperation Agency. Around the district capitals and market towns along the road where there is a great deal of economic activity related to the transportation along Route 9, villages are better off. Furthermore, the land is flat and low-lying; there are vast expanses of paddies and space for the future expansion of the paddy system. Poverty, remoteness, and the incline of the land tend to increase as you move to the north and south of Route 9; gravel roads become dirt roads that intersect with streams you must cross or be ferried across during the wet season. Eventually, you reach dirt tracks that run up into the mountains, in certain areas butting up against national protected areas.

Many villages have a mix of paddies and swidden fields across a hybrid lowland-upland landscape. Some villages practice dry swidden rice cultivation on lowland areas that can eventually be converted to paddies. Yet there are clear distinctions between villages that are more dominated by lowland terrain and have expanded paddy areas over the years and those whose landscapes are primarily dominated by sloping upland areas more conducive to swidden agriculture. The latter can only be converted to terraced paddy production through significant and prolonged technological, capital, and labor investments.

In upland villages, government officials and company managers often assumed that swidden landscapes were freely available to concede for plantation investment, a conception that was difficult for upland villages to contest. This was the case in Ban Kaengvang (introduced earlier in this chapter), a relatively small Brou village of 103 households located on the side of Route 9, a thirty-minute motorbike ride away from Xepon town. Although their village residential land is in the lowlands and they are well connected to transportation networks and markets, the rest of their village territory to the east of the road quickly slopes up into the surrounding hills. They have little paddy land. Most of their agricultural land is part of a mosaic of swidden agricultural fields, bush fallow, and secondary forest. They had rotated their swidden fields in cycles of five to six years and helped each other clear the land, plant seeds, weed, and harvest the rice through labor exchanges among households. The village chief wished the company had cleared land to the east of the road, where it is very steep, rocky, and of poor soil quality, so villagers cannot practice agriculture. Of course, the company was instead granted land by the district government on the western side, where the land is prosperous (*oudomsomboun,* in the words of the village chief).

Ban Kaengvang villagers recounted how district officials, approximately once a year prior to the concession, had told villagers to stop practicing swidden cultivation, in line with government policy. However, government officials had never enforced the policy, and so villagers kept on.[17] The Sun Paper plantation finally offered a chance for the district government to implement the policy of swidden eradication. When the district government came to the village in 2008 to promote the project, village leaders explained that "they said all of this land belongs to the state, it has to be given."[18] Villagers felt that they had little say in the matter. They did express that they had agricultural land in that area, and they were allowed to mark off their lands to prevent them from being cleared. But the company paid no attention to the signs they placed in front of their fields, clearing beyond them as if they were part of the "empty landscape" awaiting investment. Despite their complaints, villagers were not financially compensated for the land cleared, and district officials were hesitant to believe their claims. This is quite common for the clearance of swidden land—only in rare cases were villagers in other villages compensated a measly 500,000 kip (about US$62.50) per hectare.

In contrast, lowland villages, whose territories mainly comprised paddy lands, were approached and treated very differently by government officials when their land was incorporated as part of the concession area and targeted for acquisition. Generally, government officials sought to avoid the allocation of paddy, considering its outsize political importance in the history of the state's modernization programs and current government policy. In some instances, this was not possible, such as when securing land for the latex- and pulp- and paper-processing plants, which must be located on flat land and close to water sources and road and electricity infrastructure. In other cases, the government granted lowland areas that had not yet been converted to paddy or that were at the edge of a low-elevation upland area. As mentioned previously, the landscape

Figure 3.3. Swidden landscape beyond the borders of Ban Kaengvang. Photograph by Miles Kenney-Lazar.

of the areas expanding to the north and south of Route 9 in eastern Phin and western Xepon is gently sloped; the gradient increases as you travel farther away from the main road. Furthermore, many gently sloped areas are at the boundary and can be considered part of the uplands or, over time, can be converted to lowland paddy with a significant investment of energy, time, labor, and capital. These are the lands that often became contested for allocation to the plantation companies. Such contestation operated on a different terrain than in the uplands because of the potential for paddy expansion and the ability of villagers to challenge government framings of such land as empty and unproductive.

In Ban Na Khouay and Ban Chalan, negotiations over land were much different from those in Ban Kaengvang, which is eleven kilometers down the road, just over a rocky ridge that separates them. Kaengvang villagers have been unable to use this ridge for agriculture because of its inhospitable geology, soil, and slope. When Sun Paper and the district government were putting together the plans for the pulp and paper factory and surrounding eucalyptus plantations, they considered an area that covered large parts of the boundaries of both Ban Na Khouay and Chalan—the factory primarily in the latter and the plantations mainly in the former. The Na Khouay village chief was hailed to a meeting in the provincial capital, in which the company explained the benefits and impacts of the project to the villages that would be affected. He immediately refused to concede village land for the project because he said their village had a limited amount of land, most of which was paddy—only a small area of the land was used for swidden agriculture. According to the chief, this was accepted by the government and company without any pushback, and they focused on developing the factory, the most critical part of the project, in Ban Chalan.

When the land was surveyed for the factory and some surrounding eucalyptus plantations, part of the planned area covered the paddies of three to four households in Ban Na Khouay. The owners complained about the impacts and refused to allow the company to acquire their lands. Sun Paper simply conceded and cut these Na Khouay lands out of the project area, likely assuming that it would be difficult to push as the village had rejected the project already. It was only a small amount of land so the company's efforts would have been better spent in neighboring Ban Chalan, which was the heart of the project. Instead, the company approached individual farmers in Ban Na Khouay to lease lands directly from individual households, offering them a percentage of the revenue from the trees each time they were harvested, over periods of five years. The village chief was not happy with this scheme, but villagers pursued it independently and demanded he allow it to continue.

Ban Chalan villagers were also not happy to be the main target of Sun Paper's factory. A significant amount of pressure was placed on villagers to accept the project. As mentioned earlier, they refused several times because of the loss of land and the perceived impacts that it would have on their livelihoods. However, with the pressure placed on them combined with high compensation prices, they had little room to continue refusing. Their land was treated as something that was up for consultation and negotiation because it was valued lowland paddy fields. This was completely different from upland villages like nearby Kaengvang, whose swidden fields and fallows were a target for replacement as state property that could be allocated to capital. Additionally, the high compensation provided compared to the lack of payment for swidden lands speaks volumes about the value of paddy in this context.

Ban Saphang is an example of a village dominated mainly by lowland areas with a significant expanse of paddies. As discussed in the previous chapter, villagers contested the boundaries of "state land" by claiming village and household lands through the mechanism of reserved land. I raise their case again here to highlight another relevant aspect of the story. One of the reasons their contestation was so effective is that the lands allocated to Sun Paper were in a lowland area of the village that included some of their paddies and land they claimed was in the process of being converted to paddy. Saphang is a low-lying village whose ethnic minority Brou villagers have a history of clearing dry dipterocarp forest areas and transforming them into paddy, expanding the area of agricultural production within the village territory. Most of the area allocated to Sun Paper was dry dipterocarp forest, which the Lao government views as degraded and empty because of how the trees are spaced far apart from one another and how its dry climate gives the impression it is not particularly productive land. Additionally, in this area villagers practice a lowland form of swidden cultivation (figure 3.4). In Lao, the distinction between paddy and swidden as agricultural systems does not have to do with upland versus lowland terrain (even if it is broadly divided along these lines) but with whether rice is planted directly into the ground or in a constructed paddy that fills with water. In other words, swidden can also be practiced in lowlands. Yet Saphang villagers had been using lowland swidden cultivation as a temporary and intermediate phase

Figure 3.4. Lowland swidden rice fields among dry dipterocarp forest in Ban Saphang. Photograph by Miles Kenney-Lazar.

between the clearance of dry dipterocarp forests and the construction of paddies. Furthermore, they had been using this approach to quite aggressively expand their paddy system in previous years. When they received a cash grant from their involvement with the Sustainable Forestry for Rural Development project, they used the money to rent bulldozers to clear more land that eventually became paddies.

When National Assembly officials visited the village to investigate the complaint villagers had successfully lodged in Vientiane, there was tension concerning the value of the land and whether it should be retained by villagers or conceded to the company. Disappointingly, the officials claimed the project would only use unproductive land, a point that villagers contested: "The [National] Assembly said let it go, it's degraded land. We immediately responded that all this land is under production."[19] Yet National Assembly officials also gave villagers an opening for action by instructing them to fence off any paddy land yet to be cleared by the company, start farming it immediately so that it would be visibly under production, and convert any other reserved land into paddy. This corresponded with the previously described land survey conducted initially by DONRE, which was intended to mark off areas of land that villagers were using productively. Villagers thus had a potent tool in their struggle to draw the boundary between state and village land, and between "unproductive land" and land that was under production or would be in the future. Villagers ran with this idea and began planting the lands cleared for dry rice cultivation and marking off all lands that could be converted to paddies in the future, an approach that resonated with both the district government and National Assembly's guidance that land under productive use should not be expropriated.

Blurred Boundaries

There is an essential difference between how upland versus lowland ecologies, especially swidden versus paddy landscapes, are approached by the Lao state when allocating land for concessions. The state takes over the former to transform them into spaces of conservation or productive investment while the latter are socialized as spaces of peasant agriculture, also to be made productive but for the interests and benefit of peasant communities. However, the binary between these different zones does not always hold up, and the boundaries are often blurred and negotiated. This reflects how biophysical nature does not neatly fit into the categories assigned to it in the process of socialization. The materiality of rural landscapes and how they are struggled over can offer a range of surprises that confound the land's separation into distinct zones, posing problems to the claims made on them.

There is not a clear line separating upland swidden and lowland paddy landscapes. In many places, they are mixed, such as when paddies are wedged into a tiny valley between two hills where swidden rice and other vegetables are planted. Villagers often refer to these areas as "gardens" (*souan*), a term that is more politically accepted than swidden (*hai*). The blurred boundaries between upland and lowland areas are especially apt for Phin and Xepon districts, where the landscape itself blends and mixes these topographies, and many parts are not classifiable as one or the other. As the land slopes upward toward the Annamite Cordillera, and as you move away from the road to the north or the south, it becomes increasingly inclined, but there are many areas where flat and sloping lands abut one another. Additionally, there are many flat-lying or slightly sloped areas where swidden agriculture is practiced, but these areas can be transformed into paddies. In other areas, the land is mostly sloped, but a low-lying valley lies in between, where paddy land may be located or where land could be converted into a paddy.

To protect land that lies within concession boundaries, villagers can seek to take advantage of these blurred boundaries to make the case that the land is or will be transformed into paddy. Or when the land has already been cleared, they may try to get a higher rate of compensation for it. As a further example, if villagers had started to build an irrigation channel, the company must compensate them for their labor. District officials found these tactics frustrating. An agriculture and forestry official in the district complained about villagers claiming an area was paddy land when it was only a creek that could have been converted to a paddy. He said,

> If it's really paddy land then we cannot resolve it, wherever it is we have to reserve it if it's paddy land already. Only the ones that lie, sometimes they say it's a paddy because they just made a few bunds [*khan na*], but they didn't really do paddy, they just reserved the land. So we solved the issue and negotiated and compensated appropriately. If it's really a paddy with the straw after harvesting [*na feuang*] from recent production, we would leave it, whether it's in the middle or on the edge [of the plantation], we wouldn't touch it.[20]

The official was reflecting on the importance of preserving paddy land in government policy, but also the potential, in his view, that such a policy could be abused by villagers trying to protect other uses of land that had not been turned into paddies, assumed to be a higher stage of agricultural development.

In Ban Salang, villagers ran into the same problem trying to show that their land was being used productively. Under tremendous pressure, villagers had agreed to give up land that was not under production as swidden or paddy. In a focus group interview with village leaders, they recounted, "The bulldozer came close to the paddy so we rushed to put up signs, but the bulldozer reached the swidden and paddy lands. District officials arrived, and they asked, where are the bunds? If there are paddies, there must be bunds. If there are gardens, then there must be crops. Where are your banana trees? The villagers were quiet. . . . Then the company kept clearing and planting, and the village didn't know anything."[21] Villagers' inability to point to the hallmarks of sedentarized, permanent production, including any evidence of shaping the earth or planting perennial crops, invalidated their claims to be using the land in accordance with government policy. In the case of Ban Saphang, though, it was this ambiguity between current land use and potential development as paddy that the village was able to mobilize to prevent the acquisition of not only paddies under use but also those that could be used as such in the future. Therefore, the district government's strategy of excluding land that was not then being used as paddies with all of its related physical markings was limited in practice when villagers could make a convincing case about the ongoing development of a productive agricultural landscape.

Swidden landscapes are often thought of as vulnerable to land concessions for estate plantations because the government ultimately seeks to eradicate them. They are more easily claimed as empty, considering the significant areas of land left fallow each year. Yet, at the same time, the government generally seeks not to develop concessions on land that villagers are using productively. Since the revolution, Laos has pursued a "land to the tiller" policy that has emphasized the importance of ensuring that rural households have the right amount of land for their agricultural production, but not too much, and that they are productively using that land.[22] While the policy has been implemented unevenly, tending to allocate more land to lowland paddy farmers than upland swidden farmers, it is nonetheless a powerful ideology that those who use the land should retain access to it. Despite national policies, officials at the district level often recognize that swidden cultivation will remain an essential aspect of local livelihoods. The rapid elimination of swidden agriculture would create great hardship and a disastrous and ungovernable situation. If villagers are not engaged in so-called pioneering cultivation, meaning the clearing of new primary forest rather than secondary fallow and forest in a rotational system, it is often permitted.

Development projects have even been able to creatively include swidden systems in their land-use planning systems, as is the case with the Agro-Biodiversity Initiative, a joint project of the Swiss government and the Lao Ministry of Agriculture and Forestry, which has classified swidden systems in upland areas of northern Laos as rotational upland agricultural use zones. This reflects an increasing acceptance of upland cultivation as an appropriate land use if managed and not spread across an overly extensive area. This is partly a recognition that swidden fields are a type of productive land—that they are being used to actively produce rice, compared with swidden fallows, which are viewed as empty and unproductive. Villagers can thus seek to prevent the swidden fields that are in use in any particular year from being included, sometimes using their tax receipts as evidence that they have the right to use that land. Or, if such land is acquired, then they can seek to claim compensation for it.

Swidden agriculture also offers the opportunity to make rapid choices to cultivate different plots of land in different years, without putting in the significant labor to set up the infrastructure of the fields as in the case of paddy. As a result, villagers have been able to plant on land allocated to and cleared by the companies if they have not yet been planted with rubber or pulpwood trees. This occurred often on lands allocated to Sun Paper. As district-level government officials explained, the company had been slow to use the land, opening the opportunity for villagers to reclaim it, at least temporarily. One official explained that villagers only started clearing and planting after the company was allocated land in the area. "Our villagers, when no one touches the land or produce or develop, they don't do anything with the land, they only collect NTFPs [non-timber forest products], they don't do anything every day. But now, when the company has come to invest, the villagers are active and awake."[23] With this statement, he justified the allocation of land for a more "productive" use while also implying that the actions of the company had a carryover effect by inducing villagers to be more industrious, even if in a way that was antagonistic to the project.

The situation, of course, can be read very differently. It is more likely that this land lay within a swidden landscape and was left fallow as part of the rotational swidden system. Villagers were likely taking strategic advantage of the clearance of the land by the company and seeking to exert their presence on that land. However, without necessarily resisting the project outright, they may also have been using land as part of their swidden system as they would have anyway if the company had not come in. Additionally, planting rice on company land could be an excuse to allow the villagers to use the land for the rest of the year, delaying the project a bit further. This can be seen clearly in figure 3.2, in which villagers in Ban Chalan planted swidden rice on lands granted to and cleared by Sun Paper, on the area that had not yet been planted with eucalyptus trees (unlike the area in the background).

Confounding Social Materialities

The Phin district government had allocated land to Quasa in the mostly upland landscape of Ban Sokleek. However, the villagers allowed the company to acquire only 52 hectares of land (a story of resistance examined in chapter 5). One account is worth introducing here because it demonstrates how the materialities of the landscape affect the socialized natures that the plantation companies encounter. In an interview, a husband and wife recounted how the land that was eventually allocated to Quasa covered a path that they had carved out of the forest over the years to easily access their paddies from the village center. Soon after the company planted rubber seedlings, covering the path the household members had built, they ripped them out of the ground and continued to travel along the path as before. The husband remarked that it was his path because he had made it. Quasa staff were angry with him and told him to use the new, much wider plantation roads the company had recently built. However, these were constructed in a geometrical, grid-like arrangement, meaning that it would take the husband and wife much longer to get to their fields, while his smaller path provided a shortcut (figure 3.5). When the Quasa staff told the husband and wife they would bring this up with the district government, the husband angrily provoked him, "Go do it!" Eventually, the company let the issue go as it was just a small area and they had lost only a few trees.

On our way to a villager's paddy one day, we walked along this path and saw the same husband coming back the other way on his hand tractor, which had been converted into a vehicle by switching the metal, slatted paddy wheels used for plowing with rubber tires and hitching a cart to the back. Ironically, he had to turn back because the path was too muddy from recent monsoon rains, and he would need to travel along the company's roads to get to his fields. Even though the path was not always the

Figure 3.5. Household path carved into a rubber plantation. Photograph by Miles Kenney-Lazar.

best route, it was still important for him to protect it because it connected to this land that he held, constructed through his hard work.

This vignette demonstrates how the socialized ecologies and natures that plantation companies encounter are not always conducive to the development of their projects. While upland ecologies shaped by swidden agroforestry systems may be easier to acquire than lowland paddy landscapes because of their lack of political priority, other challenges lie in wait. As the previous section detailed, this is partly due to the lack of clear boundaries between upland swidden and lowland paddy landscapes. The materialities of the landscapes are not always easy to read by plantation companies and can be interpreted in different ways, framing struggles over whether they are empty lands ripe for investment or lands of potential productivity that should be driven by peasant interests and efforts.

Even in areas clearly defined by an upland swidden landscape, the social materialities of these environments can be confounding and burdensome for plantation investors. Something as simple as a villager's path to their field is inscribed onto the landscape, and villagers can challenge its erasure. Political ecologists make a case for taking the materiality of nature seriously, particularly how unruly and uncooperative natures can disrupt pathways of commodification and profit making.[24] Moreover, they highlight that it is not purely the materiality of nature that is critical but the relationship between material, nonhuman entities and collectives of humans in political-economic contexts that matters.[25] Such an approach is also referred to as post-humanist political ecology, which concerns a "*relational ontological* approach framing the human and nonhuman as mutually constituted in and through social relations."[26] It decenters the agency of the human but also sees the agency of materiality as enacted through its associations and relations with human societies. In other words, for our purposes here, the socialization of the landscape by peasant communities is a process of ascribing its material dimensions with meaning that they seek to protect. Often, companies may not be aware of these socio-ecological relations or how to navigate their complexity and importance.

Swidden landscapes seem to be an easy target for investment for the reasons described earlier: they are framed as empty, unproductive, and awaiting transformation. Furthermore, villagers are not consulted and find it more difficult to contest their allocation than paddy landscapes. However, the social materialities of upland landscapes can present a range of limitations on plantation development. As the opening vignette to this section demonstrates, uplands are complex landscapes full of different socio-ecological relations and practices, which do not always make them conducive to transformation into a uniform monoculture plantation. This is also shown in the previous section on blurred boundaries: the precise land uses and tenure patterns of the uplands are not clear-cut for both plantation companies and district officials; they can thus be difficult to determine and are open to contestation. While uplands may be politically challenging to defend for peasants, their complexity and sensitivity in Laos present challenges in their governance by outside parties. This has been argued to be one of the reasons why donor-led land titling projects in the late 1990s and early 2000s focused on urban and peri-urban areas of the lowlands.[27] These risks can appear in lowland areas, but a significant difference is how lowland areas are more permanent and well established, and risks are easier to address there. Lowlands can also site a large contiguous area where it is easier to patrol the boundaries with fences, ditches, or the employment of villagers as guards. In the uplands, smaller plots are mixed in with a heterogeneous landscape of other land uses. The upland landscape is also more volatile, dynamic, and moving.

Changing ecologies in the swidden system make it more demanding for the companies to control what is going on there.

The materiality of land in and of itself does not lead it to be acquired for plantation development or protected for peasant use. This is often influenced by how villagers demonstrate the socialization of such land, that it is under their use, occupation, and ownership. This was particularly important when plantation developers, especially Quasa, only followed a loosely defined map of the zones for their plantations. Their bulldozer operators often cleared much more than they were supposed to because they got paid for every hectare they cleared. In Ban Salang, Quasa had initially agreed to clear only land that was "empty," meaning land not under current use by villagers. This was generally defined as swidden fallow areas and secondary forest that fell within the village's reserve area for swidden expansion. Yet the unfettered bulldozer operators started clearing up to the edge of villagers' agricultural plots, including paddies. In some cases, primarily where the border was not demarcated with bunds, they cleared the agricultural land itself. District officials came to "solve" the problem by requiring that the company not clear closer than thirty meters from private land, but they continued to do so and only stopped when "villagers went and stuck poles in the ground."[28] Villagers had to occupy their fields to guard them against clearance, but in some cases the company cleared the land when they had gone for a meeting with the district government in the capital town about this specific problem. As the former village chief explained, villagers had to protect their lands aggressively: "The company listened to some villagers because they were outraged, they wanted to take a knife and cut the bulldozer operator, scaring them into stopping. Some households spoke softly, and so when they returned home, the bulldozer operators kept clearing."[29] Due to a lack of respect of villagers' land claims and uses, the villagers had little option but to resort to aggressive action.

The uplands do not always meet the material needs of plantation investors, and there can be surprises when planting there. Most companies prefer to locate their plantations closer to the road on lower-lying lands. Planting in remote upland areas creates many problems. These areas are far from roads, making it harder to transport machinery, inputs, and harvested products. It is difficult to develop large plots of connected plantation plots that would be more efficient, and it is harder to plant and use machinery efficiently on sloped lands. As discussed in chapter 1, at first Sun Paper staff planted their trees down the slope of the hills, which invites erosion, rather than across them. Moreover, not all uplands have equally fertile soil suitable for plantations, such as the rock-filled, steep mountainside to the west of Ban Kaengvang that villagers wished the company had planted on. In Ban La Ang, a village that we initially surveyed but did not select as a case study, the area that Sun Paper had been allocated in the village uplands was full of rocks and large boulders, making it almost impossible to plant on.

Plantations in the uplands run up against not only the material complexities of the geology and soil but also those related to villagers' livelihoods and land uses, particularly livestock and fire. It is well known that cattle like to munch on saplings and young trees. This has caused a significant debate on the expansion of the rubber industry in northern Laos. It is a major source of frustration for farmers when companies place the responsibility and blame on farmers: fining them when their cattle eat the trees, requiring that villagers create their own fencing to protect the plantations, and demanding that villagers sell off their livestock. Another material risk that plantation companies face in the uplands is the spread of fire from swidden fields when the bush fallow is cleared and burned during the dry season. When these fields neighbor the plantation, fire can quickly spread. Sun Paper reported that its eucalyptus plantations had burned when a fire, which was started in a neighboring swidden field to clear the brush and fertilize the soil, spread into its plantation. Whether the fire was intentional or accidental, it shows the problems of trying to fit plantations into the ecologies of the uplands.

Another socio-ecological aspect of the upland landscape that plantation companies are not prepared to face is land that Brou villagers consider sacred and inhabited by spirits. These principally include cemetery forests (*pa xa*), where they bury their dead, and spirit forests (*phi mahaesak*), where spirits reside, both of which cannot be cleared and are governed by strict rules. Most Brou villagers are animists or follow *sasana phi,* which means "belief in spirits," so that spirits are obviously an intimate part of their worldview. There are spirits associated with important material objects, such as the house, the village, the land, forests, and even rice. In the cemetery forests, the spirits are those of villagers' dead ancestors. Spirits are somewhat contradictory entities in Brou belief, as with spirit belief among other ethnic minority groups throughout the country: they can be powerful protectors of the land, but they can also harm people. Some spirits are benevolent while others are malevolent. Many are neutral: they can be beneficial or harmless if villagers pay their respects to them, but if they are offended or not respected they can create harm, leading to misfortune, sickness, or even death.

For outsiders, cemetery and spirit forests cannot be easily distinguished from the rest of the forest. Plantation companies should not be clearing dense forests whatsoever, but both Quasa and Sun Paper have cleared forests inside and outside the areas allocated to them. In some instances, this has included spirit forests, which has angered villagers. Companies have been required to pay the community for the costs of sacrificing an animal—a pig, cow, or buffalo, depending on the seriousness of the infraction—to appease the spirits. In my initial misassumptions about how the villagers' spirit beliefs operated, I wondered whether the spirits might have punished the companies somehow, sabotaging the bulldozer operators and delaying the clearance of the forest. However, the villagers told me that the spirits would not affect Vietnamese and Chinese company staff because they did not believe in the spirits. Sadly, the spirits would punish the villagers for not protecting the forest from clearance. Nonetheless, the unwelcome prospects of such punishment are part of the motivation for villagers to be enraged at companies and demand that they pay compensation to help appease the spirits when they clear spirit forests.

◆ ◆ ◆

The socialized materiality of the landscapes targeted by plantation companies and allocated by the Lao state plays an important role in shaping which lands are cleared and planted with industrial tree crops, which lands remain under the control and use of peasant communities, and which lie somewhere in between—under peasant control but effectively useless because they are impacted by the clearance of surrounding lands. The biophysical, ecological, and morphological properties of these landscapes do not matter on their own. In some cases, they are conducive to or hinder plantation expansion in and of themselves, such as steep or rocky lands that are not easily planted. For the most part, though, the biophysical materialities of rural landscapes are socialized—in how they are socially and politically treated within the complex social landscapes of the Lao polity at multiple scales—ultimately determining whether they are prioritized for peasant or capitalist usage.

Most important is how different types of land and landscape are socialized as sites of peasant potential and productivity versus being socialized as areas of emptiness, environmental destruction, and poverty, available for capital. The former, of course, are lowland landscapes of paddy production and potential conversion to paddy, the prized form of agricultural production in the socialist modernist ethos of contemporary Laos. The latter concern upland landscapes of swidden fields, bush fallows, and secondary forests, which the state wishes to leave in the past. These differences play an important role in influencing which landscapes are largely cleared, destroyed, and converted into plantations in this region and which are retained for peasant livelihoods. These were considerations that played out at multiple scales and multiple stages of decision-making. Land concessions were planned in predominantly poor and upland areas in the eastern region of Savannakhet that slopes up toward the Annamite Cordillera rather than the wealthier paddy landscapes of western and central Savannakhet. When land was sought for the allocation of the plantation at the scale of the district, areas were targeted that were not predominantly covered by paddies, not too far from road infrastructure, but not within the national protected areas—in other words, upland swidden landscapes.

This chapter has also demonstrated how the distinctions between upland and lowland landscapes are not easy to determine, as the boundaries between them are blurred. Plantation concessions have been allocated in lowland areas that appeared to be empty and unproductive because they lacked paddies—but villagers have contested this by claiming that these are sites of future paddy expansion. Furthermore, they have used those areas productively in a swidden style of agriculture: dry rice planting, but on lowlands. In the uplands, the district government officially stated that they planned to allocate only empty and unproductive land, which translates into swidden fallows and secondary forests (what district officials would consider degraded land) that were not then under production. There were many pockets of land within these landscapes that villagers were planting or planned to plant in the coming year and thus could claim to be productive land that should not be cleared—and they had the tax receipts to back up such claims. Moreover, there were pockets of land that lay at the boundary between uplands and lowlands, which villagers claimed to be paddy or in the process of conversion to paddy land, but that were difficult to categorize. These are gray zones of land categorization that affect the contestation over how landscape ecologies should be socialized—those that the state should exert control over to allocate to private capital or those that the state should ensure are used by the community.

The socialization of nature and ecologies of upland and lowland landscapes significantly impacts the characteristics of land struggles.

However, it does not determine the outcomes of such struggles and the actual processes by which people make claims and contestations over land. For that, I turn to the connections and linkages between people and the Lao state in the next chapter. This is a concern with the political and social relations that communities have with the state that enable them to enact their contestations of land acquisition, or, in the absence of such connections, limit their ability to make such claims heard and take effect. First, we turn to the controversial and sensitive context of land acquisitions within the single-party state of the Lao PDR.

Chapter 4

Resisting with the State

The Lao government hosted the ninth Asia Europe People's Forum (AEPF) in October 2012, an event intended to provide an "open, dynamic and inclusive" space for "meaningful and practical discussion for change."[1] It was a rare opportunity for civil society groups to discuss human rights and development issues with other Asian and European civil society organizations. As a requirement for the ninth Asia–Europe Meeting summit of heads of state and government to be held the next month, the AEPF put the government in an uncomfortable position because of its perceived potential to agitate anti-government dissent. Government spokespeople were planted throughout the meeting venue and often spoke up, giving rosy statements about the country's national development and progress to counter more critical presentations.[2] In a session on land issues, a young Brou woman working for an INGO in southern Laos, who would later assist with the first period of my village-level fieldwork, spoke up about the socio-environmental impacts of a rubber plantation in her home province, which were similar to those of Quasa. She spoke of how villagers were angry that they could no longer farm the land and forage the forest, forced to become reliant on wage labor for an income.

The woman's speech received enthusiastic applause, but it quickly generated backlash from government plants in the meeting. During and after the session, government officials confronted her, saying she must have made up the information in her speech and foreign organizations had paid her to do so. She received aggressive text messages to the same tune. The following week, government officials began visiting the provincial office of the INGO where she worked, questioning her participation in the meeting. The week after, local government officials visited her parents in their village and asked them where their daughter lived and worked.

The Brou woman brought her concerns to one of the main organizers and keynote speaker of the AEPF, Sombath Somphone, a prominent community development practitioner in Laos who had developed a unique philosophy of Buddhist-inspired sustainable development and was awarded the 2005 Ramon Magsaysay Award, a prestigious recognition of public leadership and service in Asia. Concerned about the harassment, Sombath met with the Ministry of Foreign Affairs to discuss this case and the harassment of others who had spoken up about critical issues at the forum. A few weeks later, in mid-December 2012, as Sombath was driving home from work, he was pulled over for a routine police check of driver's documents. As shown on CCTV footage filmed by his wife on her mobile phone at a police station afterward, a man drove off with Sombath's jeep while he was escorted into another truck. He has not been seen since.

The events of late 2012 have had a chilling effect on the nascent but flowering civil society that operates outside the umbrella of the party-state and that was becoming increasingly but only mildly critical of government development, land, and forestry policies. The enforced disappearance of Sombath sent a message to other civil society leaders. Sombath was by no means a radical anti-government activist. The disappearance of a development practitioner with a different, though not necessarily antagonistic, philosophy of development meant that the same could happen to others practicing alternative development and articulating mild criticism. This message was communicated to them quite clearly. A senior government official told a Lao director of an environmental civil society organization that if he tried to organize a civil society meeting in advance of a donor-led forestry meeting, he would "go the way of Sombath."[3] Reflecting on the changing political context, a foreign development practitioner working on land and forestry issues in Laos since the 1990s articulated a common sentiment among INGO workers: "Laos was becoming more open every year since I've been here, until the end of 2012 when it began to move back in the opposite direction."[4]

The debates around land issues at the AEPF that were so sensitive are linked to the government's granting of land in rural areas to private capital for resource extraction and infrastructure and plantation development. As set out in earlier chapters, this is often presented as a narrative in which the state has an increasing hegemonic dominance over rural land as state land. It can grant state land to resource capital and repress local land rights in the same way that anyone perceived as anti-government is repressed. Villagers are presented as having little voice or agency to contest these processes. And when they do, they are further repressed—either aggressively "reeducated" or arrested. For example, in the southern province of Sekong, villagers who had been resisting the concession of their land to a Vietnamese rubber company since 2006 were arrested multiple times. In 2017, they were arrested for cutting down rubber trees in an act of desperation to retain access to their land.[5] Similarly, a community that refused to leave its paddies to make way for a Vietnamese golf course on the outskirts of Vientiane was threatened with jail time.[6] Such cases of outward resistance and arrest are relatively rare because villagers are aware of the consequences of such actions.

Despite the increasing cases of repression at national and local levels in response to resistance, Laos is not necessarily sliding backward as the development practitioner proclaimed. In many ways, this repression responds to an increasing assertiveness of Lao citizens to confront head-on the social and environmental crises they are facing. Furthermore, an expanding field of resistance occurring across the countryside operates under the radar because it is quiet, it is not spectacular, and it does not lead to newsworthy instances of repression. This is a general trend that has been observed nationwide. As a development practitioner who has worked on land issues for more than two decades and is well respected among land rights advocates says:

> Previously, villages gave land away very easily. The village headman would accept money from the company, maybe US$1,000, and give some of it to the villagers. There was very little consultation, and a lot of village land would be given away. Now there is consultation with the village and negotiating. The villages cannot completely protect their land against expropriation, but they can negotiate so that they only give away part of their land. When the company asks for a thousand hectares, they only end up giving away a hundred.[7]

Even central-level government officials have admitted that villagers' reactions to concessions have changed over time. A MONRE official remarked, "Now villagers are not the same as before. They raise concerns to the National Assembly, to the government, and to us. They never did this before."[8] This is not to say that rural people did not lodge complaints or negotiate in the past. However, in recent years, they have become increasingly empowered within a dynamic political environment, such as the multiple moratoriums—albeit contradictory, weakened, and not well enforced—that the government has created on land concessions since 2007.

What distinguishes forms of resistance that do not lead to repression or arrest is that they operate *within* the party-state ambit of power.

For instance, villagers can call the National Assembly's telephone hotline during legislative sessions to complain about land expropriation.[9] In a particularly well-known example in southern Laos, land was even returned to a village after it had been expropriated for a coffee plantation, in part because of how villagers engaged with the state.[10] They brought their case to the National Assembly as a public grievance, setting in motion an official process of mediation with the company.[11] Villagers justified their resistance with narratives of revolutionary fraternity, such as fighting for land during the war, converting swidden rice land to cash crop production in line with state agricultural modernization goals, paying land taxes, and being awarded certificates of appreciation by the government.[12]

The operations of resistance shape whether land socialized for the peasantry can be defended and can continue to be reproduced as peasant land. Chapters 1 through 3 discussed some of the structural dynamics that affect how land is socialized for capital versus the peasantry: investor–state relations, histories of state land, and politicization of upland–lowland ecologies. This chapter demonstrates the importance of action taken by peasants within such contexts, particularly in relation to the state. The socialization of land can be exploited by the state to facilitate the granting of such lands to foreign capital. Yet precisely because it is a socialized relationship, peasants can contest this process to make the case that such land is socialized for them, the tillers. In other words, they can seek to socially re-embed land within a group of land users. The degree to which villagers can do so is not only affected by historical structures of land use and tenure but also by the relationships they have and develop with the state and its representatives, and how they enact them through spatial strategies related to the lands targeted for plantation investments. However, as elaborated in detail in the next chapter, the capacity to take such action also depends on the political cohesiveness of a village, considering their often heterogeneous and fragmented composition.

More specifically, this chapter addresses how peasants resist within a context where operating outside or against the party-state comes with inherent dangers. When authorities frame such resistance as anti-government, it is more easily repressed by the state. The idea of *resisting with the state* captures how peasants tread a careful line between antagonistic action that could lead to political repercussions and everyday peasant resistance that is not noticed by the government at all. Instead, peasants strike a middle ground when they resist with the state by engaging with complex and contradictory internal state politics. They seek to mobilize state ideologies, narratives, policies, and mechanisms to their advantage by exploiting their internal contradictions. For example, chapter 1 details how peasants took advantage of the political gap that emerged between Sun Paper and local officials. Chapter 2 shows how the contradictions of histories of socialized land were utilized, seen particularly in how notions of "state land" were overturned. Chapter 3 examines how ideologies of productive use of land were inverted to protect sites of potential productivity and areas of swidden landscapes currently in use. This chapter focuses on the strategies of resistance that peasants use in relation to the state and the personal relationships with state officials that facilitate such approaches.

Beyond the Everyday

The scholarship on resistance tends to focus on forms of protest that contest state power. Social movements are often highlighted as essential vehicles for challenging and moving beyond the development agendas of states, global development agencies, and corporations.[13] They can help marginalized resource users advance claims to lands, forests, and fisheries they had been denied access to because of land grabs and large-scale extractive investments,[14] historical land inequality and exclusion,[15] and rapid land-use changes.[16] Not only do such movements help sustain access to land and resources; they also expand spaces of democratic resource governance to include the voices of everyday resource users and civil society.[17] Furthermore, social movements and resistance can be seen as critical social forces shaping the uneven geographies of development that result from resource extraction projects.[18]

Social movements and resistance are often viewed as a type of "contentious politics" in that they create interactions with systems of power that are episodic, public, and collective and involve claims directed toward or mediated by governments.[19] They are broad-based and well organized, building on the interests and claims of a large group of people around common generalized issues rather than specific concerns of particular communities.[20] This rich body of work on social movements and direct resistance, while expanding understandings of how movements improve resource access and governance processes, focuses mainly on contexts and cases in which popular movements occur in open, direct, and confrontational ways. In this chapter, I address how resistance emerges and operates in situations "where there is no movement" or where social movements and other forms of open and confrontational protest are highly repressed.[21] In authoritarian regimes, where resources and rural communities' territories are governed in a top-down anti-democratic fashion, involving little participation by small-scale resource users and civil society, how can resistance emerge and make successful claims to land and resources? And why are some resistance efforts more effective than others?

These questions have been principally answered along the lines of James Scott's work on everyday forms of peasant resistance.[22] For Scott, oppressed subaltern groups do not consent to their domination, even if they appear to do so publicly. Instead, they engage in a critique of power via a "hidden transcript" that occurs offstage, or what Murray Last refers to as "dissent from within."[23] In everyday resistance, subaltern groups engage in "normal" acts that go against the grain of power, producing small and incremental gains that also act as forms of subversion but that do not challenge hegemonic power structures. Peasants engage in various strategies, ranging from foot-dragging to evasive protest, which can act as precursors to major riots or rebellions.[24] As theorized by Antonio Gramsci, when subaltern groups resist, they struggle against specific material and political conditions grappled with in the moment through local and place-based experiences of domination.[25] Most importantly for this chapter, subaltern groups engage in resistance that appeals to some power players to prevail against others.

Despite their differences, frameworks of social movements and everyday resistance are comparable in that they both position resistance in relation to the state. Social movements are aimed directly at state power, whereas everyday resistance aims to avoid state or elite power. In Laos, however, a common type of peasant resistance does not overtly challenge or completely avoid the state. Instead, it directly engages with the terrain of power that the state operates on without threatening state power. In other words, it is a form of resistance that seeks to align its objectives with those of the state, such as by showing that peasant use and ownership of land for productive agricultural purposes are in line with the political and developmental aims of the state. It is a form of resistance that seeks to work from within the power relations, dominant discourses, and ideologies of the state. To understand the Lao case and others like it, resistance and domination must be viewed as dialectically intertwined rather than as a binary: "Domination and resistance cannot exist independently of each other, but neither can they be reducible to one another: they are thoroughly hybrid phenomena, the one always containing the seeds of the other."[26] Therefore, when Lao peasants resist, they are accepting a certain degree of state domination, but concurrently seeking to find opportunities within that space for their own interests to be met.

I move beyond the framework of everyday resistance to understand forms of resistance that make overt claims of access to land in the face of threats of expropriation but without contesting hegemonic modes of development and state power. I am interested in forms of resistance that forge a third path, beyond the everyday but shy of broad-based social movements and contentious politics. In the literature on resistance in contemporary Southeast Asia, it has been recognized that there is much more to resistance than a dichotomy between covert everyday resistance, on the one side, and open confrontational collective action or contentious politics, on the other.[27] There are diverse forms of resistance that fall between these extremes. Moreover, these different forms of resistance can coincide, interact, or catalyze one another. Scott argues that everyday resistance can set the stage for developing more overt struggles by developing necessary counter-hegemonic consciousness.[28]

"Rightful resistance" is one conceptual approach that examines middle-ground forms of resistance, based on observations from rural China, where villagers resist within the boundaries of their legal rights.[29] Kevin O'Brien and Lianjiang Li define rightful resistance as

> a form of popular contention that operates near the boundary of authorized channels, employs the rhetoric and commitments of the powerful to curb the exercise of power, hinges on locating and exploiting divisions within the state, and relies on mobilizing support from the wider public. In particular, rightful resistance entails the innovative use of laws, policies, and other officially promoted values to defy disloyal political and economic elites; it is a kind of partially sanctioned protest that uses influential allies and recognized principles to apply pressure on those in power who have failed to live up to a professed ideal or who have not implemented some beneficial measure.[30]

Such resistance is "rightful" in two ways: based on certain norms of what is "right" or legitimate, and based on protections or rights found in the laws or implied in ideologies promoted by policymakers. Put simply, rightful resistance can emerge wherever there is a gap between rights promised and rights delivered.

In this chapter, I build on the theory of rightful resistance by examining how peasants engage with the complex and contradictory de facto internal politics and power relationships of the state, which go beyond a simple dichotomy between central-level legal rights and local-level obstructionism. Such contradictions and gaps can be conceptualized with a Gramscian perspective that views the state as a dynamic and complex web of social relations, emerging and changing with broader domestic and international social forces (see also chapter 1). This can be understood in the Gramscian scholarship of Nicos Poulantzas and Bob Jessop. For Poulantzas, the state is an outcome of the contradictions of capitalism and struggles among competing class fractions.[31] For Jessop, the state is both a social relation and a site of strategic action in which various classes and social actors struggle to influence state power and practice through what Gramsci refers to as a "war of position."[32]

While rightful resistance usefully captures how efforts at resistance in authoritarian political contexts like Laos make appeals to the state, its focus on legal rights only begins to scratch the surface of possibilities for resistance in such contexts. Instead, the practice of rightful resistance in Laos is based more on dimensions of politics and power relations among resisters, authorities, and other key actors, mediated by law, institutions, discourse, and ideology, than on rights on their own. First, the rights that peasants call upon to legitimate their resistance are framed within a narrow politics of development. Instead of being conceptualized as broad-based rights for citizens, they are more aptly viewed as forms of discursive and political power as they fit into state-defined "modern" conceptualizations of what is "right." These include state-driven norms concerning what types of lands and forests *should* be protected. Second, not all peasants can exploit the political system to their advantage; those who can almost always have some sort of political connection that enables them to engage the state. Resistance is thus unevenly available to those who are already in a position of relative political power.

In this vein, I instead focus on the concept of resisting *with* the state. When peasants are unable to protest the state directly and openly or organize a broad-based social movement, they must act within the hegemonic power relations dominated by the state. In some cases, this means they operate under the radar or with "private transcripts," as with Scott's everyday resistance. In many instances, however, they move beyond everyday resistance to operate within the politics of state-based hegemonic power relations. In resisting with the state, peasants are treading a middle ground between broad-based social movements and noisy contentious politics on the one hand, and quiet everyday resistance on the other. They use whatever connections and relations they have with the dominant power paradigm of the state without directly challenging the status quo. They work within state discourses and ideologies of productivity, ecological conservation, historical struggles over territory, and modernization. Furthermore, they go beyond just using such connections and relations to the state by refashioning them to their advantage. They exploit cracks in the relationships between different agencies and levels of the state, and between state agencies and company representatives. They appeal to personal, ethnic, kinship, and historical connections with state officials to make exceptions on their behalf. They seek to mobilize communal solidarity at the village level and the power of the village as the lowest level of government administration to make democratically based decisions about their territorial land use (see also chapter 5).

Hidden Legacies of Lao Resistance

Laos is often framed as a country of rigid or frozen politics, especially in comparison to the livelier politics of neighboring Thailand, Cambodia, and Myanmar. In the evenings, Lao people often watch Thai news channels on television to tune in to the comparatively more exciting dramas of politics there, particularly at moments of protest and upheaval, learning more about politics in Thailand than in Laos. This is not surprising as it is simply difficult to access information about politics in Laos. The party-state is notoriously secretive about its inner workings, and the state-controlled media reveals little else. Sometimes people tune in to the "opposition" Radio Free Asia station in the Lao language, a US-government-funded news media organization that presents news stories that are almost the opposite of government media narratives or reveal information that would otherwise not make it into the Lao media. I was surprised to hear a staff member of PONRE in Savannakhet openly listening to Radio Free Asia in the office one afternoon while his boss was present in the room. When I asked him about it, he simply replied that he wanted to know what they were saying. Now, Facebook, and more recently TikTok, which offer diverse sources of information and critical perspectives that do not fit into government narratives, along with much misinformation, have become the default news sources.

Grassroots politics and everyday politics are approached similarly. There is recognition that there is a politics of access to resources and power for personal gain, such as how the benefits from a development project or an investment will be distributed among government officials. Or there is a politics of who will get a permanent government job, often going to a relative of senior officials in the department or to whoever pays the most for the position. These are framed as the politics of patronage and patron–client relations, laden with corruption. Outside of these petty forms of politics, however, it is often assumed that there is a lack of grassroots politics on the part of everyday people. The repressive nature of the Lao state supposedly prevents any freedom of political expression due to the risks associated with it. Such risks include being identified as antigovernment by the state, being brought into government offices for "reeducation," or being arrested or disappeared.

This misses out on the complex but quiet politics that does occur. The politics that animates the current era, such as that described in the introduction to this chapter, is not unique but linked to longer histories of political movements in Laos. Historical political movements did not end with the establishment of the Lao PDR in 1975, and their legacy shapes the contours of contemporary politics. While political movements can be traced far back in time, most important for this discussion are those formed against French colonialism and American imperialism during the Cold War and established for the development of a socialist regime and society, as well as the countermovements to them.

Lao people are often characterized as happy, carefree, and laid-back, which is at odds with their potential to be political and resist the inequalities and injustices they face. These characterizations can be traced back to the French colonizers. While racist tropes of colonized peoples in the tropics as affable and lazy were common, the French singled out the Lao as less industrious than the Vietnamese and Khmer in French Indochina. Yet the establishment of French colonial rule in its Lao territories was not without contestation, resistance, and revolt.[33] One need only turn to the nationalist movements that began in the 1940s, the battle for independence, and later socialism to see a rich history of political struggle and movement. If politics today seems stale, it was anything but in the middle decades of the twentieth century. The civil war that dominated the country from 1959 to 1973 was a proxy conflict between the United States and the Soviet Union in the context of the Cold War and a contest within Laos for different visions of an independent country. One side retained its royalist heritage and was in line with the ideals of the capitalist world; the other side restructured its social relations and pursued a new socialist future aligned with the communist world.

With the establishment of the Lao PDR, this conflict formally ended, but its legacies carried on. Perceived enemies of the state, particularly officials and soldiers associated with the previous regime, were sent to reeducation camps in remote areas of the country, especially the northeastern provinces near Vietnam.[34] The state did not fully control some areas of the country, and there were ongoing conflicts with rebel groups aligned with the US-backed royalist regime.[35] In northern Laos, Hmong militia trained by the Central Intelligence Agency during the war continued to stay in Laos and sporadically resisted the regime they fought against, and the area has been plagued by a litany of shootings, including a shooting at a bus as recently as 2016.[36]

Although not immediately apparent, the politics of the Cold War era continues to animate Laos today. The government quickly frames critical action or protest that is perceived to be anti-government as a threat to the nation's sovereignty. There are always suspicions that these are linked with exiled Lao and Hmong living abroad who want to see the collapse of the regime. This is what happened, for example, with one of the few open instances of protest—a peaceful march in 1999 led by a group of students in downtown Vientiane who were calling for democracy. It was quickly dispersed and its leaders jailed.[37] In rural areas, political histories can influence how development projects affect different groups of people. In this regard, Michael Dwyer shows how more exploitative forms of Chinese rubber investments in northern Laos have targeted villages that fought on the side of the Royal Lao government but have not fled the country.[38] Ian Baird and Philippe Le Billon's work makes evident how villages with solid connections to the revolution are more likely to prevent the development of land concessions on their land.[39]

Yet the politics of land and development in Laos today is not only influenced by wartime linkages and Cold War associations. There are also changes occurring in the relationships between rural peoples and the state and their ability to have their grievances heard and taken seriously. Since the revolution, the party has maintained that it is the vanguard and representative of the people's interests, especially those of peasants and workers. It has emphasized Leninist principles of democratic centralism. The concerns and ideas of lower-level officials and citizens are allowed to filter up and be used as part of the basis for top-down decision-making. The party itself, while not formally democratic, tends to keep its fingers on the pulse to gain a sense of whether it maintains this legitimacy as a bearer of the people's interests. The party has shifted course or made reforms to shore up legitimacy at crucial times. The abandonment of the agricultural collectivization campaign in 1979 and the market reforms that followed in the 1980s are examples of this. And in 2016, the party selected Thongloun Sisoulith to be prime minister and tasked him with achieving reforms in areas of significant concern for Lao people—illegal logging, land issues, corruption, and the drug trade.[40] The National Assembly has also taken on the role of filtering complaints and concerns from citizens through its hotlines and as an outlet for direct complaints to the government and investigations.

While these mechanisms have always been present, they have been increasingly exercised in recent years. This is partly in response to how the country has liberalized politically and economically, allowing people to have greater control over their lives and interact with international actors and processes like never before. These mechanisms result from the wide range of socio-ecological ruptures or sudden and intense periods of adverse change that people face across the country.[41] These include resettlement for hydropower development and mining, dispossession for plantations, SEZs, road and rail infrastructure, logging of forests, and increasingly unaffordable land prices due to speculation in urban areas. Frustration and anger have built up. Consequently, people have looked to the few outlets for expressing these within the state realm while seeking to avoid being characterized as anti-government and facing political repression as a result. These are not just imported ideas from abroad about land and resource rights. They also reflect the socialist ideals of justice and equality, especially for peasants in rural areas, that the country was founded on. Such ideals are being violated by expanding capitalist relations of resource extraction and commodity production across the countryside.

Orbiting the State

Resisting with the state is a mode of orientation toward power that shaped the action of many villagers in response to land dispossession and plantation incursion. The dominance of the party-state in Lao politics, even in rural areas, and especially over project development, means that there are few options other than operating within the orbit of state power. As the cases discussed earlier demonstrate, when villagers' resistance is seen as anti-government or sabotage against company property, such as uprooting trees, this leads to repression and arrest. However, villagers often only resort to such actions when no other option is available. They first try to make appeals through the state. In both strategy and narrative, villagers seek to frame their actions as being in line with government policy and ideology, even when they are in practice contesting the implementation of government policy and projects. These can be seen as attempts to work through the state to ensure the socialization of land for the villagers rather than to enable the state to socialize it for capital.

When villagers put up a front of resistance, it is almost always through a direct engagement with the state in multiple forms. In the first instance, this is through negotiations with the state officials who first come to the village and promote the project with the company—always district officials and sometimes provincial- and central-level government officials. These are incredibly unequal negotiations—a tremendous amount of state power and pressure is exerted on villagers, and many buckle under that pressure and do not know how to respond. In other instances, however, villagers have stood up to that pressure, striving to show that they should have a say in what lands are acquired and what the village should receive in return. There are rarely any cases in which villagers reject a project or criticize government policy outright.

When villagers negotiated with district officials and company representatives, they tended to come to some sort of agreement in the end—although in some cases, only after multiple rounds of disagreement. Such agreements were always forced to a certain degree as almost every village recognized that the project would be pushed through somehow and that if they refused point-blank this would create political problems for them. Furthermore, the agreements reached were often vague, such as denoting a general area that would be developed without a clear surveyed map and some form of benefits provided to the village. They were sometimes orally agreed upon, other times written down in a note of record (*bot ban theuk*), and villagers were rarely given a copy.

Due to the vagueness of agreements, the companies often started clearing land that villagers did not believe they had conceded to the project. This was sometimes the result of a misunderstanding. In Ban Saphang, villagers thought their land was being surveyed for land registration rather than plantation development (see chapter 2). In many cases, this was because a general agreement was made first and the land surveyed later, a process that rarely included villagers. As a result, lands were included that villagers would never have agreed to give up in the first place. Finally, there were cases in which the companies were allocated clearly defined lands but cleared beyond them, a widespread practice of Quasa.

Such infractions engendered further frustration and anger among villagers and created openings for strategic resistance with the state. It gave them the chance to complain to the government about what was done wrong. Although resistance against state policy and politics is highly sensitive, there is a lot of latitude for complaints about the incorrect implementation of policy and projects, especially if in violation of legal requirements. As noted in the introduction, Laos is seeking to become a "rule of law" state and ensure that legal processes are followed in the development of projects, including land concessions. Local-level officials, like Ai Soukanh, discussed earlier, are often concerned with plantation companies' legal infractions. While it is unlikely for legal cases against the companies to make it to court, there is room for officially raising cases with the government for resolution. This might include oral complaints to district officials visiting a village. It also often includes official letters of complaint or proposals (*bai saneur*) to the district government or even going to higher administrative levels.

My experience of conducting research with government officials, who were sometimes present during the fieldwork and other times not, indicates how villagers modulated their critiques and claims based on the audience, showing how they sought to submit their complaints in relation to state policy and power. When government officials were not present, or interviews were conducted in Brou, villagers felt comfortable enough that the district officials could not understand what they were saying or had lost interest in the conversation that they vented their frustrations and grievances. When government officials were present, and interviews were being conducted in Lao, one might expect villagers to hide their complaints and toe the government line about the benefits of the project or the limited impacts. However, this was not the case. At the end of each interview, we asked whether the interviewee had any comments or questions for us. Especially when interviewing village leaders, this was taken as an opportunity to present their grievances publicly in order to get them resolved. Even with government officials present, the approach was the same. The village offered official and public statements of the wrongs yet to be righted and what the village would like to be done about them. These frequently concerned tangible changes that could be made, such as the benefits that the company promised to the village, like a new road, electric lines, or a village office. Or villagers included requests for a water pump so they would not have to drink the river water the company had polluted. Occasionally, they even included proposals for the return of land that villagers felt had been unfairly acquired or, in place of that, financial compensation. The public statements made by villagers represent how they resist with the state by negotiating the boundary between action and claims that raise the problem they are dealing with but do not come across as antagonistic. Yet they are strong enough to ensure that their claims are heard. They show deference to the state but at the same time prod it seeking to get a response.

While this predominantly occurs collectively as a village, there are also cases where it happens at an individual household level, such as for Thao Chom in Ban Salang. Although the village leaders did not resist the concession of village lands to Quasa and Sun Paper, Thao Chom did not agree with this outcome. He decided to take matters into his own hands when more than 4 hectares of his paddy, swidden fields, and forest land were cleared by the company.[42] As Quasa approached his land, he told company staff to stop, and they alerted the police, who summoned him to the district government headquarters and threatened to arrest him while the company cleared his land in the meantime. Thao Chom reported, "They said you prohibited [*huang ham*] the use of state land. I said, how is it state land? This is my land that I used since my parents' time." They then questioned that, if it was his land, why had he not expanded his paddy land, reflecting state ideologies that permanent wet rice cultivation is the only legitimate form of agriculture. He explained that he and his family did not have the capital to do so. Thao Chom continued to refuse to concede his land and was summoned to the district office twice more. The third time, provincial officials were present and eventually agreed to give back his land if he would pay the company US$5,000 for the cost of clearing. Referencing his impoverishment, Thao Chom recounted that he told them, "What can I give to you? And I didn't tell you to clear the land." They complained and wanted to arrest him, but since then he has not encountered any further problems with the company. Quasa even offered to buy the land for 20 million kip (about US$2,500), which he also refused because his family would otherwise have no source of food: "How could I take money? We have a lot of kids, we're not educated, we must do paddy like this."

Thao Chom's actions are a telling and unique case of civil disobedience. By refusing to concede his land rather than damage company property, he maintained his moral position in the negotiations that the land was rightfully his. He thus presented the actions of the company as immoral, incorrect, and potentially even illegal. Although he resisted the state-sanctioned clearance of his land, he held a disposition throughout the process that indicated he did not intend to antagonize the state. I specifically sought out Thao Chom when I heard of his resistance. When I met him at his house, I was surprised to find that he was not a hot-headed firebrand, angrily contesting government policy, unlike some other villagers in Ban Salang. Instead, he was rather meek and even apologetic. He was reticent at first and somewhat submissive, repeatedly thanking us for coming and pressing his hands together high above his head in a *nop* greeting, which symbolically lowers the speaker in relation to their interlocutor. He seemed to approach district government officials in the same way, noting, "They were very angry, they wanted to arrest me. Still, I wasn't angry. I just wanted to preserve my land." And when he was threatened with arrest, he said, "So be it if you do." Additionally, he always indicated that he sought to comply with the government's requests as much as he could. During the first meeting, they told him he must make his complaint with the provincial government in the provincial capital, 160 kilometers away. He said he could not afford to travel there but would be happy to accompany district officials there.

Although Thao Chom's resistance was antagonistic to district officials, he sought to orient his claims and actions in line with the state as much as possible, which ultimately strengthened his case and enabled him to regain access to his land. His disposition was nonthreatening but firm. His actions demonstrated that persistent, quiet disagreement and dissent can be more impactful in the Lao context than aggressive outbursts or protest. Resisting the acquisition of his lands and the actions of the company without framing this as resistance to government policy was a productive form of political action as it focused on the injustice that he faced. It showed that his actions were in line with a government policy of enabling villagers to continue using the land that was passed down to them from their families, especially if that land was productively supporting their livelihoods.

"The State Is People Too"

In resisting with the state, contestation is about not just going against state projects but finding ways in which villagers' claims can take hold within the state—to be recognized. While villagers submit complaints and proposals to the state all the time, they are often ignored. Therefore, one way to achieve village claims to land is via connections with the state. As a leader of Ban Sokleek insightfully put it, "The state is people too," reflecting on how the state comprises people and social relations. These are the ways of getting past bureaucratic obstacles. Two types of social relations with the state proved to be particularly effective. The first is ethnic and kinship connections. The second is political connections forged during the Second Indochina War and the subsequent communist revolution. In different ways, both types of relations enable villagers' obstinate willingness to go beyond the village level, beyond a simple complaint or proposal to the government, and go directly to people in power who can do something about it.

Ethnic Brou peoples inhabited most villages targeted by plantations. This is not by accident, as the Lao government guides land concessions toward areas that are viewed as degraded or undeveloped, especially the swidden landscapes more common in ethnic minority villages. As discussed in chapters 2 and 3, government officials hold biased views against the swidden agricultural practices of Brou villagers. Officials expressed that Brou people were not industrious or interested in economic improvement and instead would rather live off the natural bounty of the forest. Furthermore, although the Brou are the predominant ethnic group in Phin and Xepon districts, they make up a minority of local government staff.[43] Interviews with focus groups in ten villages show that Brou people had few if any personal or kinship links to government officials in the district government or at the provincial and national levels, except for some unique cases discussed in the following paragraphs. A lack of such connections can make it much more challenging for villagers to break through an obstinate governmental bureaucracy and have their claims and complaints taken seriously.

The only village that had close connections to government officials was Ban Phailom (noted in the introduction), inhabited mainly by Phu Thai peoples, a largely Buddhist ethnic group closely related to the lowland Lao. Additionally, most governmental positions in the district government are held by either Phu Thai or Lao people. The village elite had several close links with the district government. The deputy village head had previously worked as a district-level police officer, and he noted that he was "close with" (*leung kan*) the district governor. We ran across him twice in Xepon town, where he shared that he was participating in biannual district government planning meetings.

When district government officials approached Ban Phailom villagers to concede land for Sun Paper's project, they readily refused. They explained that they had little land left for their own agricultural livelihoods and complained that their land had been encroached on by neighboring villages. As described by the deputy village head, these decisions "depend on the village. If the village doesn't give [the land], then that's it. If the village *did* give the land, the district government couldn't stop us. It depends on our will [*chit chai*]. They don't force us."[44] He confidently stated that the decision lay with the village rather than the district or province. This is a striking difference from the experience of many ethnic Brou villages described earlier.

Kinship can be another vital form of connection with political power. However, like ethnicity, it was generally not a type of relationship that Brou villagers could call on, except in one extraordinary case. Nalao villagers were unsure how to react when they witnessed their agricultural and forest lands being cleared by Quasa bulldozers. A neighboring village had conceded land, but the company cleared beyond that village's border into Nalao territory, even clearing some of their paddies. When villagers complained to district officials, they were told that nothing could be done as the land had already been cleared. They could either receive compensation for private land lost—1 million kip (about US$125) per hectare of paddy and 200,000 kip (US$25) per hectare of reserved land—or get nothing. Although villagers accepted the compensation, they were not yet satisfied. When their complaints to the upper levels of the district and provincial governments had no effect, they began to organize with similarly affected neighboring villages to appeal to the central government. They were fortunate that a woman in a neighboring village was a relative of the then vice president of Laos, Bounnhang Vorachit, who is also ethnically Brou (he was president from 2016 to 2021). They used the compensation money to pay their way to Vientiane, where they presented their case to Vorachit, after which he ordered the district government to return the land to them. When the district government questioned why they made complaints to higher levels of government despite accepting the compensation, villagers responded, "We weren't satisfied, so what could we do? If we didn't take the money, you would still clear the land, so we had no choice."[45] When the company asked them to return the compensation money, the villagers said they had spent it all getting their land back.

In other cases, villagers mobilized connections with provincial- and central-level government officials that they had established during the war and revolution, which were particularly important for Ban Saphang (discussed earlier). When village leaders attempted to lodge a written complaint with the district and provincial governments, they were shuttled back and forth between them. Frustrated that their complaint was not being taken seriously, village leaders—several of whom had fought in the war—appealed to a veteran comrade now placed within the Savannakhet provincial branch of the National Assembly. As one villager recalled, "We studied revolution together, were comrades [*sahai*] together, but in 1977 [two years after the founding of the Lao PDR], I left to be a citizen [*paxaxon*], but he became a leader [*nai*], part of the government."[46] Their comrade helped them submit a formal complaint to the National Assembly through the correct channels and ensured that assembly members visited the village and viewed the site of conflict. The National Assembly did not directly stop the company from clearing the village land and even recommended that villagers work as laborers on the plantation. However, they encouraged villagers to mark off their paddies and begin planting rice on lands they wished to preserve. The National Assembly visit elevated pressure on Sun Paper and provided villagers with the confidence to occupy paddies and reserved lands.

Revolutionary histories, however, do not always lead to the protection of land. In some cases, as shown by Baird and Le Billon, those with the most useful revolutionary connections are also those who most enthusiastically support government policies.[47] In other cases, connections are not maintained over time and lose their de facto power. This was the case for Ban Thatham, which lost significant amounts of land to the Quasa rubber plantation. A village elder mentioned to me his old friendship with founding members and leaders of the Lao revolution, including Kaysone Phomvihane, Souphanouvong, and Khamtay Siphandone, and how he had lived and fought with them during the war in Houaphan province in northern Laos before moving to the south. Although I was skeptical, government officials who accompanied me thought it was true, but he had not maintained such political connections as he had fallen into poverty due to alcoholism.

◆ ◆ ◆

It is often assumed that there is a lack of politics in Laos, that the party and the state put a lid on all forms of political activity through propaganda, repression, and force—an assumption that shapes investors' flawed decision-making as well (see chapter 1). Furthermore, the Lao population is viewed as compliant, whether due to a cultural ethos of tranquility or a strategic response to decades of political repression. Such perspectives miss out on the rich politics active in Laos, which is not visible at first glance, yet abundant beneath the surface. Historically, Lao peoples have engaged in active struggles for independence, freedom from imperial repression, and a socialist society of equality and justice. Other peoples have fought against socialist and communist movements for a society of democracy, individual rights, free market capitalism, and royal tradition. These struggles continued after the war ended in 1973 and the Lao PDR was established in 1975, characterizing rebel movements and government counterinsurgencies across the Mekong and in remote, mountainous regions where Hmong resistance fighters continued their war against the Lao government.

There have been periodic forms of protest and critique against the government that have been swiftly repressed, such as the 1999 student democracy protests that led to five people being jailed.[48] More recently, Lao migrant workers in Bangkok were arrested, and one was disappeared, for protesting for human rights outside the Lao embassy. Such repression extends to the internet as well. When floods hit southern Laos in 2019, Houayheuang "Mouay" Xayabouly posted a Facebook Live video criticizing the government for doing too little to provide relief to stranded people due to mismanagement of public funds.[49] She was arrested on charges of defaming the government and sentenced to five years in prison. As detailed at the beginning of this chapter, the most famous case of repression is the disappearance of Sombath Somphone for the perceived action of fomenting anti-government sentiment among civil society. And in rural areas, villagers have been arrested for any perceived sabotage of resource investments, such as villagers in Sekong province detained for uprooting rubber trees.

These are the most visible forms of a politics of resistance in Laos, in large part because of how they are repressed and the attention that generates. However, other forms of politics and resistance operating across the country do not make the news because they are not manifested by outward, noisy, or visible protest. Their gains and losses due to repression are relatively quiet. They recognize the risks of repression that they face and how action perceived as anti-government can create problems for them; this form of politics, however, operates within the hegemony of state power, which I have conceptualized here as resisting with the state. To resist with the state is to strike a middle ground between everyday forms of contestation that lie utterly under the radar and outwardly acquiesce to power—seeking to make small gains—and large-scale, broad-based, organized social movements and antagonistic protests against the state. Seemingly contradictory, resisting with the state entails contesting the implementation of state projects and presenting such resistance in line with state ideology, politics, and policy. Additionally, it employs strategies in line with state procedures, such as official letters of complaint and participation in land surveys. Yet this approach to politics is not limited to a strict adherence to state rules and procedures, going by the book. There are no apparent legal or administrative pathways for contesting land dispossession. So some form of resistance is necessary, going against the grain of state power to a certain degree to ensure that claims are heard and ideally recognized but not so much as to invite repression.

The strategies and narratives that villagers use to resist with the state and the potential they have to do so based on political and social connections play an essential role in the socialization of land. Along with the relations between investors and the state (chapter 1), the formalization of property (chapter 2), and the politicization of socio-ecological relations (chapter 3), how rural communities resist with the state determines whether they can at least defend the socialization of land for the community with the protection of the state or whether the state socializes it for capital accumulation. As the next chapter shows, the potential to resist is also affected by relations within the community and the ability to produce solidarity in the face of threats and adversity—a capacity that cannot be assumed in heterogeneous and fractious groups of villagers.

Chapter 5

Solidarity in the Landed Village

State power was essential for the transfer of village lands to plantation companies, as made clear in earlier chapters. Both Quasa and Sun Paper depended on the state's legal, discursive, ideological, and coercive power from the central to the district levels. The coercion-backed consent produced by state authority and power was indispensable for convincing or forcing villagers to part with the land they relied on for their livelihoods or hoped to pass on to the next generation as their village populations expanded. The application of state power, however, was uneven over space and across time. As shown in chapter 1, the Phin and Xepon district authorities became wary of using government force to acquire land for Sun Paper throughout their investment. Eventually, it was suggested that Sun Paper negotiate its own deals with villages and then seek approval from the district government, which flipped the negotiations over land between company and village. At the beginning of the project, village officials felt they had little choice but to accept the project because it was being forced on them by the local government. When the company came on its own, village officials were empowered to strike deals that would make the concession of their land worth it.

Sun Paper experienced these dynamics when it sought land in Ban Heuang, a small ethnic Tri village in the uplands of Xepon district, about a ninety-minute drive from the district capital and close to the Vietnamese border. Company representatives approached the village without district officials, although they did bring along the village chief of Ban Chalan, hired by the company as an informal negotiator. Sun Paper had not been officially granted any land by the government in Ban Heuang; it only had the right to seek land there. It was therefore up to the company to strike a deal with the village authorities and bring it to the district and provincial governments for approval. Sun Paper had no choice but to offer a lucrative land leasing deal to the village chief: 60 million kip (about

US$7,500) to rent 3–4 hectares of upland swidden fields and secondary forest for three years to "help the villagers develop." In comparison, compensation for agricultural lands in other villages ranged from 200,000 to 1 million kip (about US$25–US$125) per hectare or none at all in some cases. After consulting the rest of the village and hearing their dissent, the village chief refused the deal, and the company officials became quiet and left. Villagers had guessed that the company's real intentions were to lease the land for sixty years and clear more than 50 hectares. The chief of a neighboring village had told them that after they signed an agreement with Sun Paper to lease out 20 hectares of village land, the company cleared 100 hectares, and Ban Heuang villagers did not want to take that risk.

Without governmental pressure bearing down on the village, Ban Heuang leaders were able to engage in a negotiation regarding a deal on their land and financial benefits for their village. They were free to reject any offers without further hassle and harassment, a radically different situation from that of many other villages. Yet even when such coercive pressure was applied in other villages, some have refused to concede land with a collective voice. We have seen cases of villages taking the issue to the National Assembly or signing everyone's name in the village to challenge the attempt to arrest a few dissenting voices. Additionally, when villages have eventually ceded to state and corporate demands, they have not necessarily done so without internal dissent and frustration with the decision they felt forced to make.

Villages that conceded large amounts of land often referred to themselves as politically weak institutions, at the very bottom of the governmental chain of power. If a decision was made by the central government and approved by the province and district, then the village authorities had no choice but to go along with it. However, to a certain degree this is only true when villagers believe it to be, when they buy into the abstract power of the central state and their comparative lack of power. When villagers, especially village authorities, act as if they have some say in the matter and have the right to make decisions regarding land within their territory, this upsets the envisioned power hierarchy. It puts into question the top-down land allocation process of the concession model. The landed power of the village should be taken seriously—by observers and practitioners and by state officials who must negotiate with it and work tirelessly with it to implement top-down projects. Centralized state territorial power over rural land is only hegemonic when the village is convinced or coerced into buying into this mode of power.

The case of Ban Heuang exhibited this power when the top-down state was not present and the power of the state was directly vested in the village, the lowest level of government. Furthermore, it demonstrated that the land sought by the company, which would normally be socialized for capital and thus treated as government land available to be leased to companies, was socialized by the village as land for the peasantry. It was up to village authorities to choose whether to lease out their land, name the conditions and price of doing so, or refuse the offer altogether. Yet, even when the state is present, villages have power within the decision-making process regarding the allocation of land, despite severe limits on such power within a top-down political system. Village authorities must ultimately agree to the concession within their territory or else the project cannot move forward, although there is significant political pressure placed on them to do so. As an element of the state structure, the village has a role to play in the socialization of the land sought by the company. It can contest the state's attempt to allocate it to plantation companies and shape decisions about how it is used, managed, and claimed.

Village power over land, as circumscribed as it can be within the structure of the Lao state, is not automatically present but must be produced through the organization and strategies of the village in relationship to its land. Villages that concede their land out of fear and promises of infrastructural development have missed the opportunity to exert and develop this power. Others that have stood up to refuse the acquisition of their land and engaged in lengthy negotiations have exerted and expanded their influence. Villages in Laos are not inherently united and cohesive social entities. Rather, they can be highly heterogeneous and fractured due to the ways in which they have been politically and socially produced over time, such as when they have been resettled or when smaller villages were combined into larger ones.

Village power depends on the ability of the villagers to unite in struggle over threats to their livelihoods, or their capacity to act in solidarity (*khwam samakkhi*). In the face of tremendous political pressure to concede land, especially when accompanied by implicit threats of violence and uneven economic opportunities for different villagers, it can be difficult to maintain village solidarity. Cracks can emerge and widen between different groups, such as between village authorities and regular households, particularly when plantation companies seek to buy off village elites. Village power is also fashioned by how the village approaches its land. It can view it as land socialized for peasant use: village land that can be managed as collective and individual agricultural and forestry lands for the development of their livelihoods. Or it can view it as state land that is only to be allocated to households as private agricultural land, the rest managed by upper levels of the government and available to be socialized for capital. This chapter engages with these dynamics by investigating the critical role the village plays in the socialization of land, affecting who ultimately controls and uses land.

The Village, Land, and Power

Believing in the collective power of communities in rural Laos to contest multinational plantation investments and centralized state power can seem to be a romantic exercise, imagining the village as a singular unit that democratically and collectively seeks to defend the integrity of its lands and resources. As the previous chapters show, however, there have been many instances when villagers put up a front of resistance, although framed within state goals, ideologies, and policies. Others have acquiesced to the expropriation of their land or their efforts to resist have faltered. The aim of this chapter is to show how that difference is crucially influenced by the relations among people at the scale of the village.

There has been a long line of thinking on the "community" or the "village," especially in Southeast Asia, and the degree to which it can be considered a bounded, coherent unit that acts singularly, compared with its internal fragmentation and conflict and its blurred external boundaries with other communities and political entities such as the state. Across the Global South, including Southeast Asia, the village has historically been seen as the organic unit of rural society, especially in the transition from colonial ethnography to academic research in the 1950s.[1] Villages were often viewed as primordial, natural units that existed before the formation of precolonial and colonial states and continue to persist to this day. This was closely linked with the idea of the village as a community, so much so that village and community became synonymous. Village communities were seen as little societies with distinct attributes, practices, and cultures contained within their boundaries. In other words, they were natural entities. Similar views have been dominant in Laos, where it can be tempting to view villages as autochthonous communities in part because there are many that have historically been small and remote, comprising a single ethnic group residing in the same location for a long period of time. W. Randall Ireson's work epitomizes this perspective: "Villages in Laos perhaps more than in any other region of Southeast Asia can be characterized as self-sustaining communities relatively unconnected with larger political or social units."[2]

These assumptions began to be deconstructed in the 1980s, when it was argued that villages were produced through colonial rule.[3] The idea of a "timeless Asian village" is "not only a cliché which lacks any real empirical base, but . . . also a construction which, for the most part, originated during colonial rule."[4] Additionally, the realities of agrarian change under emerging forms of rural capitalism—the increasing predominance of non-farm labor, out-migration leading to multiple sites of residence, and class differentiation—prompted scholars to question assumptions about the homogeneity and boundedness of the "village community."[5]

Political ecologists have been particularly critical of how the concept of "community" has been used in conservation programs. The move toward community-based natural resource management since the 1980s was a welcome transition away from top-down, state-based forms of "fortress conservation." However, it is based on an assumption that there is a community present to manage the resources that cover a small area. Or that there are a small number of individuals, a homogenous social structure, and a set of shared understandings about resource use—factors that would lead to desirable resource use and conservation outcomes.[6] Groups of people labeled as a community, however, do not always meet these idealized conditions and can vary by size, composition, norms, and forms of resource dependence. Most importantly, political ecologists point to the class and power inequalities inherent among groups of people, challenging the capacity to conceive of themselves as one community.[7] Communities have rarely emerged organically and are better understood as socially constructed. As Étienne Balibar famously writes, "*Every social community reproduced by the functioning of institutions is imaginary*, that is to say, it is based on the projection of individual existence into the weft of a collective narrative, on the recognition of a common name, and on traditions lived as the trace of an immemorial past (even when they have been fabricated and inculcated in the recent past)."[8]

Histories of Southeast Asia demonstrate the multitude of ways in which communities have been constructed, merged, and moved due to colonial rule, war, population management programs, and development projects. The imagining or construction of community is a highly political act—there is much at stake. For Tania Li, the conceptualization of a community is closely connected to control over the ownership and management of land and natural resources: "Contests over the distribution of property are articulated in terms of competing representations of community."[9] The recognition of a group of people as a community can legitimate their rights to territory, property, and resources at a policy level. It can also lead to conflicts between different communities over the same resources, displace Indigenous residents of a territory, or enable elites within a group to dominate control over resources at the expense of more marginalized members of the group.[10]

In Laos, historical disruptions to villages illustrate how they are in many cases a modern construction. During the Second Indochina War, ground fighting and especially American bombing displaced people from their villages and led to a general movement of populations along the Ho Chi Minh Trail in the east of the country toward the west. After the socialist revolution, groups allied with the royalist regime and educated classes in urban areas migrated en masse to Thailand. Upland groups allied with the Pathet Lao moved into lowland villages to take advantage of abandoned agricultural lands. When the Pathet Lao came to power in 1975, the state began resettling villages to the lowlands to assert control over groups that had some association with royalist forces and were seen as a security threat. Resettlement activities were expanded to a wide variety of upland groups under a developmental rationale, to bring them closer to government services and infrastructure. Smaller villages were combined in what were called "focal sites," in some cases putting together villagers from different ethnic groups who had never lived together. In the late 1990s, resettlement increasingly occurred for development projects, such as hydroelectric dams, mines, and SEZs along with other real estate and infrastructural projects. Due to displacement and intentional resettlement, old villages have been erased while new ones were created, putting together groups of people who had never resided in the same village together.

As these historical changes in Laos reveal, the construction of communities is not a process that can be imagined as separate from the state. In this regard, Michael Watts contends that "communities (with their attendant forms of identity, rule and territorialization) can be produced simultaneously at different spatial levels (scale politics) and may work with and against one another in complex and contradictory ways."[11] The modern concept of community is produced vis-à-vis the state, from which recognition is sought. Along these lines, Philip Hirsch criticizes the idea that the "power of the state was located outside the village, and left the village to its indigenous institutions and forms of organization."[12] Focusing on the Thai context, he argues that the state and the village are no longer mutually exclusive entities and that "the unequal power relationship is now shifted from a state–village axis to a complex of relationships that have become internal to the village, for the very reason that the village has ceased to exist independently of the state, either in a geographical or an institutional sense."[13] This is consistent with histories across Southeast Asia in which "state and village formations are part of the same process" and that villages have been constructed via processes of domination and subordination.[14]

Similarly, the Lao village is not just a community of people living together in a common space with shared associations, engaging in some degree of self-government. It is also a political-administrative unit produced by the state. Even in the precolonial era, the village was part of the mandala system, a political system prominent in precolonial Southeast Asia in which power emanated outward from a central polity, creating a sphere of influence over smaller entities.[15] In contrast to European nation-states, the mandala was defined by its center rather than its boundaries. Furthermore, polities maintained unequal tributary relationships with one another. Prior to colonialism, the Lao village had to pay tribute to local fiefdoms (*meuang*) and their rulers (*chao meuang*), who paid tribute to more powerful rulers.

More remote, upland, and especially non-Lao villages were often beyond the reaches of local fiefdoms and thus could largely govern themselves autonomously, but this began to change under the colonial system when the French switched the tributary system into taxation and corvée labor. In the post-1975 socialist era, the state has physically and spatially reorganized village geographies through resettlement land-use planning and zoning processes. New categories of forest, agricultural, and village land have been created: state categories and zones of land use that do not necessarily correspond with customary or actual land-use and ownership patterns. Additionally, the administrative and political presence of the party-state structure within the village has intensified. Immediately after the revolution in 1975, the new regime's restrictions on the movement of people and goods led villages to become "less open and more corporate," part of the process of solidifying villages as coherent entities under the state.[16]

Villages have traditionally been governed by a collective of leaders, including a village chief and often culturally and spiritually significant elders and shamans, especially in animist villages. Currently, a village chief still runs villages but is now associated with the state administrative system rather than traditional practices. These often overlap, but this is not always the case, as leaders must be elected by the village and approved by the district government. The district government may influence the process to replace a traditional leader with a younger one who is more in line with government policies and administrative procedures. The political apparatuses of the state have also increasingly infiltrated villages. It is also more and more common for village leaders to be recruited as members of the party. Additionally, the mass organizations under the Lao Front for National Construction, especially the Women's Union and Youth Union, have expanded to many, if not most, villages throughout the country. The state also plays a role in categorizing villages according to various criteria of development and improvement. This includes grouping villages according to wealth—poor, middle, or wealthy—as well as giving villages awards for achieving a certain status and being "model villages," such as a "drug-free village," "crime-free village," "model health village," "model village," "cultural village," or "developed village."[17]

Considering the multiple ways in which the village and community are fragmented, constructed, and imbricated with the state, how can their coherence as an entity that could contest the acquisition of land be approached? The construction of the village does not mean it is an artificial entity that does not have any basis in reality—there are real social processes and relations at work that are treated with significance by state officials and villagers themselves. Groups of individuals do reside, work, and act together in collective ways that, in various degrees, can resemble elements of what is considered a community. Here, I emphasize a relational approach that focuses on the social relations among members of a group and in relation to other groups and political institutions that have been historically produced over time. This is similar to Holly High's approach to studying villages in Laos, focusing on "village formation projects," which is "a means of conceiving how 'village' emerges through everyday representations, ranging from state policies to personal mobilizations in a process that is inherently mutable and incomplete."[18] In other words, she examines the production and reproduction of the village over time. We can therefore analyze how social relations among a group of people have been constructed over time and to what degree they cohere as a "village" or "community." As the rest of this chapter exemplifies, the village as a collective entity operating to defend its interests in land and resources is produced in relationship to the historical threats to the territory it occupies over time. Yet this is a constantly negotiated form of action in relation to socialist state building and governance at multiple scales, including within the village.

An important element of my approach here is to view the village as a set of contradictory relations. While it is part of the government, it can also operate as a community, albeit one that has emerged in organic and produced ways over time—a collection of social relations among people residing in the same area. As a result, there are elements of the community that are somewhat autonomous from the state. Even the village administration, while being part of the state, is also responsible for the people's livelihoods. While the Law on Local Administration of 2003 states that the village is supervised by and reports to the district administration, it also says that the role of the village is to "preserve natural resources and the environment within the village" (Article 47).[19] Furthermore, Article 53, "Authority and Duties of Village Heads," states that they are to "educate, mobilise and encourage harmony and solidarity of the people; [and] to promote the people's exercise of their rights and their compliance with their obligations." It goes on to say that village heads have the responsibility "[to] propose to higher-level authorities the suspension of orders or the cancellation of activities which are against the laws, rules and the common interests of the village."[20]

The village can thus serve the interests and needs of both the villagers and those of the state. As High argues, the concept of the cohesive, primordial village can be used by rural peoples strategically as "an essentialist vision of village as a basis for unity and strength. . . . The idea of village is closely bound up with administration, but it is not solely a tool of state intervention, and indeed state definitions and ideals of village can be used to counter or overcome state demands."[21] Although the state calls the village into being, it also emerges as a site of struggle. The interests of state and village are not necessarily mutually exclusive, such as for state-led infrastructural development (roads, electric lines), which fulfill both state and village goals. Yet they come into apparent conflict in the case of state land concessions, which are mainly in the interests of the central state and, to a lesser extent, the provincial and district governments, and in most ways go against the interests of the village. This does not necessarily have to be the case; concessions could be negotiated in ways that straddle the interests of both. Villages would often be willing to concede part of their land if they could decide which area, ensure that it is clearly demarcated and does not encroach on agricultural or other important lands, and receive proper compensation for it, such as in the development of road and electric infrastructure. Yet as clearly demonstrated in the Law on Local Administration, the village has a certain right and even responsibility to make decisions about projects and policies that will affect the interests and rights of the villagers. This also comes with a certain degree of legitimacy in that the village has as a representative of their livelihood interests in a socialist state established by and for the peasantry and working classes.

Contradictions of Solidarity

In an initial survey of twenty-three villages when selecting cases for further investigation, I conducted focus groups with a mix of villagers, including village authorities and households. Although these were one-off interviews that did not capture the full range of perspectives within the villages, no one expressed positive sentiments toward the plantation investments that had encroached on their lands. They all expressed disagreement with what had taken place and regrets regarding the poor deals that they had received: a loss of land for minimal compensation in return and, in many cases, unfulfilled promises from the company. What is remarkable is that villagers expressed these critical sentiments in front of the government officials who were present for these initial meetings, rather than presenting views in line with government policy. In some villages, though, such sentiments became more apparent with hindsight. They had been lured by the attractiveness of a development project that would bring infrastructural development, modernity, and wealth to the village in exchange for some land. However, even when they consented, they did so under tremendous pressure from the district and upper levels of government. Most expressed concern about the project's effects at the time and did not want to concede to it but either felt there was little scope to refuse or saw no easy way out. However, in a small subset of villages, most people were steadfast in their opposition to the project, especially if it did not bring any tangible and meaningful benefit to them. They pursued whatever means possible to limit the acquisition of their lands.

Despite common frustrations and anger with the plantation project, the actual practices of resistance differed significantly across the villages, in large part due to distinctions regarding how to respond to the project, which were shaped by the internal relations among villagers, often characterized as their "solidarity." In conventional views of the village, it is a cohesive entity and the appropriate unit of analysis because of the organic, communal bonds among its members. Small groups of people who live closely together over multiple generations would naturally engage in cooperation, collective action, and mutual support due to their shared identity and feelings of belonging. This is in many ways the idealized village—what many researchers, development projects, and governments envision a village should be, however far removed it may be from reality. In socialist Laos, this ideal is often envisioned through the concept of "solidarity." As High argues, the concept of solidarity has been an important ideological tool of the socialist state to encourage villagers to support state goals and offer their collective effort and even labor to support state projects.[22] This is based on socialist ideals of collective transformation of society and the notion that villages traditionally work together in solidarity, which can be mobilized to support state goals. Thus, as Grant Evans shows, the agricultural collectivization program of the late 1970s was built on the idea that villages already engaged in various forms of collective labor and mutual support, and therefore were well positioned to develop collective farms.[23]

The notion that the village is a site of communal solidarity can operate as a form of rule and a mode of oppression. This was the type of rhetoric used to enroll farmers into collective farms in the early socialist period. It continued to be employed by the state in the contemporary, late socialist period after the market reforms of the 1980s. Since the late 1990s, the government has pursued various forms of decentralization, which government instructions describe as a movement to "build the provinces as the strategic units, the districts as the planning and fiscal units, and the villages as the implementation units."[24] As has been noted, however, this is more of a process of "deconcentration" since responsibility but not decision-making power is distributed to lower administrative levels of government.[25] Appeals to solidarity can enact this agenda of mobilizing villages to implement state work as part of their responsibility within the socialist society and governing system, such as maintaining and repairing village schools.[26]

Although they can be a powerful tool of state ideology, appeals to solidarity and communal effort can be limited in their effectiveness. As Evans and High both argue, they are based on misunderstandings of collective labor and mutual support in the village. These traditional qualities of peasant communities are assumed to operate in the abstract, whereby peasants are naturally willing to work cooperatively toward a common goal. Such practices can therefore be reoriented toward societal goals directed by the state. However, the ways villagers support one another and work together are not solely a desire to tirelessly work for the common good but through individual relations of reciprocity. For example, collective work groups on a farmer's land are built on the practice of labor exchange: the labor that one household provides for another is returned on their plot of land later. The failure of the agricultural collectives in Laos and Vietnam was partly due to how they ignored these principles of reciprocity and were built upon a more abstract goal of solidarity.[27]

High similarly shows how villagers are reluctant to work on state projects, such as school maintenance and reconstruction, despite appeals to solidarity. Nevertheless, they are more than willing to work on constructing temples or helping to prepare for village festivals.[28] She writes, "The vision of 'solidarity' cannot be relied upon to produce the kind of actual cooperation and donation that decentralization policies require . . . the village as a cooperative unit is not a pre-existing unit to be exploited—it is best seen as a process and a social formation, thus characterized by conflicting representations, change, and ambiguity."[29] The difference is that such work is organized through relations of reciprocity, where labor put in to support one person's activity is returned at a later point in time. Furthermore, such actions are driven by villagers' interests rather than externally imposed on them, such as by the state. When villagers do not enthusiastically work for the state, even if it would benefit the village, state officials and village leaders often complain that villagers no longer have solidarity. However, this completely misses out on why they are not engaged in the work: because it does not match their interests and it seems their efforts will not be reciprocated. Their foot-dragging is a classic example of everyday resistance, in this case resistance against the attempt to mobilize their solidarity in a way that does not align with their interests.

Nonetheless, solidarity is not only a tool of top-down rule and oppression that is used to compel villagers to comply with state policies and projects. In the bottom-up forms of cooperation that Evans and High discuss, villagers exhibit a type of solidarity with one another as it is based on their voluntary efforts to achieve common interests. The concept of solidarity has a prominent place in the politics of radical and social and political movements, particularly those animated by labor and anticolonial struggles that emphasize how exploited groups of people work together to achieve common goals, including with the support of more privileged groups or others with different backgrounds and experiences.[30] Thus David Featherstone defines solidarity as "a relation forged through political struggle which seeks to challenge forms of oppression."[31] Solidarity can emerge among people with common experiences of struggle, but also across groups with different experiences and positionalities but common perspectives, whether subaltern groups or those with differing degrees of privilege.[32] An important emphasis of critical scholarship on solidarity is that solidarity is not a preexisting, natural quality due to assumed similarities between people that can be drawn upon by those in power or assumed by activists. Instead, it is a relationship that is developed among people and groups who may be characterized by important differences and inequalities, through shared experiences of struggle and toward common interests.

Solidarity is a concept that can be used to different ends, and so it is important to be critically aware of how it is being mobilized. On the one hand, it can emerge organically as a reflection of the struggles and interests of oppressed and exploited subaltern groups to achieve freedom, equality, or civil and economic rights. Scholars have recognized that while such forms of solidarity can exclude other groups of people from their movements or mask inequalities within, solidarity as a concept and practice is politically important and valuable.[33] Such bottom-up forms of solidarity rooted in people's lived experiences contrast significantly with top-down, imposed forms of solidarity. While the solidarity of communist parties, like the Lao People's Revolutionary Party, may have originated in their shared struggle against American imperialism during the Second Indochina War, after the war they expected villagers to express solidarity in order to follow the party's policies and pursue their goals. Imposed solidarity is not unique to the socialist state but can be pursued by any political or corporate entity seeking to instill a degree of cohesiveness in its employees or subjects to work toward interests that may not match their own.

Solidarity can thus be seen as a contradictory concept with multiple conflicting forms that can emerge at different moments and switch from one to another. Genuine organic forms of solidarity can ossify over time, no longer representing common experiences and interests. In contrast, when those in power seek to impose solidarity among subaltern groups, it may backfire on them. Frustrations amid the exploited and oppressed may forge a new solidarity against the powerful. In Laos, the state only expects a minimum degree of solidarity: just enough for villagers to cohesively accept state policies and projects and to provide their cooperation and labor to implement them. However, when villagers are dissatisfied with such policies and projects and seek different outcomes, their genuine solidarity that emerges in struggling against such impositions becomes dangerous for the state.

In the following sections, I discuss varying types of reaction among villages toward attempts to acquire their land for plantation development. For those that lost significant amounts of land, this was partly due to their limited ability to construct internal solidarity in the face of pressure; divisions that emerged among villagers, oftentimes between village leaders and households, prevented them from putting up a united front of resistance against the project. For villages that were able to resist the acquisition of significant areas of land, many were unified in their resistance and put up a strong front of solidarity, despite the pressures faced. It was not the type of state-oriented solidarity that the government typically seeks.

Villages Fall Apart

Almost all the villagers I spoke with were unhappy with the plantation projects that targeted their land as most villages had lost some land to a company and a majority were dispossessed of quite significant areas. It is not surprising that many villages could not stand up to the incredible pressure the government placed on them to concede land. This did not necessarily mean they lacked any form of solidarity—many of them did collectively oppose the projects. Rather, they did not have the unique capacity to resist projects repeatedly and collectively from the outset, vigilantly monitor and limit activities, and renegotiate the terms of their involvement along the way. Some were overrun by projects in which the plantation seemed to take over the village territory. They became absorbed into what Li calls a "plantation zone": "In these zones, it is not just crucial livelihood resources that are monopolized by plantations; law and government are also colonized by, and folded into, the plantation system."[34] In such cases, any semblance of village solidarity broke down in the face of the pressure exerted on the villagers. A divide emerged between certain sections of the village leadership and elites and the remaining households, the kind of division that so often undermines the construction of a village as a community. Two cases of villages targeted by Quasa reveal different divisions that emerged: an indebted Ban Nammak, where villagers disagreed on whether to give away land in exchange for debt relief, and Ban Salang, where the village chief was bought off by the company.

BAN NAMMAK

The tension in Ban Nammak was palpable each time we visited. In our initial focus group interview, the village authorities were hesitant to detail the negotiations over the allocation of land for Quasa's plantation. On later trips, they and other villagers began to open up about the back-and-forth between them and district officials, the intimidation they experienced, and what they had done to protect their lands. But they always remained somewhat guarded. Whereas leaders in other villages would often offer us a place to spend the night, in Ban Nammak they found ways of communicating that it would be better if we did not. The deputy village chief pushed the issue onto the village chief, whose remarks on how small his house was and how little rice they had got the message across. A district official who escorted us on a trip to Ban Nammak explained that the lack of welcome was because they were a "difficult" village, lacking in "solidarity." To district officials, a lack of solidarity within villages was characterized by the breakdown between different factions, particularly village leaders and regular households, that prevented them from cooperating with government policies to help them develop. However, lack of solidarity in Ban Nammak was about not just their inability to implement government policy but also how Quasa's land investment broke down the ties among community members and eventually produced tensions within the village that the company could exploit to acquire large areas of land.

Ban Nammak's reticence partly had to do with their frustration with the events that had led Quasa to dominate the village landscape. Although the company had told the village it would clear 400 hectares during the initial negotiations in 2008–2009, a mapping exercise conducted by an INGO in 2011–2012 showed that Quasa had cleared 795 hectares of the village's land. This was equivalent to 30 percent of the total land area and 40 percent of zoned land used for agriculture. In 2015 the district government allocated another plot of land in the village to the company to build a latex-processing facility. The school next to the factory would be handed over to the company to serve as a workers' dormitory. As a consequence, there was a great deal of sadness, anger, and desperation at what had befallen them. "We couldn't not give the land. Us leaders thought it's very difficult to preserve the land. Whatever they say is state land, so we'll give it to the state then. It's really difficult. If we don't have a place to live, then we'll just die!"[35]

Nonetheless, the story of Ban Nammak's negotiation with the district shows that they did not just hand over their land out of fear. In their first interactions, they were resistant to the concession of their land despite the intimidation and coercion they faced. In their words, "At first, Ai Somvang came from the ministry [central level government] when they came to measure land at first. He came and asked but asked for our daughters [meaning land in this context]. The village refused. He said again that if you don't give [the land] we'll still take it, we'll arrest you and take you away."[36] In a second visit, this time from district officials and Quasa staff, villagers reported, "We kept forcefully asking [*so pai so ma*], the district prosecutor was angry, saying 'you can't not give the land.' The head of the company didn't say anything, it was our Lao people who were angry."[37] Eventually, Quasa started clearing land within the village without consent, right up to the border of the Phou Xang Hae National Protected Area to the north of the village. Villagers collected 10,000 kip (US$1.25) from every household to fund a trip to the provincial capital—more than three hours away by bus—to make an appeal to the government. They were able to meet the provincial vice governor, an ethnic Brou man, which led to an order restricting Quasa from clearing land within the national protected area. The provincial administration also wrote a letter for the village.

After the company had already started clearing land, villagers were divided as to what should be done. One faction aligned with the village head felt that they should try to take advantage of the situation to get whatever they could out of the company, while another wanted to contest the clearance of their lands. The latter pushed to ask for half of the cleared land back, but Quasa would not budge. So the former faction asked Quasa to pay off a debt the village had to Électricité du Laos, the state electric utilities company, to construct power lines to the village in 2004. As village leaders put it, "They cleared the land already, so we couldn't stop them, so we asked the company to pay for the price of electricity totaling 74 million kip (US$9,250); it was like that." At the time of electrification, the village was only able to pay 20 million kip (US$2,500) of the 94 million kip (US$11,750) price tag, which they raised from logging in the village's forests. The village did not see a single kip of the payment, as it was arranged directly with Électricité du Laos. Ultimately, the appeal of having their debt paid off overpowered the concerns of other factions within the village that were worried about the long-term impact of losing access to important agricultural lands.

When the district government requested additional land for the latex-processing factory in 2012, even the village leadership that had eventually agreed to the concession of their land wanted to draw a line. Not only would the factory displace a secondary school that a Japanese donor had built, but villagers also worried about the impacts on a village health center that bordered the targeted land as construction would further clog up the stream at the site. Most important, they were concerned about the stench from the processing of latex, which is notoriously noxious before it is processed. The factory would signal one more step in the absorption of the village into the territory that Quasa was establishing. A few Vietnamese workers were already renting land in the village, setting up cafés and motorbike repair shops. The establishment of the factory would bring many more laborers to the area. However, it seemed the district government and Quasa already saw Ban Nammak as pliable. They continued to block the village's complaints until they felt nothing could be done, no matter how angered they were. All they could say to district officials, as they recounted, was "Er! If it's going to be like that, then we'll wait for there to be problems [with the factory] and let the district solve them."

Ban Nammak is not exactly a fragmented village of different factions. However, it did not act with the unified and persistent vigilance necessary to limit the actions of a ruthless company like Quasa. As Quasa cleared land without being stopped by angry villagers seeking to protect their land, the company gained control over the territory in a way that became difficult to roll back. This was especially so because it opened a divide within the village exacerbated by its debt. Ban Nammak does not have a long history of close ties. Like many other villages in Laos, it is fairly recently established, forged in 1975 as part of a government policy to combine smaller villages into larger ones (*ban noi tao hom ban nyai*) along linked roads—Ban Nammak sits on a junction between Xethamouak town and Vilabouly district as well as several other villages to the east and west. While there were no rumors of village leaders being paid off by the company, the village chief was known to receive 100,000–200,000 kip (US$12.50–US$25) at every meeting that Quasa held in the village.

BAN SALANG

Neighboring Ban Salang villagers were similarly afraid to stand up as a community to protect their land. When asked if they willingly gave up their lands to the company, they replied, "Who would be? It's the land next to our paddy fields, but if we didn't, they said they would put us in jail, so we were scared. The district [government officials] said that whoever doesn't give [land] must sign their name on the document. Who would be brave enough to sign?"[38] One of the reasons it was difficult for villagers to be brave was a lack of leadership from the former village head who was in power when the project was being developed. Two villagers had gone to the district to try to get land back, so we asked the village leaders:

MKL: Why didn't the whole village go [to the district]?
VILLAGE LEADER 1: Who would go?
VILLAGE LEADER 2: We're afraid of going to jail.
VILLAGE LEADER 3: The village chief [*nai ban*] got money from the company already.
MKL: Is that so, village committee?
VILLAGE LEADER 3: Who knows, we ourselves don't know [*they laugh*]. Ask for the record, where it says the village chief was paid. We haven't seen any record, but we're sure that the village chief got some money from the company.[39]

Although they could not confirm it, they were relatively confident that the former village chief had been paid off—a Lao staff member of an INGO with years of experience working in the village affirmed the rumor. They were particularly suspicious after a tip-off from bulldozer operators working for the Vietnamese plantation company. They had started clearing land in the village, seemingly without any prior announcement or consultation. The bulldozer operator explained, "The village sold [the land] to the Vietnamese already." Additionally, whenever the village had problems with Quasa, the village chief would go to the company alone to resolve the issue, which they suspected may have meant he was paid off each time. This may partly explain why he was no longer the village chief if it had caused tension within the village, and he did not partake in the focus groups with the leadership or other households.

We finally caught up with him at his hut near his paddy field at the edge of the rubber plantation, far outside the village's geographic center, seemingly existing at the edge of its social life. I had imagined that he might exhibit some signs of wealth from his rumored payments from Quasa, such as a new house or car. However, he did not hold any apparent material possessions that distinguished him from other villagers. As it was the end of the wet season, he was getting ready to harvest rice from his paddy fields like any other villager. I also expected that he might seek to justify the concession of village land to Quasa by mobilizing government narratives of economic development and livelihood improvement. Yet he was as critical as other village leaders and seemed genuinely conflicted about how the village had conceded its lands and his role in that process. He specifically felt that the village had little choice in the matter, which may be why he did not put up a fight and took whatever Quasa offered: "The village didn't really agree [to concede land], but it was necessary because the district came, and we had to give [the land]. . . .

At that time, we thought that if the central level already approved, then it's finished for the people. In our hearts [*chit chai*], we didn't want to."[40]

In addition to potential payments, the former village chief had also been hired as a salaried guard for the plantation to prevent villagers' cattle from eating the young rubber trees. It seemed to be a relatively laid-back position, much of which he could do from his paddy house at the edge of the plantation, because, as he explained, cattle could not eat the rubber trees anymore as they were much larger after several years of growth. His salary ranged from 700,000 to 900,000 kip (US$87.50–US$112.50) per month throughout the year (higher during the dry season, when cattle were more likely to wander into the plantation looking for food). He still complained that company managers would cut his wages when they came by and did not find him doing his work. He bemoaned that they were likely to ask him to fix a broken fence without paying him anything extra. Despite the cushy job, he also lamented the personal losses that the plantation had brought to him: his income had decreased since the establishment of the plantation by several million kip per year because he could no longer find NTFPs to sell, but this ignores the significant increase in cash income that his plantation job provided. Moreover, he reflected on how there was no longer any swidden land left in the village, but he had already transitioned to paddy production and none of his lands had been absorbed into the plantation.

In both Ban Nammak and Ban Salang, there was deep resentment with how Quasa, aided by local government, had acquired village land. Such indignation may have hardened after the full effects of the plantation project had been felt, but there was clearly a strong current of resistance from the beginning. The problem was not that villagers' views and positions were completely fragmented but that they were not entirely united in common cause—the type of tight-knit, bottom-up solidarity necessary to contest the weight of coercion they faced. In Ban Nammak the opportunity to use the project to relieve a collective debt swayed a faction of the village, while in Ban Salang the village elite were swayed by cash payments and job opportunities. Effective resistance requires a degree of collective commitment and persistence that is not easy to achieve.

Building Solidarity

Consistent across all villages that effectively resisted partial acquisition of their land was their development of a high degree of bottom-up solidarity, rather than the top-down solidarity with government policies and projects that the state sought to achieve. They were firmly opposed to the project, at least in how it was initially proposed, and rejected it from the beginning. They only conceded if they could negotiate the terms of the project: what lands would be conceded, how they would be compensated financially, or the company's construction of electric lines and roads to the village. And when these promises were broken, they receded to their former position of opposition, rescinding their earlier offers or refusing to concede any more land.

Instances of resistance based on villagers' solidarity were recounted in previous chapters, and so these cases are only worth briefly reviewing here. Ban Saphang's success in limiting the extent of Sun Paper's plantation was aided by the villagers' ability to make their case heard and be taken seriously by the government (see chapter 4). However, they could only achieve this by rejecting the plantation project in solidarity and working together to prevent it as soon as they learned of it. Whenever the company and government approached them to acquire land, a communal meeting was held and the villagers consistently refused the project due to a lack of perceived benefits. When they traveled to Vientiane to appeal to the National Assembly, each household chipped in cash to raise 4 million kip (about US$500) to pay for it. When contesting the clearance of their lands, they organized themselves so that a few villagers would always be physically in the fields to occupy and defend them. Later, another plantation company offered to lease village land, proposing to pay US$350 per hectare for a thirty-year concession. Although the village chief was impressed by the offer, he repeatedly emphasized that he lacked the authority to decide without the support of all villagers.

The rest of this section focuses on two additional cases; in both, villages were targeted by Quasa. Ban Phoulao struck a deal with Quasa to exchange infrastructure for land and resisted later attempts to acquire more land when Quasa did not keep to its end of the bargain. Ban Sokleek conceded a small amount of land and negotiated with Quasa based on their history of dealing with earlier resource extraction projects in the village.

BAN PHOULAO

Ban Phoulao is worth investigating further because heavy pressure was placed on the villagers by the government and Quasa, but they still put up a fight and were able to prevent a large area of land from being acquired. Their case exemplifies the tensions and challenges that villages face when a state-sponsored plantation targets their land, and the collective nerve it takes to contest it. At first glance, it may seem that they were unsuccessful in defending their lands as Quasa acquired 492 hectares within the village, but this only resulted from extended negotiation and was much less than the company sought to develop within the village territory. Ban Phoulao was united in opposing the project since it was first proposed to them. District officials and Quasa staff visited the village six times before they could pressurize them to concede any land for the project. At first, government officials from every level of government, and even the district chief, approached villagers and told them that they had the right to decide whether to concede land—villagers took this offer literally and refused. They said, "This rubber plantation depends on the village, which area is conserved, which area would be given, but don't give a lot of land, only the land that is not being used. We agreed with what they said. . . . They said if you don't give the land then that's it. The land that the company wants is land that villagers don't use. But don't give dense forest land [*pa dong*] . . . when they came to inform us it was good."[41]

The company and government kept returning, more demanding each time. Their tune changed with each visit, and they eventually declared that the company would develop the plantation project regardless of village dissent. Despite this, Ban Phoulao villagers continued to refuse, confidently asserting their land rights, despite the complexities of landownership in the Lao context. "This isn't only village land, it also belongs to the state, but we live here, we protect it [*pok pak haksa*], we are the owners [*hao pen chao*]."[42] Village leaders recounted their solidarity in response to state pressure: "The way they did it was not normal. They started writing down people's names. Whoever won't give land, write your name down. So everyone in the village wrote their name down. They asked, 'Who's the chief here?' and we responded, 'The whole village is the chief.' So they stopped. If it were just one or two of us, they would have taken us away."[43] An agreement was only reached when the company met the demands set by villagers to pay for the extension of power lines to the village and to fix and maintain a dirt access road each year.

Villagers were skeptical from the beginning that Quasa would fulfill its promises. They consistently tried to get the company to start honoring the "contract" between them by building a road before clearing land for their plantation. "They came to inform us that they were going to clear a road for the village, but they didn't do it following the contract. I immediately took our villagers [*ai nong*, literally "siblings"] and went to protect the land, to tell them to stop because they didn't clear the road for the village." The company called the district prosecutor, who asked the village what was going on. The village stopped the company again when it had cleared about half the land, but when the company said it would make the road, the district prosecutor let the company continue.

Quasa failed to deliver on its road-building promise, even after the land had been cleared and trees planted. On top of that, the company dared to come again and ask for another 300 hectares, this time in the eastern section of the village. The village chief immediately refused "because they lied to us." Quasa then reduced its request to 100 hectares, but as the village chief recounted, "I said we're also not giving 100 hectares. Our land was taken already, and we didn't get anything." In that manner, they effectively ended plantation expansion within their village territory.

Although 492 hectares is a significant amount of land, Ban Phoulao covers a large area. Not only did the village authorities prevent Quasa from acquiring another 300 hectares; they also influenced where the 492 hectares would be located. They did not know how much land would be acquired at the time and were only informed later how much had been cleared. However, they did direct the company's project to the northwest region of the village territory, bordering another village that had also agreed to give land to Quasa. This was an area that they used less intensively than others, but it included swidden fields and fallows of the village. Be that as it may, they intervened as much as possible to prevent the company from expanding further into village agricultural lands, though they had difficulty communicating with the Vietnamese bulldozer operators who did not speak Lao. The village chief recollected, "I was so busy at that time that I wasn't around at all. One moment, this person's land was impacted, another moment, it affected that person's land. Sometimes, I went to tell them [the company], but then they would still go clear at nighttime." Company staff told villagers that if any land was cleared beyond the boundary of the allocated area, villagers could plant any crops they liked in that area, "but in the end, the company cleared everything, they wouldn't allow us to touch it." Villagers couldn't find certain NTFPs anymore, like cardamom, rattan, and lady palm (*san*). However, they reported that they could still collect firewood and timber for house construction and, more importantly, there was still enough agricultural land in the village for everyone.

Ban Phoulao exhibited strong resistance to the clearance of their land without their demands being met. They felt and responded to the pressure of the state. Village leaders explained, "We couldn't not give the land, the state wanted development. Ow! It was necessary to give it." But within this constrained environment, villagers only agreed to give up some of their land in exchange for suitable compensation: electric lines and yearly road maintenance. When such compensation was not provided, they closed off their land frontier. Almost all of the villagers gathered together at every meeting. The village chief wanted to make it clear to us that the company hadn't paid him anything: "If I took from the company then the villagers would complain about me, so I'm honest, I didn't take anything. They tried to give to me, but I didn't take anything."

BAN SOKLEEK

Ban Sokleek is perhaps an even more remarkable case, as villagers put up the most potent resistance to Quasa's project, limiting its acquisition to "three hills" covering only 52 hectares. It is a remarkable case considering how ruthless Quasa could be in its tactics and its ability to mobilize the full coercive power of the state, including at the provincial and district levels, to acquire land within village borders. As the cases of Ban Salang and Ban Nammak illustrate, it is easy for any semblance of village cohesiveness to collapse in the face of such violent pressure. Ban Sokleek leaders recognized how different their village was from others in the area: "Look at other villages, they've completely fallen apart [*taek yaek mot*], they don't get along with the village chief. Look at our village, we're poor, but we're together, and we have solidarity. If anyone is sick or hurt, then we go to visit them together."[44]

Villagers did not want to concede any land to Quasa. But they felt that they could not refuse the project outright because the state demanded that they make a shared sacrifice for the country's development, which other villages were also making. At a meeting in the district capital, officials told them, "It's not just your village, it's the whole district where more than 4,000 [hectares] will be allocated," so the village authorities allowed them to clear land. On top of that, there was the heavy weight of state power: "We couldn't *not* give [land] because the party-state was doing it." In response, they selected a site for the company to clear that they described as dry dipterocarp forest and secondary forest that did not have large trees or many NTFPs, and that villagers were not using for agriculture. Furthermore, they prevented the company from clearing household swidden and paddy fields adjacent to the allocated plantation area, as had happened in other villages. They had been told that the company would provide them with whatever they wanted for compensation. They asked for a groundwater pump but never received it.

When the company came to ask for more land, the village authorities agreed but only if the company paid the village 15 million kip (US$1,875) in compensation. Company representatives kept a record of their proposal, which they said required approval from their parent company, VRG, in Vietnam. Thinking that the village had already agreed to more land clearance, the company started clearing land on a fourth hill. Villagers went to protest (*tuang kheun*) with the company manager at the company's office in Phin district, demanding that they receive financial compensation before land clearance could continue. When the company continued to equivocate, the village decided not to take any chances and told them to stop clearing land immediately. Villagers reoccupied the fourth hill: "When the boss came to the village, we told him that if the company plants [rubber trees], we'll take it back." The lack of compensation for the first three hills and the hesitancy to provide compensation for the fourth convinced the village that they needed to take control of the land: "If there's no compensation, how can we give [the land]?"

It is somewhat incredible that Ban Sokleek had this capacity to stand up to immense pressure from a company with deep and strong connections with the government and that sought to acquire significant amounts of land, especially when compared to other villages. As with other villages, I wondered if village leaders had unique political connections with different governmental agencies at various scales through kinship, ethnicity, veteran, or other personal links. However, Ban Sokleek is an upland village consisting of all ethnic Brou households, with very little paddy land located only in some small areas in valleys between hills; most of the village landscape comprises swidden fields, fallows, and secondary forest. In these circumstances, all that was left was village solidarity and strategic tactics for preventing the acquisition of their lands.

Even when the village authorities acceded to state demands and conceded three hills to the company, they emphasized that it was their choice to do so and their right to make that decision. Reflecting customary power over the territory, they made the case that the government had to get their permission before the company could use any land within the village's borders. We asked, "Before the company wanted to take land, did the company and government ask the opinion of the people?" They responded, "They sure did ask! Following tradition [*hit khong bapeni*]." This tradition entails the right of the whole village to make decisions regarding the land, not only the village leadership. They explained that they had an intensive and lengthy discussion with all villagers; even "divorcées and widows came to consult." This delayed Quasa's project because "it was a long time before they came to clear." The village chief was adamant about consulting with villagers on essential matters like this and ensuring that everyone was on board: "Let's put it like this. If you are the village chief [*nai ban*], you have to consult with the people, or they will blame the *nai ban*. . . . If you don't inform them in detail, soon the villagers will think that the *nai ban* has sold the land. Villagers will complain and attack you, and you'll have to move to another village [much like the former village chief of Ban Salang]."

Village leaders also explained that they were unified in their campaign to reclaim the fourth hill that Quasa started clearing without their permission. When we asked them how they were able to get the land back when other villages could not, they emphasized that it was because they never conceded that land and would never let the company have it: "We didn't give it! Who would take it? They would have to arrest the whole village, make the place where they'd keep us full [*followed by laughter*]." Their collective defiance gave the village much confidence in their negotiations with the company, so much so that they felt "the company is afraid of us" rather than the more common inverse sentiment.

Solidarity in Ban Sokleek has been produced over a long period in relation to various processes that have affected the village, creating its ability to retain control over their lands. The village has a long history in its current location. They're not exactly sure when—"our generation doesn't know"—but they estimate it was at least since 1930: "Look at all of the big mango and jackfruit trees," they explain. But they trace back their lineage in the area to the early nineteenth century, as they say the village moved due to the Thai invasion of Laos in 1828, or what they referred to as *Tai kuat* or the "Thai sweep," because they swept up and took everything away, including people who were repatriated. The village name can be seen in the same location on a 1954 topographic map of the area created by the US Army Map Service in the lead-up to the Second Indochina War. Like other villages in the area, they evaded US bombing during the war in the forest but returned to the village after the establishment of the Lao PDR in 1975.

Not only is Ban Sokleek ethnically homogenous, it is also a small village of sixty-one households with practically no in-migration over the past half century. The area's small size, ethnic homogeneity, and long-term settlement are factors that one would expect to contribute to solidarity by engendering a close connection between village leadership and the rest of the village. A Lao staff member of an INGO working with these villages on land and forest issues and rural livelihoods felt this was a crucial difference. Although the INGO started working in the area after the negotiations with Quasa and the government had primarily finished, through their engagements across a range of villages they had unique insights into the internal social relations of each community. The staff contended that Ban Sokleek had stronger village leadership. They could effectively mobilize villagers to cooperate with them and negotiate with the government collectively, especially compared to the weak leadership of Ban Nammak and Ban Salang. And the small size of the village allowed for close connections between leadership and villagers.[45] While a small population does not inherently produce solidarity, it can be a useful social resource when advancing a unified position in struggle.

These conditions support Ban Sokleek's solidarity in opposition to Quasa's acquisition of more land than villagers were comfortable conceding without proper compensation. However, perhaps the most important element shaping the consciousness of the village to only concede their territory and resources if they were appropriately compensated was a history of engagement with resource-extractive projects in the village. In the 1980s, logging was undertaken by state timber companies without any compensation or benefits to the village. Then, in the late 1990s, two mining companies, one private and the other state-owned, were given the rights to quarry stones used for construction on a total of 20 hectares within the village. In exchange, a deal was negotiated that provided compensation to the village of 5 million kip (US$625) per year per company. Additionally, village authorities often negotiated various aspects of the benefits and impacts of the project on the village. Company trucks, which drove through the village on the way from the quarry to the main road every few hours, kicked up a lot of dust. When village authorities complained, the companies agreed to spray water on the dirt road in the mornings and evenings to reduce the dust. These engagements with prior investments and the lack of compensation from Quasa for the first three hills taught them a great deal about how to concede land and resources only if they received something substantive in return. "We requested compensation because our land was lost. It's the state, so we don't blame them, but there must be compensation. It's the same with the stone quarries." Half-jokingly, villagers remarked that they had a unique ability to make demands on resource investors: "It has to do with our intelligence [*laughter*]. Those villages don't feel like developing. Our village wants to develop." Therefore, they also contested state narratives that land concessions could generate development. For them, development was best achieved through a strong-willed and crafty village that determined its destiny within the range of possible opportunities.

♦ ♦ ♦

The notion of the village in Southeast Asia and its capacity to act as a coherent community is highly polarized. Villages have historically been imagined as natural primordial units that are the bedrock of Southeast Asian societies and polities. From this perspective, they have only begun to mutate and become unequal, stratified, and depopulated due to forces of modernity, nation building, and capitalism. More contemporary scholarship, however, has recognized how villages are presented as constructed artifacts, imagined communities produced by historical processes, such as colonialism. Characterizing them as coherent and focusing on the village as the critical unit of analysis more generally mask important realities about the human geographies of rural Southeast Asia, like the inequalities and divisions within so-called communities and how people's connections to place extend far beyond the village. It has also been well argued that the village does not exist autonomously as a social and political unit but is deeply integrated into other political units and relations—for example, the state.

Critiquing and questioning assumptions about the coherence of the village also raise questions about the basis for community action. Critical scholarship in political ecology and cognate fields on community-based natural resource management has demonstrated how problematic it can be to assume a "community" to manage natural resources or that such a group of people will manage them in equitable ways for the good of all members. This also raises questions about how collective resistance operates, such as in response to threats of land grabbing. Without a coherent community, is it possible for a so-called village to stand up to the immense pressure of top-down land acquisition, as faced by the villages discussed in this book? Or, if a front of resistance is created, then to what degree is it representative of the political voice of all members versus merely the village elite? Furthermore, is it possible for coherent communities to act with one voice, despite how constructed they may be?

In this chapter, I have staked out an argument that addresses how agency operates within a village in response to land grabbing. My position takes a constructivist approach to community seriously while also considering how a community, as an agent of change, can be formed in ways that unite but also fall apart. I take a relational approach that considers how social relations among members of a group of people living together are constructed over time and fashion degrees of cohesiveness and common perspective, like whether to contest or accept a state concession of village land. This includes a consideration of how that community is produced in relation to the state and other political-economic forces, as well as the role that members of that group play in such a process of production—in other words, the dialectical relation between external and internal processes in shaping the type of collective formation that emerges. The construction of villages is thus a complex and conjunctural process that emerges over time, not produced by a single actor but through cooperation and contestation among them. In many cases, this generates fractured and divided villages, as seen when multiple smaller villages of different ethnic groups are resettled into one larger village. In other cases, though, cohesive villages may be produced over time as a reaction to external threats, as with Ban Sokleek, described previously, whose demands hardened in response to their engagements with resource extractive companies over time.

This framing of solidarity in Laos captures the contradictory nature of how communities are produced. This concerns the production of solidarity because of the dialectical relation between external forces, especially the state, and the social relations of the village. Moreover, it shows how solidarity can be employed for top-down control of communities, but it can also offer a way for communities to express their bottom-up refutation of policies and projects imposed on them. The various cases covered in this chapter reveal how whether a village "has solidarity" or not does not determine whether that solidarity is with the state and its policy of granting land concessions to foreign plantation companies or focuses on the village's immediate and direct interests in defending its access to land and forest resources. Solidarity is hence a tool of village cohesion that can be oriented toward different interests and objectives. Ironically, it was an abundance of solidarity in some instances, such as for Ban Saphang, Ban Phoulao, and Ban Sokleek, that enabled them to collectively resist the granting of their lands and not fall directly in line with government-endorsed projects. In other cases, such as Ban Nammak and Ban Salang, a lack of solidarity enabled the government to allocate village lands to companies. Yet the disintegration of village cohesiveness made them difficult to work with and created problems down the line—for instance, the burning of rubber trees. Therefore, government appeals to solidarity sought to produce the right kind and right amount of solidarity—enough to implement their projects and maintain a governable community that would not threaten the future of the plantations.

Concerning the book's central argument, this chapter has shown that contradictory processes of socializing land in Laos—for capital or the peasantry—are manifested and molded by the social relations of solidarity and cohesiveness at the community level. As the introductory case of this chapter established, without state power involved, communities are more than willing to strike hard bargains and negotiations surrounding the concession of their lands and what they would need to receive in return for the loss of something so crucial to their livelihoods. They have vital interests and demands at work but are limited by the imposition of state control and management of their lands. As covered in chapter 2, control over the territories that villagers use and occupy is a shared relationship between village and state. Villages have a great degree of power in that relationship—much more than is often recognized—but they must demand their rights with the full strength and weight of a united community. So how their solidarity is constructed and the direction it takes affect the purposes and direction of socializing land.

Conclusion

I returned to eastern Savannakhet province in July and August of 2022 for a brief follow-up visit, seven years after completing the bulk of my research. Not surprisingly, much had changed during the time I was gone. Arriving in the capital of Phin district, I sought out my former governmental interlocutor, Ai Soukanh, which was more difficult than I had expected, as I had lost his phone number in the interim. The DONRE office had moved back to the old district government headquarters where Quasa staff had previously been living (see chapter 1). Ai Soukanh was not in and it was challenging for his staff to get in touch with him, as he had recently lost his phone. They finally reached him after contacting one of his family members through Facebook. Close to retirement, he met me at his home near the old district market. Though he had received various financial payouts from companies like Quasa over the years, the state of his small house suggested that he had not become a particularly wealthy man. His daughter, who had studied in Vietnam to take up a job with Quasa, was dissatisfied with the work and eventually left for another job in Bangkok, where two of his other daughters had migrated earlier. Ai Soukanh was considering moving there to live with them in retirement.

Although my research permits had long expired and I was visiting the district on a tourist visa, Soukanh was happy to use his connections to take me around the district hinterlands one last time and show me what changes had taken place. We visited Ban Nammak, the village where Quasa had acquired 30 percent of its land and planned to build a latex-processing factory. To my surprise, a plantation of acacia trees stood on the land that had originally been cleared for the factory. Further, the secondary school that would have been displaced by the project had not been demolished. When we met the former village chief, he explained that village authorities continued to complain to district officials about the likely smell from the factory, and surrounding village committees had expressed discontent over potential impacts on water quality. They said if the factory were built then the whole village would move. "Where would you move to?" Soukanh asked rhetorically during our conversation. In a meeting the next day, Quasa managers explained that the company had moved the factory site due to these concerns about environmental impacts on nearby villages, choosing instead a site in Xepon district that was far from any settlements. Although this was a success for Ban Nammak, unfortunately the company retained control of the land for the acacia plantation, intending to use the trees as raw material for packing and transporting its products.

Several days later we visited Xepon district to check up on Sun Paper's project. After speaking with government officials and a Sun Paper representative, I was surprised to learn that the amount of land the company had cleared and planted within its granted concession area had not increased since 2015. It had never been able to solve its land access problems via the concession model and instead expanded its system of contracts with individual households, who provided their land in exchange for a share of the value of the cut wood at harvesttime. Sun Paper gained access to 70 percent more land through this approach than via concessions, which demonstrates that working with rather than against farmers had become the superior model of plantation development. Sun Paper also distributed almost 20 million eucalyptus seedlings to farmers for them to plant so they could sell the mature trees back to the company, a different form of contract farming. Finally, Sun Paper made a strategic purchase of Birla Lao Pulp and Plantations Company Limited, an Indian company with a struggling plantation project. In this manner Sun Paper gained control over an additional 17,000 hectares of plantations in western Savannakhet. Incredibly, this significant increase in production area still does not provide nearly enough raw material for the company's pulp and paper mill, which came online in 2017. Requiring 1.5 million tons of raw wood material annually, Sun Paper imports more than 1 million tons from Thailand and Vietnam each year.

Returning to this region revealed that the land frontier that both companies played important roles in over the past decade and a half had largely closed. This coincided with a broader closure of the resource frontier across eastern Savannakhet. Having been a site of heavy logging since the 1980s, the district had little valuable timber left, even in the national protected areas, by the time I conducted my fieldwork. Villagers who had admitted to being involved in illegal logging in nearby territories were traveling to other parts of southern Laos to log for

Vietnamese traders. Reserves at the Sepon gold and copper mine in a neighboring district, one of the largest in Laos, had been steadily declining. Route 9, the main road crossing the province that had consistently been pummeled by logging and mining trucks, had finally been completely repaired and smoothed out, representing a new era of frontier closure, albeit one with ongoing resource commodity production.

However, this frontier closure does not mean that relations to land have become solidified, settled, and unchanging. While they may be less fluid during the period of frontier formation, land continues to have complex social lives, as it is not simply a material entity but a set of dynamic social relations. This remains the case when land has been transformed into exclusively owned private property or, more specifically for the Lao case, into state property leased to foreign companies. Despite being dispossessed of land, villagers' ties and relations to land have not completely disappeared. They bitterly remember where their customary land is located and how it was taken from them. Some conflicts have yet to be completely resolved as villagers wait for surveying teams to mark off boundaries between village and company land. Lasting disputes over land have prompted villagers to avoid working for the company or to do so only when in need of cash income. Those who have worked for Quasa have been deeply dissatisfied, and many have left due to the mismatch between low pay and backbreaking work. In 2021, a group of laborers protested to the company after they were not paid wages they were owed. While not directly related to land, labor conflicts reflect on Quasa's broader lack of legitimacy among rural villagers who remember the violent acquisition of their lands.

Company relations to land are also not static. Quasa needed to move the construction of its factory to another site after villagers' concerns over environmental and health impacts became trenchant. Due to its inability to acquire sufficient land through a concession model, Sun Paper switched to new modes of accessing land and planting trees. It has also acquired the land of other companies and is seeking to make deals with the government to secure lands within national production forests, areas historically zoned for timber harvesting. When expanding the land area for the factory, Sun Paper bought up large amounts of land from households in Ban Chalan and worked with the government to transform this into state land that the company could lease. Ultimately, the land both companies acquired through concessions belonged to the state, and the Lao government could decide to use it for other purposes, especially at the end of the concession period. Under the right political conditions—widespread protests, movements, and heavy political pressure—the land could even be returned to villagers or they could be enrolled in plantation shareholding schemes to benefit from the revenues. While these scenarios are unrealistic in the current context, the point is that the future of land remains open.

I have argued that not only is there a dense sociality to land but that land can be socialized toward different ends, especially toward the interests and aims of capital compared to those of the peasantry. Both processes have been at work as industrial tree plantations expanded across eastern Savannakhet while constantly running into a landscape populated with rural land users. In many ways, the governmental project of seeking to turn land into capital or, more specifically in this case, to turn land over to capital has won out. Large swaths of land peasants used for farming, used for hunting and harvesting forest products, or reserved for the next generation's use have been expropriated by the state and allocated to plantation companies. Combinations of coercive threats, ideological promotion, intense negotiation, and underhand corporate tactics have been used to separate people from their lands. The most vulnerable groups of people have been hit hardest—ethnic minority villagers practicing forms of agriculture that the government seeks to replace, who lack political connections, and whose village politics have been divided by conflict.

Yet land has also been further socialized for the peasantry through this process. Villagers have used whatever political and personal means possible to make claims to land and defend it from acquisition. This has often led to small gains, preventing a couple of plots of land or a small section of village forests from being acquired, or more generally pushing back the boundaries of an expanding plantation area. In some cases, larger losses have been prevented. In reclaiming land granted to companies, villagers shaped the boundaries between state and village land in practice. This was constituted by a loss of land to plantations for many villages, but it also more securely marked out where their village land, for their use, was located, not to be further encroached upon in the future. It is because of this peasant defensiveness of land, and the push to protect it going forward, that plantation companies, especially Sun Paper, encountered limits on the amount of land they could acquire. As a result, it is widely recognized by government officials that there is little land left for concessions. This explains the turn to new areas such as national production forests.

Although these dynamics operated unevenly across different groups of peasants, ultimately the efforts to socialize land for the peasantry were effective in limiting the extent of land dispossession in general.

This conclusion addresses these contrasting and contradictory forms of socializing land, how they have had variegated impacts on different groups of peasants, and what this says about how power over land is asserted and how land relations are likely to continue changing. The next section investigates what types of social relations affect how control over land is placed and how land changes hands. I then reflect on the implications of different types of socializing land for uneven agrarian change in Laos. Finally, I speculate about what these transformations mean for the future sociality of land in Laos and other sites of intense land grabbing.

Intersecting Land Relations

Socializing land is a process of producing and changing social ties and relations to land. This includes the embedding of land within the control of localized groups of people for their continued use, occupation, management, and cultural practice—what I have referred to as socializing land for the peasantry. It also addresses the weakening of those ties, enabling the state to assert control over land and allocate it to plantation companies—socializing land for capital. What is particularly valuable about this approach is that it can be used to analyze how power over land is produced—to examine which relations to land are the strongest and can withstand external threats that seek to unravel them. Other ties are more vulnerable and more easily undone. A focus on the socialization of land also concerns how projects of dispossession, regardless of how effective they are, change social ties and relations to land, often producing new forms of land relations in the process.

To understand how power over land operates, it is important to examine how the various relations to land described in this book intersect with and overlay one another, ultimately affecting how land is socialized in different and contradictory ways. A variety of factors have played a role in determining who accesses, controls, and owns land in eastern Savannakhet (captured in table 1 in the introduction). However, these indicators cannot be simply added up to determine what type of outcome they produced. Rather, it is essential to analyze the ways in which they interact with one another to shape power and control over land. I therefore examine the multiple layers of relations and forces that combine and interact to produce specific outcomes rather than viewing them in isolation.

A critically important starting point for understanding how land becomes socialized for capital, and what limits are reached, is the relationships between plantation companies and the state, covered in chapter 1. The state, as the legitimate manager of land as a national resource in Laos, can make crucial decisions regarding what it is used for and by whom. When companies are able to develop strong political and economic relations with the state from the central to the district and even village levels, not only can they be granted a large concession but they can also exert significant pressure on villagers to concede land, thus restricting opportunities for resistance and disempowering peasant relations to land. Villagers targeted by Quasa's project were up against heavy and coercive state forces bearing down on them that tore through their social ties to land in many cases, violently dispossessing them. This was due to Quasa's ability to not only mobilize the ideological and coercive power of the state but also to operate extralegally without accountability or punishment—clearing lands with impunity outside zoned boundaries and into prohibited forests. The three villages that had some way of contesting the company's project effectively (Ban Phoulao, Ban Sokleek, and Ban Kaengchee) had to concede some land to Quasa and could not prevent the company from acquiring some of their lands.

Sun Paper mobilized some of the same state power as Quasa in the early days of its project before the company's relations with the district government waned. During that initial period, it was nearly impossible for villagers in Ban Xaylom to stop the project due to the presence of security personnel. However, Sun Paper followed state regulations more closely than Quasa, which slowed the implementation of the company's project and created time and space for villagers to resist and push back the encroachment. And with limited district support, Sun Paper was less effective at finding ways to sever the social relations between villagers and their land. More importantly, it enabled villagers to lodge their claims with the state, creating an environment in which their social relations and ties to land could be protected. Two villages that contested Sun Paper's project—Ban Na Khouay and Ban Phailom—prevented the acquisition of any of their lands.

As Quasa and Sun Paper mobilized state power to acquire land, they had to operate within a complex landscape of property relations and politicized ecologies, dealt with in chapters 2 and 3. Such lands were discursively constructed by the state as open, empty, and underutilized, belonging to the state rather than private property holders. Government officials directed Quasa's and Sun Paper's projects away from the low-lying plains of western Savannakhet and toward the sloping and upland territories of the eastern region. And within those areas, provincial and district officials sought to zone out lands outside their lowland paddy territories along Route 9 and near district centers. They allocated lands farther away, mainly comprising shifting cultivation fields, fallows, and secondary forest, up to the boundaries of national protected areas and national production forests. However, the social and ecological reality of this landscape was much more complex and offered opportunities for peasants to resist acquisition of lands considered productive and worthy to be registered property. As discussed at length in chapter 3, though, the boundary between upland swidden landscapes and lowland paddy is not clear-cut. Instead, there is an expansive indeterminate area between them. Furthermore, lowland paddy areas were sometimes allocated due to poor surveying or, in other cases, the companies cleared them without permission.

When it came to negotiation and contestation, the geographies and ecologies of landscapes across the province were critical in (dis)empowering the social ties and relations that villagers used to make claims to land. The socio-ecological relations of swidden agriculture are not in any way a weaker tie than those of wet rice agriculture. However, as documented in chapter 3, swidden cultivation is demonized across Southeast Asia, including by the Lao government, which aims to stabilize and eliminate the practice. Swiddeners' rich social relations to land are ignored or discounted by the government. When land is left fallow, it is perceived to be empty because it does not fit into the productivist vision of the Lao state. A further consideration is that most government officials are ethnic Lao from the lowlands and so may not appreciate the socio-ecological relations of upland systems. Swidden agricultural lands have therefore been much harder for villagers to protect. Some villages have been able to do so by focusing on the swidden lands in use that villagers pay taxes on, while other lands might be framed as land in reserve for future use, emphasizing its productive potential. Nonetheless, seeking to defend swidden landscapes is a largely losing battle, one that can only be fought on the fringes of such a landscape, especially in more hilly, upland terrain that lacks potential for conversion to paddy. Like Ban Phoulao and Ban Sokleek, mentioned previously, upland villages had to concede some swidden areas to protect others.

Paddy land, in contrast, has a socio-ecological set of relations that is prioritized by the state, despite not being more critical to livelihoods in the area than swidden lands. While claims to swidden areas must be treated as if they are not swidden land, claims to paddy land are valid in and of themselves. The district government took cases seriously when paddy land was inadvertently cleared, which was not supposed to happen. They even returned those lands to the villages in some cases. In other cases, high rates of compensation were provided, especially if that land was highly sought after, like the paddies in Ban Chalan wanted for the Sun Paper factory. So when villagers seek to protect their paddy lands for clearance, they do not need to rely on unique government connections or fight against a company with weak connections with the government. Just the potential for land to be converted into paddy is powerful in itself. Lowland areas on which dry swidden rice is planted are framed by villagers, such as in Ban Saphang, as areas that will later be converted to paddy land and thus are paddies in the making. These areas are harder to protect and villagers may need to deploy other strategies, but they provide more potential than upland swidden landscapes.

As Quasa and Sun Paper developed their projects within a complex landscape of unclear and developing property relations and indeterminate boundaries between different and highly politicized socio-ecological types of land uses, villagers sized up the opportunities they had to make claims to land. They especially considered their connections to and strategic engagement with the state, as discussed in chapter 4, to limit the socialization of land for capital and ensure it remained socialized for the villagers. While the dynamics of property and politicized ecologies influenced what types of lands were easier to protect, villagers' political relationships with the state affected the potential for them to have their claims heard or to enact them. Most villagers in this area had weak connections with the state and were only able to negotiate with district officials, which often did not get them anywhere. In a few cases, however, those connections were essential and sometimes helped strengthen a case or provided an opportunity that would otherwise not have been available. The Phu Thai village Ban Phailom maintained ethnic links with the district government, especially with village leaders who had previously worked as government officials. These helped them more easily refute the project than if they had to rely on claims that there was no available land in the village, which is mostly lowland. Comparatively, Ban Saphang may have had more trouble resisting Sun Paper's incursions if they did not have a veteran connection with the National Assembly. This allowed them to bring more attention to their case and strategically protect lands under use and others framed as future paddy land. Then, in the unique case of Ban Kaengchee, an indirect connection to the vice president helped them push the government to force Quasa to return cleared paddy lands that the company may have otherwise put up more of a fight to protect.

For villagers to make strong claims over land, they need to be strategic and tenacious, which requires them to put forward a united front of resistance and action, as addressed in chapter 5. When all the dimensions of socializing land favor the interests of capital—when they are up against a company with strong relations with the state, their lands are not considered potential household property, their land-use practices are viewed as unproductive and in need of replacement, and they have no kinship or political connections with the state—villagers' ability to stand strong in solidarity is critical, although not a guarantee of success. The only way that Ban Sokleek could protect its lands against the demands made on Quasa's behalf was through its early, consistent, and united defense of its lands and territory. In contrast, when Ban Nammak villagers were debating how to respond to attempts to acquire land because of the temptation of having their debts to the electric company settled, the divisions within the village limited their ability to resist.

On the other hand, even if all the dimensions of socializing land for the peasantry work in their favor—if they are up against a company whose relations with the government are weak, they are using their lands in line with state property schemes and visions of productive agricultural development, and they have political connections with the government—villagers struggle to prevent the acquisition of their land without internal solidarity. For example, in the case of Ban Chalan, solidarity against the project broke down as the high benefits of land compensation were presented to individual villagers. Solidarity in action against dispossession is a fundamental element of ensuring land remains socialized within the village, an ingredient without which the rest of the land relations matter little.

Examining the interactions of these layers of social relations to land across multiple actors, scales, and levels of government demonstrates the complexity of socializing land in relationship to projects of (dis)possession. The granting and development of land concessions in Laos can seem hegemonic in the capacity of the state to control land and provide it for capital. However, the seeming ease of doing so belies the challenges of relying on a range of different capital, state, propertied, geographical, and ecological relations to fall into place to produce state land that can be used for plantation capital. When the constellation of these relations breaks down, and other community and state relations are empowered in their place, then the hegemonic regime of dispossession falls apart and peasant relations to land are strengthened.

Unequal Transformations

One of the central aims of this book has been to understand how power and control over land have been produced, leading to uneven geographies of (dis)possession. I have revealed the limits to corporate and centralized state control over land. However, a more important objective has been to understand why and how rural peoples and environments are devastated by loss of land and environmental degradation associated with widespread monoculture plantation development. How land is socialized prior to, during, and after the granting of land concessions is critically important for dynamics of rural wealth, development, agrarian change, and environmental sustainability. In the villages where plantation companies oriented the socialization of land to their interests with the aid of the state, and villagers were effectively dispossessed of large amounts of agricultural and forest land, their livelihood prospects and quality of life more generally were greatly diminished. Where villagers were able to prevent companies from acquiring all the land allocated to them, the negative effects of land dispossession and plantation incursion were felt but to a lesser degree than in the more heavily affected villages. As a result, the difference was the degree of underdevelopment experienced, which is explored here.

Villages that were subjected to extensive dispossession and destructive socio-environmental transformation include Ban Nammak, Ban Phoulao, Ban Salang, Ban Kaengvang, and Ban Xaylom, where large portions of the village territory were converted into rubber and pulpwood plantations, dramatically altering how the villagers make a living and relate to rural space. In each of these villages, dispossession also radically transformed villagers' rural livelihoods and relationship to nature. Most immediately, many villagers lost access to their agricultural lands, primarily used for planting rice. Swidden landscapes were acquired, including the land cleared each year to grow rice and other vegetables intercropped in the field, such as chili, eggplant, and cucumber. This is not only a loss of productive agricultural land in one year but also the restriction of a whole swidden system. With less fallow land accessible, farmers who still had access to some land (but considerably less) had to practice swidden cultivation in shorter rotations of two to three years, which invited more weeds and reduced the productivity of the harvest. In some cases, households lost "reserved land" (*din chap chong*). This did not affect their agricultural productivity each year but limited the amount of land they would be able to pass on to their children and grandchildren and generally restricted the availability of land for a village growing in population.

The loss of swidden fields and fallows is also part of a broader pattern of deforestation, especially of bush fallow and young secondary forest, and including older growth secondary forest and potentially some primary forest. This is a continuation of trends started in the 1980s with logging by state-owned forestry enterprises, which robbed Phin district of much of its valuable hardwood. It also eliminates wildlife in the area, although some wild boars, birds, and rodents can still be hunted. Most important for villagers, though, it has severely restricted the availability of NTFPs, which are essential for both subsistence and sale for supplementary income. Villagers collect and consume a wide range of wild vegetables for edible consumption, such as bamboo shoots and mushrooms, and certain herbs for medicinal use. Some NTFPs are also valuably sold on the market, such as the malva nut (*mak chong*), used for medicinal purposes. But all these NTFPs are increasingly difficult to collect. Villagers must search farther and spend more time yet find less of them. When asked about the availability of NTFPs in these villages, a common refrain was "They're all gone."

The socio-ecological effects of forest clearance and plantation development go beyond the loss of access to resources to include environmental destruction impactful in other ways. The careless clearance of land often bulldozed debris like brush and soil into creeks and streams, clogging them up and disrupting natural water flows in the area. At other times, debris ended up in paddies, rendering them uncultivable. The use of agrochemicals was also a significant concern for many villagers. Heavy use of fertilizers is common in any agro-industrial plantation. Most alarming for villagers were the high levels of herbicides that both Quasa and Sun Paper used to kill weeds and grasses that normally grow between the rows of trees, saving on labor costs. These chemicals can easily leach into the soil and waterways surrounding the village, flowing into the streams and rivers that villagers use for bathing, washing, and drinking. In Ban Phoulao and Ban Salang, villagers felt something was wrong with the water and requested that the company build a groundwater pump, which it never did.

Indirect effects of land and forest loss are as important as direct impacts. With less land available, villagers have been driven to search out new lands, clearing their reserved areas or, in other cases, clearing old-growth forests in neighboring villages (as discussed in chapter 3). Those with access to lowlands have transformed them into paddies, in some cases taking on debt to pay hired tractors to clear the land and shape the paddies. Some villagers have been enticed to get involved in cash-cropping schemes, such as planting cassava for traders from nearby towns, which have been exploitative and fraudulent. In Ban Phoulao, villagers were defrauded by a trader from town who convinced them to take on large loans from the Agricultural Promotion Bank to grow cassava. When the crop was ready to harvest, the trader never showed up, the cassava rotted in the field, and the villagers ended up in debt. Some villagers sought to compensate for a loss of land by taking up wage labor, but the opportunities were limited. There were fewer jobs with the companies than expected, and villagers often were not satisfied with the work. They felt they were worked too hard for too little pay, and they did not like the disciplined work schedule that did not allow them to take time off for other work or social events in the village. While there is always some other wage work in the village or the region with other households, it is limited. Still, villagers have not migrated to other parts of the country or to Thailand for work, which is a more common practice among Lao villages near the Mekong that have been dispossessed of land.[1]

Another indirect impact was the trauma that land clearance created within villages. There was palpable anger and frustration in the villages that had lost large areas of land. When I first visited Ban Salang with government officials as part of the Swiss-funded "quality of investment" project, villagers raised their voices at government officials when asked about the project's impacts. Although their frustrations had been heightened after drinking at a funeral reception earlier in the day, it is rare for anger to be on such public display in an official setting in Laos. In villages that had not put up much resistance, in part due to internal disagreements over the project, such as Ban Nammak and Ban Kaengvang, the legacy of the conflicts that the plantation had exacerbated could still be felt in the village. It might be seen in the lack of warmth, the pointing of fingers, or the expressions of distrust. Many interviewees conveyed a lack of optimism about a future in which they had few resources to build on. Then there were the less common cases, where spirit and cemetery forests had been cleared, and villagers placed blame on themselves for not protecting them, worrying that they would be harmed or otherwise penalized by the spirits as a result.

These transformative impacts felt by the most affected villages were sometimes not even within the village. In some cases, a few villagers benefited from the investment, such as the leaders who brokered the deals and received money from the company or had cushy jobs as plantation guards. For the most part, the difference concerned how negative the impacts were—who was less worse off because of the plantation development. In some ways, this unevenness was arbitrary, based on how the plantation borders were negotiated between the company and the district government. As documented throughout this book, the village had some say in this, but more powerful villagers did not have enough influence to guide the project away from specific plots of land, such as their own. Unequal access to different types of land meant that wealthier villagers were less impacted than poorer ones. While access to land in most villages was relatively equal, some households had more plots than others and in different areas, so a loss of some land to the plantation still left them with other areas to rely on. Wealthier households were also more likely to have access to paddy lands or resources to develop lowland areas into paddies, which were less likely to be acquired for the project. Alternatively, when paddy land was acquired, they could get it back in some instances or get a higher rate of compensation.

Poorer households are not only more likely to have less land and be entirely reliant on swidden agriculture without access to any paddy lands; they are also more likely to rely on the collection of NTFPs for subsistence and as a source of income. The disappearance of NTFPs from swidden fallows and secondary forests therefore has a devastating impact on their livelihoods. Women are particularly affected by this change as they are often the ones in the household responsible for social reproductive activities, including collecting subsistence NTFPs and firewood. They must spend more time and energy foraging, on top of all the other household tasks they are expected to undertake. The more significant impacts that poorer households and women faced from the plantation projects help explain why they were often more defiant in their resistance in villages where sentiments were divided as village elites favored such investments.

As with how some households within villages heavily affected by plantation investments were spared the worst impacts, there was significant variation in the livelihood, agrarian, and environmental changes across villages. None of the villages was better off or significantly benefited from plantations in the region as the government envisioned. The difference is that some villages are now less underdeveloped than others. Moreover, they still retain lands and resources that can be mobilized to generate social wealth and improve their lives and the lives of their children and grandchildren. Some villages have been almost completely spared these impacts, such as Ban Phailom and Ban Na Khouay, which were both able to prevent Sun Paper from acquiring any land within their territory. Others were able to stave off some of the worst impacts of the project by limiting the amount of land acquired, such as Ban Sokleek, Ban Kaengchee, Ban Chalan, and Ban Saphang. Even Ban Phoulao, which was significantly affected, prevented the concession of another large plot of land to Quasa, thereby avoiding worsening the situation.

Across all these cases, various social relations came together that enabled villagers to prevent the acquisition of large areas of land and avert or partially limit the worst impacts of the plantation projects. Yet villagers are not wholly excluded from the investments' effects, as there are all sorts of indirect consequences, though some of these were beneficial. They could work part-time to gain some extra income, although this was not so common. For example, in villages that had resisted Sun Paper's land acquisition, villagers reported that the company refused to hire them as wage laborers. But for the most part, the indirect impacts were harmful. In some cases, villagers lost access to NTFPs in forest lands in neighboring villages, previously shared as a commons. It is also possible that the company could expand its project at the borders of the village in the coming years. Or villagers are subjected to the polluting impacts of the project, which do not respect village borders. For instance, Ban Na Khouay will have to deal with the dust, noise, and dangers associated with Sun Paper trucks coming to and from the factory on the road that passes through their village. Nonetheless, these are minor disturbances compared with the destructive transformations other villages faced.

Social Futures of Land

The global privatization of land is often seen as an expanding process of land enclosures that marks the end of older forms of communal, collective, and even public lands. Under neoliberal globalization, there is only one form of property: private. The phenomenon of land grabbing across the Global South can be seen as indicative of this process—enclosing the commonly used lands of peasants, pastoralists, forest dwellers, and fisherfolk, turning them into large tracts of land and territory owned by multinational investors. Alternatively, in places where large-scale land grabbing is not taking place, rural peoples are enclosing their common lands and turning them into private property to produce cash crops, like cacao trees in upland Sulawesi.[2]

One of the main aims of this book has been to show that the advance of private property-based forms of land and resource investment does not spell the end of social land but is rather one episode in the changing social relations of land over time. It is premature to claim an end to social land as property relations shift over time; while relations may stabilize for long periods, disruptive events or evolutionary changes can always alter them. Private property systems can and have dramatically changed due to efforts to socially re-embed land in more democratic, equitable, and less commodified ways. Land reforms in the Global South throughout the twentieth century redistributed unequal landholdings inherited from the colonial era.[3] In socialist countries, there was the nationalization and collectivization of land. Today, there are contemporary social movements to redistribute control over land, such as by the Movimento dos Trabalhadores Rurais Sem Terra (Landless Workers' Movement) in Brazil or in the Land Back movement that seeks to reestablish Indigenous control over land in North and South America, Australia, and New Zealand, among other places. These are examples of how the social relations of land can change, even if the land itself remains stuck in place. The same can be said for land grabbing when understood not just as a transfer of property but as a transformation of property relations that has multiple effects on the land acquired and other lands that remain in peasant control.

A key argument is that socializing land is an ongoing process. The socialization of land in Laos is not only something occurring before the incursion of foreign investments, shaping how they were developed. It is not only something established in a precapitalist context, in which rural communities form communal, customary modes of using and managing their lands over long periods, or a mode of land use influenced by the socialist revolution in Laos that treated some agricultural lands as a collective asset for a short period and imposed limits on its commodification, sale, and accumulated ownership for several decades. The creation of land concessions is also part of the socialization of lands. Such lands are granted to plantation capital as a long-term land lease and are partially privatized. However, they have also been created as state lands through this process, carved out of the rural landscape of customarily used community and household lands. Such state lands still belong to the "national community," which the government represents. Land concessions can be revoked by the state—and have been when companies have sat on land without productively using it. When concession periods are up, the government can decide to use the land for other purposes or even return it to the community, however unlikely this may be in practice.

Concessions are also not the end of socializing land because of the reaction among the peasantry that they produce. This is akin to what Karl Polanyi calls a countermovement, in which there is an effort to re-embed land, labor, money, or the economy more broadly back into society, putting them under social protections.[4] In the Lao case, peasants have quickly learned how damaging large-scale land concessions and plantations can be for their livelihoods and rural environments. When concessions were first proposed to rural communities in a rosy light as projects that would lift them out of poverty and provide permanent jobs, villagers accepted them as a type of development project, like those from the state and international aid projects. However, as they gained more experience with concessions and plantations, and word spread through kinship and ethnic networks in a region about their impacts, villagers became resistant to the acquisition of their lands. A Brou research assistant with a long record of working in these villages remarked, "Villagers no longer believe in the government as they did after the war [after 1975]. At that time, the villagers really loved and trusted the government. They did everything the government wanted. Now they have lost faith."[5] As plantations expanded across eastern Savannakhet, villagers increasingly sought ways to protect their lands from acquisition, to socialize them for their use.

In some ways, the advance of plantation concessions and the peasant reactions they elicit have privatized rural landscapes in Laos. Erik Harms has written about how new urban development projects in Ho Chi Minh City (Saigon) have reduced popular resistance to a form of atomized dissent, in which residents are solely focused on their claims to compensation to the land they are being evicted from.[6] The dynamics are different in rural areas where villages have access to and manage large areas of collectively used land, but similar effects can be seen across eastern Savannakhet. As has been shown, collective claims to land are ineffective against plantation concessions—it is precisely these village lands that are not exclusively used by any one household that the government seeks to transform into state land. In attempts to protect these lands, villagers have had to resort to individual claims, to make the case that a swidden fallow or communally used forest area is exclusively theirs and reserved for future use. This may have the effect of driving villagers to privatize village land further to ensure that each household has enough for itself and future generations, and protect it from any later acquisition attempts by showing that they are using it productively. Further, attempts to gain financial compensation are focused on the amount paid for individual land.

Nevertheless, the use of private claims to protect land should not be seen as an end in and of itself. Instead, these claims are part of a broader process of communities seeking to assert control over their lands in the face of external investments. Private claims are strategically used as it is understood that only land under productive agricultural use by villagers can be excluded from plantation boundaries. They recognize that collectively used village land can be claimed as belonging to the state. Moreover, villages advance these claims collectively by making the case that certain areas are in use by villagers, rather than individual villagers negotiating on their own with state officials and company representatives for their land to be protected. The villages where collective negotiations broke down due to lack of internal solidarity had a much harder time defending claims to land, including individual claims. Villages negotiate territories of land use, and when they do concede to the loss of land, they not only want individual landowners to be compensated but also seek collective forms of compensation. In conceding their lands, most villages negotiated for the companies to build roads, electric lines, health clinics, or village offices, even though the companies denied these agreements and had no written records.[7]

Village reactions against plantation concessions asserted their power within the social relations of the state. As discussed in chapter 2, "state land" in Laos is governed by a complex relationship among multiple levels of the state, including the village. The central state primarily grants concessions, apart from some granted by provincial and district governments. Nonetheless, some villages increasingly asserted their right to shape such projects, to outright refuse them, or to negotiate their conditions. As covered in chapters 1 and 5, because of Sun Paper's challenges in acquiring land and the company's deteriorating relationship with the district government, the company's representatives had to negotiate land deals with villages before presenting the results to the district government for approval. This enabled villages to negotiate better deals for themselves, collecting a communal rent on the land that met their expectations of its value or ensuring that the company built infrastructure for them, and rejecting a deal when their conditions were not met.

Other plantation companies were developing similar strategies to navigate the limits of state power to expropriate land for them. For example, Stora Enso, a Scandinavian pulp and paper company that was operating in eastern Savannakhet, had started courting villagers in Phin and Xepon districts to expand the area of their plantations. Ban Saphang, which so vehemently resisted Sun Paper's incursions into its lands, was willing to consider Stora Enso's proposal because they offered to pay the community a rent of US$350 (2.8 million kip) per hectare per year for a thirty-five-year concession. Villagers felt that they were able to negotiate which areas of the village could be conceded—ideally those where they do not collect NTFPs—rather than be forced into deals. Similar dynamics are at work in northern Laos. Chinese banana plantation companies have opted to lease land directly from villages and farmers rather than working through the state to acquire land concessions.[8] Making deals and leasing from villages or farmers do not necessarily solve the problems of concessions. Village leaders can exploit this process and receive payouts from companies in exchange for conceding land. Chinese banana plantations are infamous for their environmental destruction due to heavy chemical and plastic use and their degradation of the land and soil, which is challenging to rehabilitate. Moreover, migrant laborers on the plantations have been abused and exposed to toxic levels of pesticides. At the same time, when villages get to negotiate their own deals, there are more opportunities for them to financially benefit from such projects rather than only have their land expropriated with little to show for it.

The Lao government continues to grant land concessions, although this has slowed following the series of moratoriums since 2007. Outside the plantation sector, concessions are still rampant, especially for hydropower projects, SEZs, and infrastructure like expressways and the Laos–China railway. Many of these high-profile projects are developed with the full backing of the Lao state and seem to steamroll any resistance. Much of the politics of resisting these projects has been concerned with compensation: households refuse compensation to demonstrate their dissatisfaction and ultimately negotiate higher prices.[9] On top of that, the early plantation concessions, especially those granted to Vietnamese companies, have been fully developed. There has thus been a bifurcation between the socialization of lands—by and for the central state versus peasant communities.

What does this all mean for the future of land in Laos and other countries subjected to land investments and grabbing? The privatization of land continues apace across the world in many forms and variations.

This is not a universal and teleological process or the end of history. Social claims to land do not just degrade into private property. Instead, they can become reasserted, strengthened, and transformed. The privatization of land can prompt a backlash that seeks its redistribution. This is the case with movements to create community or conservation land trusts or other attempts to put land back into the hands of communities and the public. Social relations to land are never static, even if they are stabilized for some time. They are constantly changing or have the potential to change. It is essential to reflect on how land is socialized—by and for whom. Historical social processes in many places have ensured that land is placed in the control of communities and publics rather than private entities or exclusive use of the state. It is critically important to continue struggling to socialize land for the people, especially for Indigenous peoples, ethnic and racialized minorities, and the rural poor and working classes. The earth, and the land that people use, belongs to both no one and everyone and hence should be treated as a common and public social good for all.

Notes

Introduction

1. *Ban* is Lao for village. Pseudonyms are used for all villages and people, including research assistants and government officials, to protect their identity.
2. *Nai ban* is sometimes referred to as the village chief, but here I follow the government's official English terminology.
3. Xaylom villagers, focus group interview with the author and a research assistant, March 10, 2014.
4. Village leaders, interview with the author and a research assistant, Ban Xaylom, February 19, 2015.
5. Village leaders, interview with the author and a research assistant, Ban Xaylom, March 10, 2014.
6. Borras et al., "Towards a Better Understanding of Global Land Grabbing"; McMichael, "The Land Grab and Corporate Food Regime Restructuring"; Rulli et al., "Global Land and Water Grabbing"; Zoomers, "Globalisation and the Foreignisation of Space."
7. Schoenberger et al., "What Happened When the Land Grab Came to Southeast Asia?"
8. Barney, "Laos and the Making of a 'Relational' Resource Frontier."
9. Borras et al., "Towards a Better Understanding of Global Land Grabbing"; De Schutter, "How Not to Think of Land Grabbing"; Mousseau et al., *Driving Dispossession*; Franco et al., *The Global Land Grab*; Zoomers, "Globalisation and the Foreignisation of Space."
10. GRAIN, *Seized.*
11. Borras et al., "Towards a Better Understanding of Global Land Grabbing"; McMichael, "Land Grabbing as Security Mercantilism in International Relations."
12. Zoomers, "Globalisation and the Foreignisation of Space"; McMichael, "Land Grabbing as Security Mercantilism in International Relations"; Sassen, "Land Grabs Today."

13. Wolford et al., "Governing Global Land Deals."
14. Cambodian League for the Promotion and Defense of Human Rights, *Land Grabbing and Poverty in Cambodia*; Makki, "Power and Property"; Oliveira, "Land Regularization in Brazil"; Visser and Spoor, "Land Grabbing in Post-Soviet Eurasia."
15. Lay et al., *Taking Stock of the Global Land Rush.*
16. Hett et al., *Land Leases and Concessions in the Lao PDR*. This does not include the area of land granted for a range of other types of projects, such as logging, hydropower, tourism, infrastructure, SEZs, and urban real estate.
17. For example, plantation and mining deals have been granted for up to fifty years. Some other projects, such as SEZs, have been granted for up to ninety-nine years.
18. Marx, *Capital,* vol. 1, p. 875.
19. Perelman, *The Invention of Capitalism*; De Angelis, "Marx and Primitive Accumulation"; Harvey, *The New Imperialism.*
20. Lay et al., *Taking Stock of the Global Land Rush.*
21. Hett et al., *Land Leases and Concessions in the Lao PDR.* If mining concessions are included, then the total amount of land granted by the government is over 1 million hectares, 62 percent of which has been developed.
22. Baird, "The Global Land Grab Meta-narrative"; Edelman, "Messy Hectares"; Fairbairn, "Indirect Dispossession"; Kenney-Lazar, "Relations of Sovereignty"; Oya, "Methodological Reflections on 'Land Grab' Databases and the 'Land Grab' Literature 'Rush'"; Peluso and Lund, "New Frontiers of Land Control"; Wolford et al., "Governing Global Land Deals"; Woods, "Ceasefire Capitalism."
23. Baird, "The Global Land Grab Meta-narrative."
24. Schoenberger et al., "What Happened When the Land Grab Came to Southeast Asia?"
25. Baird, "Problems for the Plantations"; Gagné and Fent, "The Faltering Land Rush"; Nolte, "Doomed to Fail?"
26. Hall, *Land,* p. 18.
27. Temper, "From Boomerangs to Minefields and Catapults"; Hall et al., "Resistance, Acquiescence or Incorporation?"; Sändig, "Contesting Large-Scale Land Acquisitions in the Global South."
28. Fairbairn, *Fields of Gold*, chap. 4.
29. Lough, "Madagascar's New Leader."
30. Chakrya and Baliga, "Boeung Kak: A Disastrous Decade."

31. Glassman, "Primitive Accumulation."
32. Levien, "The Land Question," p. 940.
33. Wolford et al., "Governing Global Land Deals."
34. Özsu, "Grabbing Land Legally"; Alden Wily, "Looking Back to See Forward."
35. Lund, *Nine-Tenths of the Law.*
36. Hall et al., *Powers of Exclusion.*
37. Lund, *Nine-Tenths of the Law.*
38. Baka, "The Political Construction of Wasteland"; Ferguson, "The Scramble for the Waste Lands."
39. Harms and Baird, "Wastelands, Degraded Lands and Forests."
40. Dwyer, *Upland Geopolitics.*
41. The concept of "socialized land" is not new, even if it is not commonly used. Most recently, Nikita Sud has written about socialized land in ways that are similar to the broad conceptualization I offer (Sud, *The Making of Land*). Sud uses the term to capture how land is fundamentally socio-natural in the ways that it is worked into social systems. I take the concept further to address the different orientations of socializing land and its various contentions. It is also important to note that the idea of socialized land has a much longer history. It was first proposed by the Socialist Revolutionary Party, agrarian socialists, and supporters of a democratic socialist Russian republic at the beginning of the twentieth century. In their agrarian program of 1906, they proposed land socialization as the redistribution of all agricultural land, of large landholders and peasants, to bodies of self-government that would distribute it equally to peasant laborers based on their labor contributions or consumption needs. These ideas are similar to those of postcolonial movements for land reform throughout the twentieth century that sought to expropriate land from large landlords and redistribute to small peasant cultivators, commonly framed as "land to the tiller." Lenin and the Bolsheviks were opposed to this notion of socialization as they argued that the redistribution of land to smallholders would still result in the development of capitalist relations in agriculture and class differentiation among the peasantry. However, because the idea of egalitarian land tenure was still popular among the peasantry, the Decree on Land passed by the Bolsheviks in 1917 included a clause on the "socialization of the land." In this version, though, the land owned by the people was managed by the estate, meaning that it was essentially nationalized. Land has been socialized in various ways

across socialist regimes. In the most extreme cases, private land in agriculture was abolished and land was collectivized as cooperatives or state farms from which the state extracted grain surpluses.

42. Li, "What Is Land?"
43. Castree and Braun, *Social Nature*; Goldman et al., "Introduction: The Social Lives of Land"; Smith, *Uneven Development*; Taylor, *The Political Ecology of Climate Change Adaptation.*
44. Bridge, "Material Worlds."
45. Li, "What Is Land?"
46. Sud, *The Making of Land.*
47. Li, *Land's End.*
48. MacPherson, "The Meaning of Property."
49. Ribot and Peluso, "A Theory of Access."
50. Hall et al., *Powers of Exclusion.*
51. Lund, *Nine-Tenths of the Law.*
52. Cotula, "The New Enclosures?"
53. Hall et al., "Resistance, Acquiescence or Incorporation?"
54. Alden Wily, "Looking Back to See Forward."
55. See a clear definition of contradictory relationships in Halvorsen, "Spatial Dialectics and the Geography of Social Movements," p. 445.
56. See Baird, "The Global Land Grab Meta-narrative"; Fairbairn, "Indirect Dispossession"; Wolford et al., "Governing Global Land Deals"; and Woods, "Ceasefire Capitalism."
57. Peck, "For Polanyian Economic Geographies."
58. MacPherson, "The Meaning of Property."
59. Blomley, "The Territory of Property."
60. Marx, *Capital,* vol. 1, p. 928, my emphasis.
61. Gramsci, *Selections from the Prison Notebooks.*
62. Emel et al., "Extracting Sovereignty"; Jurkevics, "Land Grabbing and the Perplexities of Territorial Sovereignty"; Kenney-Lazar, "Relations of Sovereignty"; Sud, "Land-Making as State-Making."
63. Brown and Zasloff, "Laos 1976," p. 107.
64. Evans, *Lao Peasants under Socialism*, pp. 49–50.
65. Evans, *Lao Peasants under Socialism.*
66. Evans, *A Short History of Laos*; Yamada, "Legitimation of the Lao People's Revolutionary Party."
67. Yamada, "Legitimation of the Lao People's Revolutionary Party."
68. Anonymous, "Aspects of Forestry Management in the Lao PDR"; Dwyer, "Territorial Affairs."

69. Evans, *Lao Peasants under Socialism and Post-Socialism*, p. xi.
70. High, *Projectland.*
71. Yamada, "Legitimation of the Lao People's Revolutionary Party."
72. *Vientiane Times,* "Laos Striving for Rule of Law State."
73. Vandergeest, "Land to Some Tillers."
74. *Vientiane Times,* "Govt Aims to Issue 220,000 Land Titles."
75. Fujita and Phanvilay, "Land and Forest Allocation in Lao People's Democratic Republic."
76. St. John, "The Political Economy of Laos."
77. Baird, "Land, Rubber and People."
78. Middleton et al., "Old and New Hydropower Players in the Mekong Region."
79. Kenney-Lazar et al., *Turning Land into Capital.*
80. Schönweger et al., *Concessions and Leases in the Lao PDR.*
81. Hett et al., *Land Leases and Concessions in the Lao PDR.*
82. Many bombs failed to detonate upon impact. Referred to as unexploded ordnances, they injure, maim, and kill villagers when they strike them while farming or take them apart to sell the scrap metal.
83. These challenges are similar to those of researchers working across socialist countries in Asia, as documented in the chapters of Sarah Turner's edited volume *Red Stamps and Gold Stars.*

Chapter 1. Landing Plantation Capital

1. Pang, "*Same-Same but Different.*"
2. Lyttleton and Nyíri, "Dams, Casinos and Concessions."
3. *Al Jazeera,* "Laos: On the Borders of the Empire."
4. Lintner, "Little Laos Risks Losing It All to China."
5. Wolford et al., "Governing Global Land Deals."
6. Fairbairn, "Indirect Dispossession."
7. Woods, "Ceasefire Capitalism."
8. Emel et al., "Extracting Sovereignty."
9. Stuart-Fox, "The French in Laos."
10. Toro, "Coffee Markets, Smallholder Credit, and Landscape Change," pp. 26–28.
11. Macan-Markar, "Thailand Challenges Laos Dam Building Spree"; Smirnov, *Assessment of Scope of Illegal Logging in Laos.*
12. Barney, "Laos and the Making of a 'Relational' Resource Frontier."
13. Singh, "Understanding Changes for Forest-Dependent Communities."
14. Lu and Schönweger, "Great Expectations."

15. Tsing, *Friction*; Blomley, "Law, Property, and the Geography of Violence"; McCarthy, *The Fourth Circle*; Jepson, "Producing a Modern Agricultural Frontier"; Cleary, "After the Frontier."
16. Tsing, *Friction,* pp. 27–28.
17. Barney, "Laos and the Making of a 'Relational' Resource Frontier," p. 151.
18. Sikor and Lund, "Access and Property."
19. Marx and Engels, *The Communist Manifesto*, p. 33.
20. This is the critique that Nicos Poulantzas made of Ralph Miliband, which became a key point of contention in the Miliband-Poulantzas debate. See Poulantzas, "The Problem of the Capitalist State," and Miliband, "Poulantzas and the Capitalist State."
21. Poulantzas, *State, Power, Socialism*, p. 128; emphasis in original.
22. Jessop, *State Power.*
23. Jessop, "Poulantzas's *State, Power and Socialism* as a Modern Classic," p. 43.
24. Hameiri and Jones, "Theorising Political Economy in Southeast Asia."
25. Bridge, "Global Production Networks and the Extractive Sector."
26. Lee, *The Specter of Global China.*
27. Lu, "Grounding Chinese Investment."
28. Lao PDR, "Why Laos."
29. Lund, "Fragmented Sovereignty."
30. Stuart-Fox, *A History of Laos.*
31. "Degraded forestland" is an ambiguous category, discussed further in chapter 3. For more on this topic, see Baird, "Degraded Forest." For more information about the legal framework for granting concessions, see Wellmann, *The Legal Framework of State Land Leases;* Hett et al., *Land Leases and Concessions in the Lao PDR*; and Lao PDR, *Khou Mu Ne Nam Kan Pap Poung Than Kho Moun Kan Khun Ban Xi Khong Kan Xao Le Samphathan Thi Din Khong Lat*, pp. 14–15.
32. Lu and Schönweger, "Great Expectations."
33. Baird, "Problems for the Plantations."
34. Lu and Schönweger, "Great Expectations."
35. Zurflueh, "Vietnamese Rubber Investments in the South of the Lao PDR."
36. Stuart-Fox, *A History of Laos.*
37. Stuart-Fox, "Laos: The Chinese Connection."
38. Baird and Shoemaker, *People, Livelihoods and Development.*
39. Baird and Le Billon, "Landscapes of Political Memories."
40. Dwyer, *Upland Geopolitics.*

41. Zeller, "A World Safe for Revolution."
42. Stuart-Fox, *A History of Laos.*
43. Evans, *A Short History of Laos.*
44. Stuart-Fox, "Laos: The Chinese Connection."
45. Stuart-Fox, "Laos: The Chinese Connection."
46. Schönweger and Messerli, "Land Acquisition, Investment, and Development."
47. Shi, *Rubber Boom in Luang Namtha*; Dwyer, "That Luang Marsh Project Timeline"; Friis and Nielsen, "Small-Scale Land Acquisitions, Large-Scale Implications."
48. Hirsch, "The Changing Political Dynamics of Dam Building."
49. Lyttleton and Nyíri, "Dams, Casinos and Concessions."
50. Lee, *The Specter of Global China*; Lu, "Grounding Chinese Investment."
51. Tran et al., *Vietnam Rubber Industry.*
52. Obein, *Assessment of the Environmental and Social Impacts.*
53. Obein, *Assessment of the Environmental and Social Impacts.*
54. Baird, *Quotas, Powers, Patronage, and Illegal Rent-Seeking.*
55. Stuart-Fox, *A History of Laos.*
56. International pulp and paper industry expert, personal notes shared with the author, July 18, 2018.
57. DONRE official, interview with the author and a research assistant, Xepon district, February 2, 2015.
58. DONRE official, interview with the author and a research assistant, Xepon district, November 27, 2011.
59. Several moratoria have been issued by the Lao government since 2007, varying in their extent and limitations. The most recent moratorium was issued in 2012 and prohibited the development of new land concessions in mining and for rubber and eucalyptus plantations. In 2019, the government issued a decree that opened production forests for plantation investments as a means of increasing forest cover in areas that had been heavily logged. See Kenney-Lazar et al., "Governing Land Concessions in Laos."
60. Radio Free Asia, "Laos: Land Dispute Villagers Released."
61. Pulpwood company manager, interview with the author and a research assistant, Vientiane, July 4, 2014.
62. *VietNamNet*, "Experts Warn."
63. DONRE official, interview with the author and a research assistant, Phin district, November 21, 2013.
64. Lu and Schönweger, "Great Expectations."

65. Ban Salang village committee, focus group interview with the author and a research assistant, March 1, 2014.
66. Scott, *Weapons of the Weak.*

Chapter 2. State Land?

1. Ministry of Planning and Investment official, interview with the author and a research assistant, Vientiane, December 9, 2014.
2. Verdery, *The Vanishing Hectare*; Strugeon and Sikor, "Post-socialist Property in Asia and Europe."
3. Deininger, "Challenges Posed by the New Wave of Farmland Investments."
4. Deininger and Byerlee, *Rising Global Interest in Farmland.*
5. Sun Paper manager, interview with the author and a research assistant, Xepon district, November 26, 2013.
6. MacPherson, "The Meaning of Property"; Blomley, "Performing Property."
7. Yamada, "Legitimation of the Lao People's Revolutionary Party."
8. Vandergeest, "Land to Some Tillers"; Lestrelin et al., "Territorialising Sustainable Development."
9. MacPherson, "The Meaning of Property."
10. De Soto, *The Mystery of Capital.*
11. Hirsch, "Titling against Grabbing?"; Varley, "Private or Public."
12. Ribot and Peluso, "A Theory of Access."
13. Sikor and Lund, "Access and Property."
14. Beban et al., "From Force to Legitimation."
15. In comparison, land-use planning maps produced in villages throughout much of the rest of the country result in hand-drawn or painted signboards and maps that are poorly maintained. The signboards are often falling and damaged, while the paper maps collect dust and grow mold in some corner of a district office. See Dwyer, "Territorial Affairs."
16. Baird, "Degraded Forest."
17. See, for example, Hutt, "Laos Democrats Fight a Lonely Losing Struggle."
18. Lao PDR, Law on Land, October 21, 2003, art. 3.
19. Lao PDR, Constitution of the Lao PDR, May 6, 2003, art. 17.
20. Evans, *Lao Peasants under Socialism*, p. 81.
21. BBC Summary of World Broadcasts: Far East, February 25, 1988, cited in Evans, *Lao Peasants under Socialism,* p. 91.
22. Scott, *Weapons of the Weak*; Dwyer, *Upland Geopolitics.*

23. Deininger and Byerlee, *Rising Global Interest in Farmland*; Food and Agriculture Organization et al., *Principles for Responsible Agricultural Investment*; US Agency for International Development, *USAID Country Profile.*
24. Scott, *Seeing Like a State.*
25. Hetherington, "Promising Information."
26. Borras and Franco, "Contemporary Discourses and Contestations around Pro-Poor Land Policies and Land Governance"; Dwyer, "The Formalization Fix?"; Hirsch, "Titling against Grabbing?"; Wolford, "Land Reform in the Time of Neoliberalism."

Chapter 3. Socializing Nature

1. Évrard and Baird, "The Political Ecology of Upland/Lowland Relationships in Laos since 1975."
2. Barney, "Laos and the Making of a 'Relational' Resource Frontier."
3. Fox et al., "Policies, Political-Economy, and Swidden in Southeast Asia"; McElwee, "Shifting Policies for Shifting Cultivation."
4. Peluso and Vandergeest, "Genealogies of the Political Forest."
5. Ferguson, "The Scramble for the Waste Lands."
6. Scott, *Seeing Like a State.*
7. McElwee, *Forests Are Gold.*
8. Vandergeest and Peluso, "Empires of Forestry."
9. Vandergeest and Peluso, "Empires of Forestry," p. 376.
10. FAO, *Tropical Forestry Action Plan*, sec. 1.2.
11. Baird, "Degraded Forest."
12. Cited in Lao PDR, *Forestry Strategy to the Year 2020 of the Lao PDR*, p. i.
13. McElwee, *Forests Are Gold.*
14. Baird and Shoemaker, "Unsettling Experiences."
15. Delang and Toro, "Hydropower-Induced Displacement and Resettlement"; Sayatham and Suhardiman, "Hydropower Resettlement and Livelihood Adaptation"; Green and Baird, "Capitalizing on Compensation."
16. See Rigg, *Living with Transition in Laos*; Chamberlain, *Participatory Poverty Assessment II*; and High, *Fields of Desire.*
17. Ban Kaengvang households, focus group interview with the author and a research assistant, June 25, 2014.
18. Ban Kaengvang leaders, focus group interview with the author and a research assistant, March 6, 2014.

19. Ban Saphang leaders, focus group interview with the author and a research assistant, March 5, 2014.
20. Xepon district Agriculture and Forestry Office official, interview with the author and a research assistant, November 27, 2013.
21. Ban Salang leaders, focus group interview with the author and a research assistant, March 1, 2014.
22. Vandergeest, "Land to Some Tillers."
23. Xepon DONRE official, interview with the author and a research assistant, November 27, 2013.
24. Bakker, "Neoliberalizing Nature?"
25. Bakker and Bridge, "Material Worlds?"; Braun, "Taking Earth Forces Seriously."
26. Sundberg, "Diabolic *Caminos* in the Desert," p. 321; emphasis in original.
27. Dwyer, *Upland Geopolitics*.
28. Former village chief of Ban Salang, interview with the author and a research assistant, October 17, 2014.
29. Former village chief of Ban Salang interview.

Chapter 4. Resisting with the State

1. AEPF, *People's Solidarity against Poverty and for Sustainable Development*, p. 1.
2. The account of this meeting comes from a foreign NGO director who attended the meeting, personal communication with the author, August 2013; the Brou woman who spoke at the forum, personal communication with the author; and Asian Forum for Human Rights and Development (FORUM-ASIA) and International Organising Committee of the Asia-Europe People's Forum (AEPF-ICO), *Universal Periodic Review Second Cycle—Lao PDR*.
3. FORUM-ASIA and AEPF-ICO, *Universal Periodic Review Second Cycle—Lao PDR*.
4. Foreign development practitioner, personal communication with the author, August 2013.
5. Radio Free Asia, "Lao Villagers Arrested."
6. Smith, "Golf and the Great Lao Land Grab."
7. Representative of a Lao nonprofit association, interview with the author and a research assistant, March 3, 2015.
8. MONRE official, interview with the author and a research assistant, December 5, 2014.
9. *Vientiane Times*, "Land Issues Top Public Concerns."

10. Smith, "Coffee Colonialism."
11. NGO staff, interview with the author and a research assistant, February 2015.
12. Land Issues Working Group, *Coffee Plantation in Paksong District, Champasak.*
13. Escobar, *Encountering Development*; Escobar, *Territories of Difference.*
14. Perreault, "From the Guerra del Agua."
15. Wolford, *This Land Is Ours Now.*
16. Rocheleau and Ross, "Trees as Tools, Trees as Text."
17. Bebbington et al., "Mining and Social Movements."
18. Bebbington et al., "Mining and Social Movements."
19. McAdam et al., *Dynamics of Contention.*
20. Tilly, *Social Movements, 1768–2004*; Della Porta and Tarrow, *Transnational Protest and Global Activism.*
21. Malseed, "Where There Is No Movement."
22. Scott, *Weapons of the Weak*; Scott, *Domination and the Arts of Resistance.*
23. Last, "Aspects of Administration and Dissent."
24. Adas, "From Footdragging to Flight"; Walker, "From Covert to Overt."
25. Gramsci, *Selections from the Prison Notebooks.*
26. Sharp et al., "Entanglements of Power," p. 20.
27. Caouette and Turner, *Agrarian Angst and Rural Resistance.*
28. Scott, *Domination and the Arts of Resistance.*
29. O'Brien and Li, *Rightful Resistance in Rural China.*
30. O'Brien and Li, *Rightful Resistance in Rural China*, pp. 2–3.
31. Poulantzas, *State, Power, Socialism.*
32. Jessop, *State Theory.*
33. Gunn, *Rebellion in Laos.*
34. Stuart-Fox, *A History of Laos.*
35. Evans, *A Short History of Laos*; Baird, "Party, State and the Control of Information."
36. Radio Free Asia, "Lao Authorities Arrest 30 Suspects in Bus Shootings."
37. Radio Free Asia, "Exiled Lao Activist Recalls 1999 Protest."
38. Dwyer, "Micro-Geopolitics."
39. Baird and Le Billon, "Landscapes of Political Memories"; Pholsena, *Post-war Laos.*
40. Tappe, "On the Right Track?"
41. Mahanty et al., "Rupture."

42. Thao Chom household, interview with the author and a research assistant, October 17, 2014.
43. Pholsena, "The (Transformative) Impacts of the Vietnam War."
44. Deputy village chief of Ban Phailom, interview with the author and a research assistant, March 6, 2014.
45. Deputy village chief of Ban Phailom interview.
46. Ban Saphang villagers, focus group interview with the author and a research assistant, October 21, 2014.
47. Baird and Le Billon, "Landscapes of Political Memories."
48. Radio Free Asia, "Exiled Lao Activist Recalls 1999 Protest."
49. International Federation for Human Rights, "Woman Detained for Criticizing the Government Online."

Chapter 5. Solidarity in the Landed Village

1. Vandergeest and Rigg, "The Restudy 'Problem' and Agrarian Change."
2. Ireson, "Invisible Walls," p. 221.
3. Breman, *The Village on Java*; Kemp, *Seductive Mirage.*
4. Breman, *The Shattered Image*, p. 10.
5. Rigg, "Land, Farming, Livelihoods, and Poverty"; Hirsch "The State in the Village."
6. Agrawal and Gibson, "Enchantment and Disenchantment."
7. Brockington, "Community Conservation, Inequality and Injustice"; Dressler et al., "From Hope to Crisis and Back Again?"; Li, "Engaging Simplifications."
8. Balibar, "The Nation Form," p. 93; emphasis in original.
9. Li, "Images of Community," p. 502.
10. Li, "Engaging Simplifications."
11. Watts, "The Sinister Political Life of Community," p. 3.
12. Hirsch, "The State in the Village."
13. Hirsch, "The State in the Village," p. 54.
14. High, "'Join Together, Work Together,'" p. 36.
15. Wolters, *History, Culture and Religion in Southeast Asian Perspectives.*
16. Evans, *Lao Peasants under Socialism*, p. 188.
17. High, *Projectland.*
18. High, "'Join Together, Work Together,'" p. 25.
19. Lao PDR, Law on Local Administration, October 21, 2003, art. 47.
20. Lao PDR, Law on Local Administration, October 21, 2003, art. 53.
21. High, "'Join Together, Work Together,'" p. 38.
22. High, "'Join Together, Work Together,'" p. 38.

23. Evans, *Lao Peasants under Socialism.*
24. Lao PDR, Instruction No. 01/PM/2000.
25. United Nations Development Program, *National Human Development Report.*
26. High, "'Join Together, Work Together.'"
27. Evans, *Lao Peasants under Socialism*; Kerkvliet, *The Power of Everyday Politics.*
28. High, *Fields of Desire.*
29. High, "'Join Together, Work Together,'" pp. 31–32.
30. Kelliher, "Historicising Geographies of Solidarity."
31. Featherstone, *Solidarity*, p. 5.
32. Sundberg, "Reconfiguring North–South Solidarity."
33. Featherstone, *Solidarity*; Kelliher, "Historicising Geographies of Solidarity"; Sundberg, "Reconfiguring North–South Solidarity."
34. Li, "After the Land Grab."
35. Village committee, focus group interview with the author and a research assistant, Ban Nammak, February 28, 2014.
36. Village committee, focus group interview.
37. Village committee, focus group interview.
38. Ban Salang villagers, focus group interview with the author and a research assistant, March 1, 2014.
39. Village committee, focus group interview with the author and a research assistant, Ban Salang, March 1, 2014.
40. Former village chief, interview with the author and a research assistant, Ban Salang, October 17, 2014.
41. Village committee, focus group interview with the author and a research assistant, Ban Phoulao, February 28, 2014.
42. Ban Phoulao villagers, focus group interview with the author and a research assistant, February 28, 2014.
43. Ban Phoulao villagers focus group interview.
44. Village committee, focus group interview with the author and a research assistant, Ban Phoulao, March 4, 2014.
45. Field notes, July 16, 2014.

Conclusion

1. Barney, "Land, Livelihoods, and Remittances."
2. Li, *Land's End.*
3. Cousins, "Land Reform, Accumulation and Social Reproduction."
4. Polanyi, *The Great Transformation.*
5. Field notes, February 28, 2014.

6. Harms, "Beauty as Control in the New Saigon."
7. Villagers claimed that records of the agreements had been written down but the companies kept them and did not provide copies to the village.
8. Friis and Nielsen, "Small-Scale Land Acquisitions, Large-Scale Implications."
9. Suhardiman et al., "(Re)constructing State Power and Livelihoods."

References

Adas, Michael. "From Footdragging to Flight: The Evasive History of Peasant Avoidance Protest in South and South-East Asia." *Journal of Peasant Studies* 13, no. 2 (1986): 64–86.

Agrawal, Arun, and Clark C. Gibson. "Enchantment and Disenchantment: The Role of Community in Natural Resource Conservation." *World Development* 27, no. 4 (1999): 629–649.

Alden Wily, Liz. "Looking Back to See Forward: The Legal Niceties of Land Theft in Land Rushes." *Journal of Peasant Studies* 39, nos. 3–4 (2012): 751–775.

Al Jazeera. "Laos: On the Borders of the Empire." May 25, 2017. Accessed January 27, 2024. https://www.aljazeera.com/programmes/peopleandpower/2017/05/laos-borders-empire-170522105221541.html.

Anonymous. "Aspects of Forestry Management in the Lao PDR." *Watershed* 5, no. 3 (2000): 57–64.

Asia-Europe People's Forum (AEPF). *People's Solidarity against Poverty and for Sustainable Development: Challenging Unjust and Unequal Development, Building States of Citizens for Citizens*. Vientiane: AEPF. Accessed March 2, 2024. https://aseminfoboard.org/wp-content/uploads/2022/10/2012_-_AEPF_-_Call_for_Participation_mUGD5Xs.pdf.

Asian Forum for Human Rights and Development (FORUM-ASIA) and International Organising Committee of the Asia-Europe People's Forum (AEPF-ICO). *Universal Periodic Review Second Cycle—Lao PDR: Stakeholders' Submission*. Bangkok: FORUM-ASIA, 2014. Accessed March 6, 2024. https://forum-asia.org/wp-content/uploads/2015/02/ForumLaoUPR_241114.pdf.

Baird, Ian G. "Degraded Forest, Degraded Land and the Development of Industrial Tree Plantations in Laos." *Singapore Journal of Tropical Geography* 35, no. 3 (2014): 328–344.

———. "The Global Land Grab Meta-narrative, Asian Money Laundering and Elite Capture: Reconsidering the Cambodian Context." *Geopolitics* 19, no. 2 (2014): 431–453.

———. "Land, Rubber and People: Rapid Agrarian Changes and Responses in Southern Laos." *Journal of Lao Studies* 1, no. 1 (2010): 1–47.

———. "Party, State and the Control of Information in the Lao People's Democratic Republic: Secrecy, Falsification and Denial." *Journal of Contemporary Asia* 48, no. 5 (2018): 739–760.

———. "Problems for the Plantations: Challenges for Large-Scale Land Concessions in Laos and Cambodia." *Journal of Agrarian Change* 20, no. 3 (2020): 387–407.

———. *Quotas, Powers, Patronage, and Illegal Rent-Seeking: The Political Economy of Logging and the Timber Trade in Southern Laos.* Washington, DC: Forest Trends, 2010.

Baird, Ian G., and Bruce Shoemaker. *People, Livelihoods and Development in the Xekong River Basin, Laos.* Bangkok: White Lotus Press, 2008.

———."Unsettling Experiences: Internal Resettlement and International Aid Agencies in Laos." *Development and Change* 38, no. 5 (2007): 865–888.

Baird, Ian G., and Philippe Le Billon. "Landscapes of Political Memories: War Legacies and Land Negotiations in Laos." *Political Geography* 31, no. 2 (2012): 290–300.

Baka, Jennifer. "The Political Construction of Wasteland: Governmentality, Land Acquisition and Social Inequality in South India." *Development and Change* 44, no. 2 (2013): 409–428.

Bakker, Karen. "Neoliberalizing Nature? Market Environmentalism in Water Supply in England and Wales." *Annals of the Association of American Geographers* 95, no. 3 (2005): 542–565.

Bakker, Karen, and Gavin Bridge. "Material Worlds? Resource Geographies and the 'Matter of Nature.'" *Progress in Human Geography* 30, no. 1 (2006): 5–27.

Balibar, Étienne. "The Nation Form: History and Ideology." In *Race, Nation, Class: Ambiguous Identities,* by Étienne Balibar and Immanuel Wallerstein, pp. 86–105. London: Verso, 1991.

Barney, Keith. "Land, Livelihoods, and Remittances: A Political Ecology of Youth Out-migration across the Lao–Thai Mekong Border." *Critical Asian Studies* 44, no. 1 (2012): 57–83.

———. "Laos and the Making of a 'Relational' Resource Frontier." *Geographical Journal* 175, no. 2 (2009): 146–159.

Beban, Alice, Sokbunthoen So, and Kheang Un. "From Force to Legitimation: Rethinking Land Grabs in Cambodia." *Development and Change* 48, no. 3 (2017): 590–612.

Bebbington, Anthony, Denise Humphreys Bebbington, Jeffrey Bury, Jeannet Lingan, Juan Pablo Muñoz, and Martin Scurrah. "Mining and Social Movements: Struggles over Livelihood and Rural Territorial Development in the Andes." *World Development* 36, no. 12 (2008): 2888–2905.

Blomley, Nicholas. "Law, Property, and the Geography of Violence: The Frontier, the Survey, and the Grid." *Annals of the Association of American Geographers* 93, no. 1 (2003): 121–141.

———. "Performing Property: Making the World." *Canadian Journal of Law and Jurisprudence* 26, no. 1 (2013): 23–48.

———. "The Territory of Property." *Progress in Human Geography* 40, no. 5 (2016): 593–609.

Borras, Saturnino M., and Jennifer C. Franco. "Contemporary Discourses and Contestations around Pro-Poor Land Policies and Land Governance." *Journal of Agrarian Change* 10, no. 1 (2010): 1–32.

Borras, Saturnino M., Ruth Hall, Ian Scoones, Ben White, and Wendy Wolford. "Towards a Better Understanding of Global Land Grabbing: An Editorial Introduction." *Journal of Peasant Studies* 38, no. 2 (2011): 209–216.

Braun, Bruce. "Taking Earth Forces Seriously." In *Viscosity—Mobilizing Materialities,* edited by Karen Lutsky, Ozayr Saloojee, and Emily Eliza Scott, pp. 47–61. Minneapolis: University of Minnesota Press, 2019.

Breman, Jan. *The Shattered Image: Construction and Deconstruction of the Village in Colonial Java.* Dordrecht: Foris Publications, 1988.

———. *The Village on Java and the Early-Colonial State.* Rotterdam: Erasmus University, 1980.

Bridge, Gavin. "Global Production Networks and the Extractive Sector: Governing Resource-Based Development." *Journal of Economic Geography* 8, no. 3 (2008): 389–419.

———. "Material Worlds: Natural Resources, Resource Geography and the Material Economy." *Geography Compass* 3, no. 3 (2009): 1217–1244.

Brockington, Dan. "Community Conservation, Inequality and Injustice: Myths of Power in Protected Area Management." *Conservation and Society* 2, no. 2 (2004): 411–432.

Brown, Macalister, and J. J. Zasloff. "Laos 1976: Faltering First Steps toward Socialism." *Asian Survey* 17, no. 2 (1977): 107–115.

Cambodian League for the Promotion and Defense of Human Rights. *Land Grabbing and Poverty in Cambodia: The Myth of Development.* Phnom Penh: Cambodian League for the Promotion and Defense of Human Rights, 2009.

Caouette, Dominique, and Sarah Turner, eds. *Agrarian Angst and Rural Resistance in Contemporary Southeast Asia.* New York: Routledge, 2009.

Castree, Noel, and Bruce Braun, eds. *Social Nature: Theory, Practice, and Politics.* Malden, MA: Blackwell, 2001.

Chakrya, Khouth Sophak, and Ananth Baliga. "Boeung Kak: A Disastrous Decade." *Phnom Penh Post,* February 3, 2017. Accessed February 2, 2024. https://www.phnompenhpost.com/national-post-depth-politics/boeung-kak-disastrous-decade.

Chamberlain, James R. *Participatory Poverty Assessment II (2006): Lao People's Democratic Republic.* Vientiane: National Statistics Center and the Asian Development Bank, 2007.

Cleary, David. "After the Frontier: Problems with Political Economy in the Modern Brazilian Amazon." *Journal of Latin American Studies* 25, no. 2 (1993): 331–349.

Cotula, Lorenzo. "The New Enclosures? Polanyi, International Investment Law and the Global Land Rush." *Third World Quarterly* 34, no. 9 (2013): 1605–1629.

Cousins, Ben. "Land Reform, Accumulation and Social Reproduction: The South African Experience in Global and Historical Perspective." Public lecture, Cape Town, South Africa, 2019. Accessed March 1, 2024. https://www.plaas.org.za/land-reform-accumulation-and-social-reproduction-public-lecture-by-prof-ben-cousins/.

De Angelis, Massimo. "Marx and Primitive Accumulation: The Continuous Character of Capital's 'Enclosures.'" *Commoner* 2, no. 1 (2001): 1–22.

Deininger, Klaus. "Challenges Posed by the New Wave of Farmland Investment." *Journal of Peasant Studies* 38, no. 2 (2011): 217–247.

Deininger, Klaus, and Derek Byerlee. *Rising Global Interest in Farmland: Can It Yield Sustainable and Equitable Benefits?* Washington, DC: World Bank, 2011.

Delang, Claudio O., and Matthew Toro. "Hydropower-Induced Displacement and Resettlement in the Lao PDR." *South East Asia Research* 19, no. 3 (2011): 567–594.

Della Porta, Donatella, and Sidney G. Tarrow, eds. *Transnational Protest and Global Activism.* Lanham, MD: Rowman and Littlefield, 2005.

De Schutter, Olivier. "How Not to Think of Land-Grabbing: Three Critiques of Large-scale Investments in Farmland." *Journal of Peasant Studies* 38, no. 2 (2011): 249–279.

de Soto, Hernando. *The Mystery of Capital: Why Capitalism Triumphs in the West and Fails Everywhere Else.* London: Bantam Press, 2000.

Dressler, Wolfram, Bram Büscher, Michael Schoon, Dan Brockington, Tanya Hayes, Christian A. Kull, James McCarthy, and Krishna Shrestha. "From Hope to Crisis and Back Again? A Critical History of the Global CBNRM Narrative." *Environmental Conservation* 37, no. 1 (2010): 5–15.

Dwyer, Michael Benjamin. "The Formalization Fix? Land Titling, Land Concessions and the Politics of Spatial Transparency in Cambodia." *Journal of Peasant Studies* 42, no. 5 (2015): 903–928.

———. "Micro-Geopolitics: Capitalising Security in Laos's Golden Quadrangle." *Geopolitics* 19, no. 2 (2014): 377–405.

———. "Territorial Affairs: Turning Battlefields into Marketplaces in Postwar Laos." PhD diss., University of California, Berkeley, 2011.

———. "That Luang Marsh Project Timeline and Associated Timeline of the Turning Land into Capital Policy." PhD diss. annex, University of California, Berkeley, 2013.

———. *Upland Geopolitics: Postwar Laos and the Global Land Rush.* Seattle: University of Washington Press, 2022.

Edelman, Marc. "Messy Hectares: Questions about the Epistemology of Land Grabbing Data." *Journal of Peasant Studies* 40, no. 3 (2013): 485–501.

Emel, Jody, Matthew T. Huber, and Madoshi H. Makene. "Extracting Sovereignty: Capital, Territory, and Gold Mining in Tanzania." *Political Geography* 30, no. 2 (2011): 70–79.

Escobar, Arturo. *Encountering Development: The Making and Unmaking of the Third World.* Princeton, NJ: Princeton University Press, 1995.

———. *Territories of Difference: Place, Movements, Life, Redes.* Durham, NC: Duke University Press, 2008.

Evans, Grant. *Lao Peasants under Socialism.* New Haven, CT: Yale University Press, 1990.

———. *Lao Peasants under Socialism and Post-Socialism.* Chiang Mai: Silkworm Books, 1995.

———. *A Short History of Laos: The Land in Between.* Sydney: Allen and Unwin, 2002.

Évrard, Olivier, and Ian G. Baird. "The Political Ecology of Upland/Lowland Relationships in Laos since 1975." In *Changing Lives in Laos: Society, Politics, and Culture in a Post-socialist State*, edited by Vanina Bouté and Vatthana Pholsena, pp. 165–191. Singapore: NUS Press, 2017.

Fairbairn, Madeleine. *Fields of Gold: Financing the Global Land Rush.* Ithaca, NY: Cornell University Press, 2020.

———. "Indirect Dispossession: Domestic Power Imbalances and Foreign Access to Land in Mozambique." *Development and Change* 44, no. 2 (2013): 335–356.

Featherstone, David. *Solidarity: Hidden Histories and Geographies of Internationalism.* London: Zed Books, 2012.

Ferguson, Jane M. "The Scramble for the Waste Lands: Tracking Colonial Legacies, Counterinsurgency and International Investment through the Lens of

Land Laws in Burma/Myanmar." *Singapore Journal of Tropical Geography* 35, no. 3 (2014): 295–311.

Food and Agriculture Organization. *Tropical Forestry Action Plan.* Rome: Food and Agriculture Organization, 1985.

Food and Agriculture Organization, IFAD, UNCTAD, and World Bank Group. *Principles for Responsible Agricultural Investment that Respects Rights, Livelihoods and Resources: Extended Version.* Washington, DC: World Bank, 2010.

Fox, Jefferson, Yayoi Fujita, Dimbab Ngidang, Nancy Peluso, Lesley Potter, Niken Sakuntaladewi, Janet Sturgeon, and David Thomas. "Policies, Political-Economy, and Swidden in Southeast Asia." *Human Ecology* 37, no. 3 (2009): 305–322.

Franco, Jennifer, Saturnino Borras Jr., Alberto Alonso-Fradejas, Nick Buxton, Roman Herre, Sylvia Kay, and Timothé Feodoroff. *The Global Land Grab: A Primer.* Amsterdam: Transnational Institute, 2013.

Friis, Cecilie, and Jonas Ø. Nielsen. "Small-Scale Land Acquisitions, Large-Scale Implications: Exploring the Case of Chinese Banana Investments in Northern Laos." *Land Use Policy* 57 (2016): 117–129.

Fujita, Yayoi, and Khamla Phanvilay. "Land and Forest Allocation in Lao People's Democratic Republic: Comparison of Case Studies from Community-Based Natural Resource Management." *Society and Natural Resources* 21 (2008): 120–133.

Gagné, Marie, and Ashley Fent. "The Faltering Land Rush and the Limits to Extractive Capitalism in Senegal." In *The Transnational Land Rush in Africa: A Decade After the Spike,* edited by Logan Cochrane, and Nathan Andrews, pp. 55–85. Cham: Palgrave Macmillan, 2021.

Glassman, Jim. "Primitive Accumulation, Accumulation by Dispossession, Accumulation by 'Extra-Economic' Means." *Progress in Human Geography* 30, no. 5 (2006): 608–625.

Goldman, Michael, Nancy Lee Peluso, and Wendy Wolford. Introduction to *The Social Lives of Land,* edited by Michael Goldman, Nancy Lee Peluso, and Wendy Wolford, pp. 1–20. Ithaca, NY: Cornell University Press, 2024.

GRAIN. *Seized: The 2008 Landgrab for Food and Financial Security.* Barcelona: GRAIN, 2008. Accessed March 6, 2024. https://grain.org/article/entries/93-seized-the-2008-landgrab-for-food-and-financial-security.

Gramsci, Antonio. *Selections from the Prison Notebooks.* New York: International Publishers, 1971.

Green, W. Nathan, and Ian G. Baird. "Capitalizing on Compensation: Hydropower Resettlement and the Commodification and Decommodification of

Nature–Society Relations in Southern Laos." *Annals of the American Association of Geographers* 106, no. 4 (2016): 853–873.

Gunn, Geoffrey. *Rebellion in Laos: Peasant and Politics in a Colonial Backwater.* London: Routledge, 2019. First published 1990.

Hall, Derek. *Land.* Cambridge: Polity Press, 2013.

Hall, Derek, Philip Hirsch, and Tania Murray Li. *Powers of Exclusion: Land Dilemmas in Southeast Asia.* Singapore: NUS Press, 2011.

Hall, Ruth, Marc Edelman, Saturnino Borras, Ian Scoones, Ben White, and Wendy Wolford. "Resistance, Acquiescence or Incorporation? An Introduction to Land Grabbing and Political Reactions 'From Below.'" *Journal of Peasant Studies* 42, nos. 3–4 (2015): 467–488.

Halvorsen, Sam. "Spatial Dialectics and the Geography of Social Movements: The Case of Occupy London." *Transactions of the Institute of British Geographers* 42, no. 3 (2017): 445–457.

Hameiri, Shahar, and Lee Jones. "Theorising Political Economy in Southeast Asia." In *The Political Economy of Southeast Asia: Politics and Uneven Development under Hyperglobalisation,* edited by Toby Carroll, Shahar Hameiri, and Lee Jones, pp. 3–34. London: Palgrave Macmillan, 2020.

Harms, Erik. "Beauty as Control in the New Saigon: Eviction, New Urban Zones, and Atomized Dissent in a Southeast Asian City." *American Ethnologist* 39, no. 4 (2012): 735–750.

Harms, Erik, and Ian G. Baird. "Wastelands, Degraded Lands and Forests, and the Class(ification) Struggle: Three Critical Perspectives from Mainland Southeast Asia." *Singapore Journal of Tropical Geography* 35 (2014): 289–294.

Harvey, David. *The New Imperialism.* New York: Oxford University Press, 2003.

Hetherington, Kregg. "Promising Information: Democracy, Development, and the Remapping of Latin America." *Economy and Society* 41, no. 2 (2012): 127–150.

Hett, Cornelia, Vong Nanhthavong, Savanh Hanephom, Anongsone Phommachanh, Boungnong Sidavong, Ketkeo Phouangphet, Juliet Lu, Annie Shattuck, Micah Ingalls, Rasso Bernhard, Souphaphone Pathitmixay, Chanthavone Phomphakdy, Andreas Heinimann, and Michael Epprecht. *Land Leases and Concessions in the Lao PDR: A Characterization of Investments in Land and Their Impacts.* Bern: University of Bern, 2020.

High, Holly. *Fields of Desire: Poverty and Policy in Laos.* Singapore: NUS Press, 2014.

———. "'Join Together, Work Together, for the Common Good—Solidarity': Village Formation Processes in the Rural South of Laos." *Sojourn: Journal of Social Issues in Southeast Asia* 21, no. 1 (2006): 22–45.

———. *Projectland: Life in a Lao Socialist Model Village.* Honolulu: University of Hawai'i Press, 2021.

Hirsch, Philip. "The Changing Political Dynamics of Dam Building on the Mekong." *Water Alternatives* 3, no. 2 (2010): 312–323.

———. "The State in the Village: Interpreting Rural Development in Thailand." *Development and Change* 20, no. 1 (1989): 35–56.

———. "Titling against Grabbing? Critiques and Conundrums around Land Formalisation in Southeast Asia." Paper Presented at the International Conference on Global Land Grabbing, University of Sussex, April 6–8, 2011.

Hutt, David. "Laos Democrats Fight a Lonely Losing Struggle: International Community Muted amid Another Anti-democratic Clampdown in Communist-run Laos." *Asia Times,* November 27, 2019. Accessed January 27, 2024. https://asiatimes.com/2019/11/laos-democrats-fight-a-lonely-losing-struggle/.

International Federation for Human Rights. "Woman Detained for Criticizing the Government Online." September 16, 2019. Accessed March 8, 2024. https://www.fidh.org/en/region/asia/laos/woman-detained-for-criticizing-the-government-online.

Ireson, W. Randall. "Invisible Walls: Village Identity and the Maintenance of Cooperation in Laos." *Journal of Southeast Asian Studies* 27, no. 2 (1996): 219–244.

Jepson, Wendy. "Producing a Modern Agricultural Frontier: Firms and Cooperatives in Eastern Matto Grosso, Brazil." *Economic Geography* 82, no. 3 (2006): 289–316.

Jessop, Bob. "Poulantzas's *State, Power and Socialism* as a Modern Classic." In *Reading Poulantzas,* edited by Alexander Gallas, Lars Bretthauer, John Kannankulam, and Ingo Stützle, pp. 41–55. London: Merlin Press, 2011.

———. *State Power: A Strategic-Relational Approach.* Cambridge: Polity Press, 2007.

———. *State Theory: Putting the Capitalist State in Its Place.* Cambridge: Polity Press, 1990.

Jurkevics, Anna. "Land Grabbing and the Perplexities of Territorial Sovereignty." *Political Theory* 50, no. 1 (2022): 32–58.

Kelliher, Diarmaid. "Historicising Geographies of Solidarity." *Geography Compass* 12, no. 9 (2018): 1–12.

Kemp, Jeremy. *Seductive Mirage: The Search for the Village Community in Southeast Asia.* Dordrecht: Foris Publications, 1988.

Kenney-Lazar, Miles. "Relations of Sovereignty: The Uneven Production of Transnational Plantation Territories in Laos." *Transactions of the Institute of British Geographers* 45, no. 2 (2020): 331–344.

Kenney-Lazar, Miles, Michael B. Dwyer, and Cornelia Hett. *Turning Land into Capital: Assessing a Decade of Policy in Practice.* Vientiane: Land Information Working Group, 2018.

Kenney-Lazar, Miles, Oliver Schönweger, Peter Messerli, and Vong Nanhthavong. "Governing Land Concessions in Laos." In *Routledge Handbook of Global Land and Resource Grabbing,* edited by Andreas Neef, Chanrith Ngin, Tsegaye Moreda, and Sharlene Mollett, pp. 96–109. London: Routledge, 2023.

Kerkvliet, Benedict J. T. *The Power of Everyday Politics: How Vietnamese Peasants Transformed National Policy.* Ithaca, NY: Cornell University Press, 2005.

Land Issues Working Group. *Coffee Plantation in Paksong District, Champasak.* Vientiane: Land Issues Working Group, 2012.

Lao PDR, Government of the. Constitution of the Lao People's Democratic Republic, National Assembly, No. 25/NA, May 6, 2003. Accessed March 7, 2024. http://www.asianlii.org/la/legis/const/2003/1.html.

———. *Forestry Strategy to the Year 2020 of the Lao PDR.* Vientiane: Ministry of Agriculture and Forestry, 2005.

———. Instruction of the Prime Minister Regarding the Policies to Build the Province as the Strategic Unit, the District as the Budget-Planning Unit, and the Village as the Implementation Unit. Instruction No. 01/PM/2000, March 11, 2000.

———. *Khou Mu Ne Nam Kan Pap Poung Than Kho Moun Kan Khun Ban Xi Khong Kan Xao Le Samphathan Thi Din Khong Lat Yang Pen Labop To Nuang You Sor Por Por Lao* [Guidebook on the systematic and continuous updating the state land leases and concessions database in the Lao PDR]. Vientiane: Ministry of Natural Resources and the Environment, Ministry of Planning and Investment, Ministry of Agriculture and Forestry, Ministry of Energy and Mines, Ministry of Finance, and the Centre for Development and Environment, University of Bern, Switzerland, 2021.

———. Law on Land, National Assembly, No. 04/NA, October 21, 2003. Accessed March 7, 2024. https://data.opendevelopmentmekong.net/dataset/440bda62-4042-43f3-98a4-c99ca05edd41/resource/c26fd9a7-cf74-434d-80b7-ca41f1c22536/download/lao77471.pdf.

———. Law on Local Administration, National Assembly, No. 47/NA, October 21, 2003. Accessed March 18, 2024. https://www.rcrc-resilience-southeastasia.org/wp-content/uploads/2017/12/2003_law_on_local_administration.pdf.

———. "Why Laos." Vientiane: Investment Promotion Department, Ministry of Planning and Investment, n.d. Accessed January 27, 2024. http://www.investlaos.gov.la/index.php/why-laos.

Last, Murray. "Aspects of Administration and Dissent in Hausaland, 1800–1968." *Africa* 40, no. 4 (1970): 345–357.

Lay, Jann, Ward Anseeuw, Sandra Eckert, Insa Flachsbarth, Christoph Kubitza, Kerstin Nolte, and Markus Giger. *Taking Stock of the Global Land Rush: Analytical Report III*. Bern: University of Bern, 2021.

Lee, Ching Kwan. *The Specter of Global China: Politics, Labor, and Foreign Investment in Africa*. Chicago: University of Chicago Press, 2017.

Lestrelin, Guillaume, Jean-Christophe Castella, and Jeremy Bourgoin. "Territorialising Sustainable Development: The Politics of Land-Use Planning in Laos." *Journal of Contemporary Asia* 42, no. 4 (2012): 581–602.

Levien, Michael. "The Land Question: Special Economic Zones and the Political Economy of Dispossession in India." *Journal of Peasant Studies* 39, nos. 3–4 (2012): 933–969.

Li, Tania Murray. "After the Land Grab: Infrastructural Violence and the 'Mafia System' in Indonesia's Oil Palm Plantation Zones." *Geoforum* 96 (2018): 328–337.

———. "Engaging Simplifications: Community-Based Resource Management, Market Processes and State Agendas in Upland Southeast Asia." *World Development* 30, no. 2 (2002): 265–283.

———. "Images of Community: Discourse and Strategy in Property Relations." *Development and Change* 27, no. 3 (1996): 501–527.

———. *Land's End: Capitalist Relations on an Indigenous Frontier*. Durham, NC: Duke University Press, 2014.

———. "What Is Land? Assembling a Resource for Global Investment." *Transactions of the Institute of British Geographers* 39, no. 4 (2014): 589–602.

Lintner, Bertil. "Little Laos Risks Losing It All to China." *Asia Times,* May 13, 2018. Accessed January 27, 2024. https://asiatimes.com/2018/05/little-laos-risks-losing-it-all-to-china/.

Lough, Richard. "Madagascar's New Leader Says Daewoo Land Deal Off." Reuters, March 19, 2009. Accessed January 27, 2024. https://www.reuters.com/article/idUSTRE52H56E/.

Lu, Juliet. "Grounding Chinese Investment: Encounters between Chinese Capital and Local Land Politics in Laos." *Globalizations* 18, no. 3 (2021): 422–440.

Lu, Juliet, and Oliver Schönweger. "Great Expectations: Chinese Investment in Laos and the Myth of Empty Land." *Territory, Politics, Governance* 7, no. 1 (2019): 61–78.

Lund, Christian. "Fragmented Sovereignty: Land Reform and Dispossession in Laos." *Journal of Peasant Studies* 38, no. 4 (2011): 885–905.

———. *Nine-Tenths of the Law: Enduring Dispossession in Indonesia*. New Haven, CT: Yale University Press, 2021.

Lyttleton, Chris, and Pál Nyíri. "Dams, Casinos and Concessions: Chinese Megaprojects in Laos and Cambodia." In *Engineering Earth: The Impacts of Megaengineering Projects,* edited by Stanley D. Brunn, pp. 1243–1265. New York: Springer, 2011.

Macan-Markar, Marwaan. "Thailand Challenges Laos Dam Building Spree on Mekong River." *Nikkei Asia,* January 30, 2021. Accessed January 27, 2024. https://asia.nikkei.com/Politics/International-relations/Thailand-challenges-Laos-dam-building-spree-on-Mekong-River.

MacPherson, C. B. "The Meaning of Property." In *Property: Mainstream and Critical Positions,* edited by C. B. MacPherson, pp. 1–14. Toronto: University of Toronto Press, 1978.

Mahanty, Sango, Sarah Milne, Keith Barney, Wolfram Dressler, Philip Hirsch, and Phuc Xuan To. "Rupture: Towards a Critical, Emplaced, and Experiential View of Nature-Society Crisis." *Dialogues in Human Geography* 13, no. 2 (2023): 1–20.

Makki, Fouad. "Power and Property: Commercialization, Enclosures, and the Transformation of Agrarian Relations in Ethiopia." *Journal of Peasant Studies* 39, no. 1 (2012): 81–104.

Malseed, Kevin. "Where There Is No Movement: Local Resistance and the Potential for Solidarity." *Journal of Agrarian Change* 8, nos. 2–3 (2008): 489–514.

Marx, Karl. *Capital.* Volume 1. New York: Penguin, 1976. First published 1867.

Marx, Karl, and Friedrich Engels. *The Communist Manifesto.* Peking: Foreign Languages Press, 1970. First published 1848.

McAdam, Doug, Sydney Tarrow, and Charles Tilly. *Dynamics of Contention.* Cambridge: Cambridge University Press, 2001.

McCarthy, John F. *The Fourth Circle: A Political Ecology of Sumatra's Rainforest Frontier.* Stanford, CA: Stanford University Press, 2006.

McElwee, Pamela D. *Forests Are Gold: Trees, People, and Environmental Rule in Vietnam.* Seattle: University of Washington Press, 2016.

———. "Shifting Policies for Shifting Cultivation: A History of Anti-Swidden Interventions in Vietnam." *Journal of Southeast Asian Studies* 53, nos. 1–2 (2022): 153–182.

McMichael, Philip. "The Land Grab and Corporate Food Regime Restructuring." *Journal of Peasant Studies* 39, nos. 3–4 (2012): 681–701.

———. "Land Grabbing as Security Mercantilism in International Relations." *Globalizations* 10, no. 1 (2013): 47–64.

Middleton, Carl, Jelson Garcia, and Tira Foran. "Old and New Hydropower Players in the Mekong Region: Agendas and Strategies." In *Contested Waterscapes in the Mekong Region: Hydropower, Livelihoods and Governance,* edited by François Molle, Tira Foran, and Mira Käkönen, pp. 23–54. London: Earthscan, 2009.

Miliband, Ralph. "Poulantzas and the Capitalist State." *New Left Review* I/82 (1973): 83–92.

Mousseau, Frédéric, Andy Currier, Elizabeth Fraser, and Jessie Green. *Driving Dispossession: The Global Push to "Unlock the Economic Potential of Land."* Oakland, CA: Oakland Institute, 2020.

Nolte, Kerstin. "Doomed to Fail? Why Some Land-Based Investment Projects Fail." *Applied Geography* 122 (2020): 102268.

Obein, François. *Assessment of the Environmental and Social Impacts Created by the VLRC Industrial Rubber Plantation and Proposed Environmental and Social Plans.* Vientiane: Agence Française de Développement, 2007.

O'Brien, Kevin J., and Lianjiang Li. *Rightful Resistance in Rural China.* Cambridge: Cambridge University Press, 2006.

Oliveira, Gustavo de L. T. "Land Regularization in Brazil and the Global Land Grab." *Development and Change* 44, no. 2 (2013): 261–283.

Özsu, Umut. "Grabbing Land Legally: A Marxist Analysis." *Leiden Journal of International Law* 32, no. 2 (2019): 215–233.

Oya, Carlos. "Methodological Reflections on 'Land Grab' Databases and the 'Land Grab' Literature 'Rush.'" *Journal of Peasant Studies* 40, no. 3 (2013): 503–520.

Pang, Edgar. *"Same-Same but Different": Laos and Cambodia's Political Embrace of China.* ISEAS Perspective no. 66. Singapore: ISEAS–Yusof Ishak Institute, 2017.

Peck, Jamie. "For Polanyian Economic Geographies." *Environment and Planning A* 45, no. 7 (2013): 1545–1568.

Peluso, Nancy Lee, and Christian Lund. "New Frontiers of Land Control: Introduction." *Journal of Peasant Studies* 38, no. 4 (2011): 667–681.

Peluso, Nancy Lee, and Peter Vandergeest. "Genealogies of the Political Forest and Customary Rights in Indonesia, Malaysia, and Thailand." *Journal of Asian Studies* 60, no. 3 (2001): 761–812.

Perelman, Michael. *The Invention of Capitalism: Classical Political Economy and the Secret History of Primitive Accumulation.* Durham, NC: Duke University Press, 2000.

Perreault, Thomas. "From the Guerra del Agua to the Guerra del Gas: Resource Governance, Neoliberalism and Popular Protest in Bolivia." *Antipode* 38, no. 1 (2006): 150–172.

Pholsena, Vatthana. *Post-war Laos: The Politics of Culture, History and Identity.* Singapore: Institute of Southeast Asian Studies, 2006.

———. "The (Transformative) Impacts of the Vietnam War and the Communist Revolution in a Border Region in Southeastern Laos." *War and Society* 31, no. 2 (2012): 163–183.

Polanyi, Karl. *The Great Transformation: The Political and Economic Origins of Our Time.* Boston: Beacon Press, 2001. First published 1944.

Poulantzas, Nicos. "The Problem of the Capitalist State." *New Left Review* I/58 (1969): 67–78.

———. *State, Power, Socialism.* New York: Verso, 2014. First published 1978.

Radio Free Asia. "Exiled Lao Activist Recalls 1999 Protest, Says Democracy Still Attainable." October 29, 2014. Accessed February 1, 2024. https://www.rfa.org/english/news/laos/exiled-activist-10292014185811.html.

———. "Lao Authorities Arrest 30 Suspects in Bus Shootings." April 21, 2016. Accessed February 1, 2024. https://www.rfa.org/english/news/laos/lao-authorities-arrest-30-suspects-in-bus-shootings-04212016165419.html.

———. "Laos: Land Dispute Villagers Released." June 28, 2012. Accessed February 1, 2024. https://www.rfa.org/english/news/laos/land-concessions-06282012173323.html.

———. "Lao Villagers Arrested in 11-Year-Old Land Dispute in Sekong Province." August 1, 2017. Accessed February 1, 2024. https://www.rfa.org/english/news/laos/lao-authorities-arrested-in-11-year-old-land-dispute-in-sekong-province-08012017155944.html.

Ribot, Jesse, and Nancy Lee Peluso. "A Theory of Access." *Rural Sociology* 68, no. 2 (2003): 153–181.

Rigg, Jonathan. "Land, Farming, Livelihoods, and Poverty: Rethinking the Links in the Rural South." *World Development* 29, no. 6 (2006): 945–960.

———. *Living with Transition in Laos: Market Integration in Southeast Asia.* London: Routledge, 2005.

Rocheleau, Dianne, and Laurie Ross. "Trees as Tools, Trees as Text: Struggles over Resources in Zambrana-Chacuey, Dominican Republic." *Antipode* 27, no. 4 (1995): 407–428.

Rulli, Maria Cristina, Antonio Saviori, and Paolo D'Odorico. "Global Land and Water Grabbing." *Proceedings of the National Academy of Sciences of the United States of America* 110, no. 3 (2013): 892–897.

Sändig, Jan. "Contesting Large-Scale Land Acquisitions in the Global South." *World Development* 146, no. 2 (2021): 105581.

Sassen, Saskia. "Land Grabs Today: Feeding the Disassembling of National Territory." *Globalizations* 10, no. 1 (2013): 25–46.

Sayatham, Mayvong, and Diana Suhardiman. "Hydropower Resettlement and Livelihood Adaptation: The Nam Mang 3 Project in Laos." *Water Resources and Rural Development* 5 (2015): 17–30.

Schoenberger, Laura, Derek Hall, and Peter Vandergeest. "What Happened When the Land Grab Came to Southeast Asia?" *Journal of Peasant Studies* 44, no. 1 (2017): 1–29.

Schönweger, Oliver, Andreas Heinimann, Michael Epprecht, Juliet Lu, and Palikone Thalongsengchanh. *Concessions and Leases in the Lao PDR: Taking Stock of Land Investments.* Vientiane: Ministry of Natural Resources and Environment and Centre for Development and Environment, 2012.

Schönweger, Oliver, and Peter Messerli. "Land Acquisition, Investment, and Development in the Lao Coffee Sector: Successes and Failures." *Critical Asian Studies* 47, no. 1 (2015): 94–122.

Scott, James C. *Domination and the Arts of Resistance: Hidden Transcripts.* New Haven, CT: Yale University Press, 1990.

———. *Seeing Like a State: How Certain Schemes to Improve the Human Condition Have Failed.* New Haven, CT: Yale University Press, 1998.

———. *Weapons of the Weak: Everyday Forms of Peasant Resistance.* New Haven, CT: Yale University Press, 1987.

Sharp, Joanne P., Paul Routledge, Chris Philo, and Ronan Paddison. "Entanglements of Power: Geographies of Domination/Resistance." In *Entanglements of Power: Geographies of Domination/Resistance,* edited by Joanne P. Sharp, Paul Routledge, Chris Philo, and Ronan Paddison, pp. 1–42. London: Routledge, 2000.

Shi, Weiyi. *Rubber Boom in Luang Namtha: A Transnational Perspective.* Vientiane: Deutsche Gesellschaft für Technische Zusammenarbeit (GTZ), 2008.

Sikor, Thomas, and Christian Lund. "Access and Property: A Question of Power and Authority." *Development and Change* 40, no. 1 (2009): 1–22.

Singh, Sarinda. "Understanding Changes for Forest-Dependent Communities in Upland Laos." *Human Ecology* 48, no. 2 (2020): 189–198.

Smirnov, Denis. *Assessment of Scope of Illegal Logging in Laos and Associated Trans-boundary Timber Trade.* Vientiane: WWF, 2015.

Smith, Beaumont. "Coffee Colonialism: Olam Plantation Displaces Lao Farmers." *CorpWatch,* June 4, 2012. Accessed February 1, 2024. https://www.corpwatch.org/article/coffee-colonialism-olam-plantation-displaces-lao-farmers.

———. "Golf and the Great Lao Land Grab." *Asia Times Online,* January 21, 2010. Accessed March 6, 2024. https://ki-media.blogspot.com/2010/01/golf-and-great-lao-land-grab.html.

Smith, Neil. *Uneven Development: Nature, Capital, and the Production of Space.* Athens: University of Georgia Press, 2008. First published 1984.

St. John, Ronald Bruce. "The Political Economy of Laos: Poor State or Poor Policy?" *Asian Affairs* 37, no. 2 (2006): 175–191.

Stuart-Fox, Martin. "The French in Laos, 1887–1945." *Modern Asian Studies* 29, no. 1 (1995): 111–139.

———. *A History of Laos.* Cambridge: Cambridge University Press, 1997.

———. "Laos: The Chinese Connection." *Southeast Asian Affairs* (2009): 141–169.

Sturgeon, Janet C., and Thomas Sikor. "Post-socialist Property in Asia and Europe: Variations on 'Fuzziness.'" *Conservation and Society* 2, no. 1 (2004): 1–18.

Sud, Nikita. "Land-Making as State-Making." In *The Oxford Handbook of Land Politics,* edited by Saturnino M. Borras Jr. and Jennifer C. Franco. Oxford: Oxford University Press, 2023.

———. *The Making of Land and the Making of India.* Oxford: Oxford University Press, 2021.

Suhardiman, Diana, Jessica DiCarlo, Oulavanh Keovilignavong, Jonathan Rigg, and Alan Nicol. "(Re)constructing State Power and Livelihoods through the Laos–China Railway Project." *Geoforum* 124 (2021): 79–88.

Sundberg, Juanita. "Diabolic *Caminos* in the Desert and Cat Fights on the Río: A Posthumanist Political Ecology of Boundary Enforcement in the United States–Mexico Borderlands." *Annals of the Association of American Geographers* 101, no. 2 (2011): 318–336.

———. "Reconfiguring North–South Solidarity: Critical Reflections on Experiences of Transnational Resistance." *Antipode* 39, no. 1 (2007): 144–166.

Tappe, Oliver. "On the Right Track? The Lao People's Democratic Republic in 2017." In *Southeast Asian Affairs 2018,* edited by Malcolm Cook and Daljit Singh, pp. 169–184. Singapore: ISEAS–Yusof Ishak Institute, 2018.

Taylor, Marcus. *The Political Ecology of Climate Change Adaptation: Livelihoods, Agrarian Change and the Conflicts of Development.* London: Routledge, 2015.

Temper, Leah. "From Boomerangs to Minefields and Catapults: Dynamics of Trans-local Resistance to Land-Grabs." *Journal of Peasant Studies* 46, no. 1 (2019): 188–216.

Tilly, Charles. *Social Movements, 1768–2004.* New York: Routledge. 2004.

Toro, Matthew. "Coffee Markets, Smallholder Credit, and Landscape Change in the Bolaven Plateau Region, Laos." Master's thesis, University of Miami, 2012.

Tran Thi Thuy Hoa, To Xuan Phuc, Nguyen Ton Quyen, and Cao Thi Cam. *Vietnam Rubber Industry: Current Status and Sustainable Development Solutions.* Ho Chi Minh City: Vietnam Rubber Association, Vietnam Timber and Forest Product Association, Handicraft and Wood Industry Association of Ho Chi Minh City, Forest Products Association of Binh Dinh, and Forest Trends, 2018.

Tsing, Anna Lowenhaupt. *Friction: An Ethnography of Global Connection.* Princeton, NJ: Princeton University Press, 2004.

United Nations Development Program. *National Human Development Report. Lao PDR 2001: Advancing Rural Development.* Vientiane: United Nations Development Program, 2001.

US Agency for International Development. *USAID Country Profile: Property Rights and Resource Governance—Lao People's Democratic Republic.* Washington, DC: USAID, 2013.

Vandergeest, Peter. "Land to Some Tillers: Development-Induced Displacement in Laos." *International Social Science Journal* 55, no. 175 (2003): 47–56.

Vandergeest, Peter, and Nancy Lee Peluso. "Empires of Forestry: Professional Forestry and State Power in Southeast Asia, Part 2." *Environment and History* 12, no. 4 (2006): 359–393.

Vandergeest, Peter, and Jonathan Rigg. "The Restudy 'Problem' and Agrarian Change: Revisiting Rural Places in Southeast Asia." In *Revisiting Rural Places: Pathways to Poverty and Prosperity in Southeast Asia,* edited by Jonathan Rigg and Peter Vandergeest, pp. 1–24. Singapore: NUS Press, 2012.

Varley, Ann. "Private or Public: Debating the Meaning of Tenure Legalization." *International Journal of Urban and Regional Research* 26, no. 3 (2002): 449–461.

Verdery, Katherine. *The Vanishing Hectare: Property and Value in Postsocialist Transylvania.* Ithaca, NY: Cornell University Press, 2018.

Vientiane Times. "Govt Aims to Issue 220,000 Land Titles by End of 2023." November 9, 2023.

———. "Land Issues Top Public Concerns." July 13, 2012.

———. "Laos Striving for Rule of Law State." February 6, 2014.

VietNamNet. "Experts Warn about Hoang Anh Gia Lai's Plan to Sell Land." September 29, 2016. Accessed March 6, 2024. https://vietnamnet.vn/en/experts-warn-about-hoang-anh-gia-lais-plan-to-sell-land-E164300.html.

Visser, Oane, and Max Spoor. "Land Grabbing in Post-Soviet Eurasia: The World's Largest Agricultural Land Reserves at Stake." *Journal of Peasant Studies* 38, no. 2 (2011): 299–323.

Walker, Kathy Le Mons. "From Covert to Overt: Everyday Peasant Politics in China and the Implications for Transnational Agrarian Movements." In *Transnational Agrarian Movements Confronting Globalization,* edited by Saturnino M. Borras, Marc Edelman, and Cristóbal Kay, pp. 295–322. Malden, MA: Wiley-Blackwell, 2008.

Watts, Michael. "The Sinister Political Life of Community: Economies of Violence and Governable Spaces in the Niger Delta, Nigeria." Working Paper 3, Institute of International Studies, University of California, Berkeley, 2004.

Wellmann, Dominik. *The Legal Framework of State Land Leases and Concessions in the Lao PDR*. Vientiane: Deutsche Gesellschaft für Internationale Zusammenarbeit (GIZ), 2012.

Wolford, Wendy. "Land Reform in the Time of Neoliberalism: A Many-Splendored Thing." *Antipode* 39, no. 3 (2007).

———. *This Land Is Ours Now: Social Mobilization and the Meanings of Land in Brazil*. Durham, NC: Duke University Press, 2010.

Wolford, Wendy, Saturnino Borras, Ruth Hall, Ian Scoones, and Ben White. "Governing Global Land Deals: The Role of the State in the Rush for Land." *Development and Change* 44, no. 2 (2013): 189–210.

Wolters, Oliver W. *History, Culture, and Religion in Southeast Asian Perspectives*. Singapore: Institute of Southeast Asian Studies, 1982.

Woods, Kevin. "Ceasefire Capitalism: Military–Private Partnerships, Resource Concessions and Military–State Building in the Burma–China Borderlands." *Journal of Peasant Studies* 38, no. 4 (2011): 747–770.

Yamada, Norihiko. "Legitimation of the Lao People's Revolutionary Party: Socialism, *Chintanakan Mai* (New Thinking) and Reform." *Journal of Contemporary Asia* 48, no. 5 (2018): 717–738.

Zeller, Nicholas R. "A World Safe for Revolution: China, Laos, and the Possibility of Revolutionary Nationalism." PhD diss., University of Wisconsin, Madison, 2021.

Zoomers, Annelies. "Globalisation and the Foreignisation of Space: Seven Processes Driving the Current Global Land Grab." *Journal of Peasant Studies* 37, no. 2 (2010): 429–447.

Zurflueh, Joel. "Vietnamese Rubber Investments in the South of the Lao PDR: Key Factors Influencing Decision Making in Large-Scale Land Acquisitions by Vietnamese Investors in the Agro-Forestry Sector of the Lao PDR." Master's thesis, University of Bern, 2013.

Index

Page numbers in **boldface** refer to illustrations and tables

About the Author

MILES KENNEY-LAZAR is a senior lecturer in the School of Geography, Earth and Atmospheric Sciences at the University of Melbourne and has previously held positions at the National University of Singapore and Kyoto University.